# The Maglemose Culture

## The reconstruction of the social organization of a mesolithic culture in Northern Europe

## Ole Grøn

BAR International Series 616

1995

Published in 2019 by
BAR Publishing, Oxford

BAR International Series 616

*The Maglemose Culture*

© Ole Grøn and the Publisher 1995

ISBN  9780860547976  paperback
ISBN  9781407349213  e-book

DOI  https://doi.org/10.30861/9780860547976

A catalogue record for this book is available from the British Library

This book is available at www.barpublishing.com


BAR Publishing is the trading name of British Archaeological Reports (Oxford) Ltd.
British Archaeological Reports was first incorporated in 1974 to publish the BAR
Series, International and British. In 1992 Hadrian Books Ltd became part of the BAR
group. This volume was originally published by Tempvs Reparatvm in conjunction
with British Archaeological Reports (Oxford) Ltd / Hadrian Books Ltd, the Series
principal publisher, in 1995. This present volume is published by BAR Publishing,
2019.

# BAR
PUBLISHING

BAR titles are available from:

BAR Publishing
122 Banbury Rd, Oxford, OX2 7BP, UK
EMAIL   info@barpublishing.com
PHONE   +44 (0)1865 310431
FAX     +44 (0)1865 316916
www.barpublishing.com

# Preface and acknowledgements

This work is essentially my PhD. The discussion of methods of analysis and of the use of statistics has been made more elaborate (chapter 1), and a few of the illustrations have been improved.

The large body of ethnographical data relevant for the interpretation of the spatial organization of the settlements of hunter-gatherers is referred to only through references, as the focus of this work is the implementation of behavioural ideas from ethnography (eg. Grøn 1989;1991) into the practical analysis of a concrete material.

The catalogue contains the most important distributions from the sites analysed, shown as contour lines. Since the innumerable artefact distributions which form the basis of this study will be of little interest to the majority of the readers, I have chosen not to publish these data in this book, but to make them available to those interested as data files for 'SURFER' from Golden Software (1).

It should be noted that an understanding of the typological aspects of the materials as well as of the excavation circumstances is a prerequisite for sound results in any distribution analysis.

The basic point of view promoted in this book is that the sites have to be regarded as dynamic units, and that the possibilities for understanding their basic spatial configuration are closely linked to success in distinguishing spatial 'fixpoints' which can form the basis for further analysis. The fixpoints used in this analysis are the concentrations of microliths and the hearth zones. Other cultures than the Maglemose Culture may require *quite different strategies, and some may even be impossible to 'decipher'*.

My work with analysis of the Maglemosian sites started in 1979. It developed through excavation of sites, extensive studies of hunter-gatherer literature, discussion with colleagues working with related problems such as Raymon R. Newell, Dick Stapert, Leo Verhart, Nikolai Praslov, Michail Anikovich, Andrei Sinitsin, Peter Rowley-Conwy and with numerous hunter-gatherer ethnographers among whom Galina N. Grachova from St. Petersburg maybe was in possession of the most valuable treasure of unpublished information from her 50 years of study of the Siberian people. Unfortunately she was killed in a helicopter accident in the spring 1993, and a comprehensive manuscript on the spatial organization of dwellings and the mythology connected to it, which she had then finished on the basis of her old field notes, has never been found.

Peder Mortensen and Paul Mellars have shown supportive interest in the project, and Tjeerd H. van Andel's encyclopaedic mind also turned out to contain information on and interest in its archaeological as well as its ethnographical aspects. Knud Andersen, the excavator of the Ulkestrup Huts, showed a rare helpfulness and interest even when it came to the discussion of alternative interpretations of the material. Erik Jørgensen, Flemming Rieck, Axel Johansson, Jens Bech, Jørgen Holm, Klaus Bokelmann, Niels-Axel Boas, Søren H. Andersen and Per Ethelberg gave me access to their excavated materials. The latter together with Inge Birthe Welling, Sussanne Klingenberg and Orla Madsen were members of our student group where the discussion of repeated patterns on the Maglemosian settlements started. The amateur archaeologist Frederik Klestrup Hansen led our way through the Svanemose Bog often with his attention directed at more interesting features in the landscape than the road his car was supposed to follow. Svend Erik Hansen and John Cronshaw helped correct the language of the manuscript. As supervisor on my PhD, Erik Brinch Petersen served as a good partner for discussion, also in matters where our opinions diverged.

In 1983 The Danish Research Council for the Humanities financed the excavation of the Maglemose dwelling Svanemosen 28 and in 1984 furthermore yielded a grant which made it possible for two years to concentrate on the analysis of the Maglemosian sites, which had until then been carried out as a supplement to fieldwork for Haderslev Museum. During my following attachment to Langelands Museum The Council financed an international conference on 'Social Space in Dwellings and Settlements' and the publication of the conference report (Grøn, Engelstad and Lindblom 1991) in 1987. My PhD was accepted in the Spring 1993.

This book is dedicated to my wife, Elsebeth, and my children, Tue and Ida, who have been living with this project for so many years.

# Contents

7.    Notes

8.    References

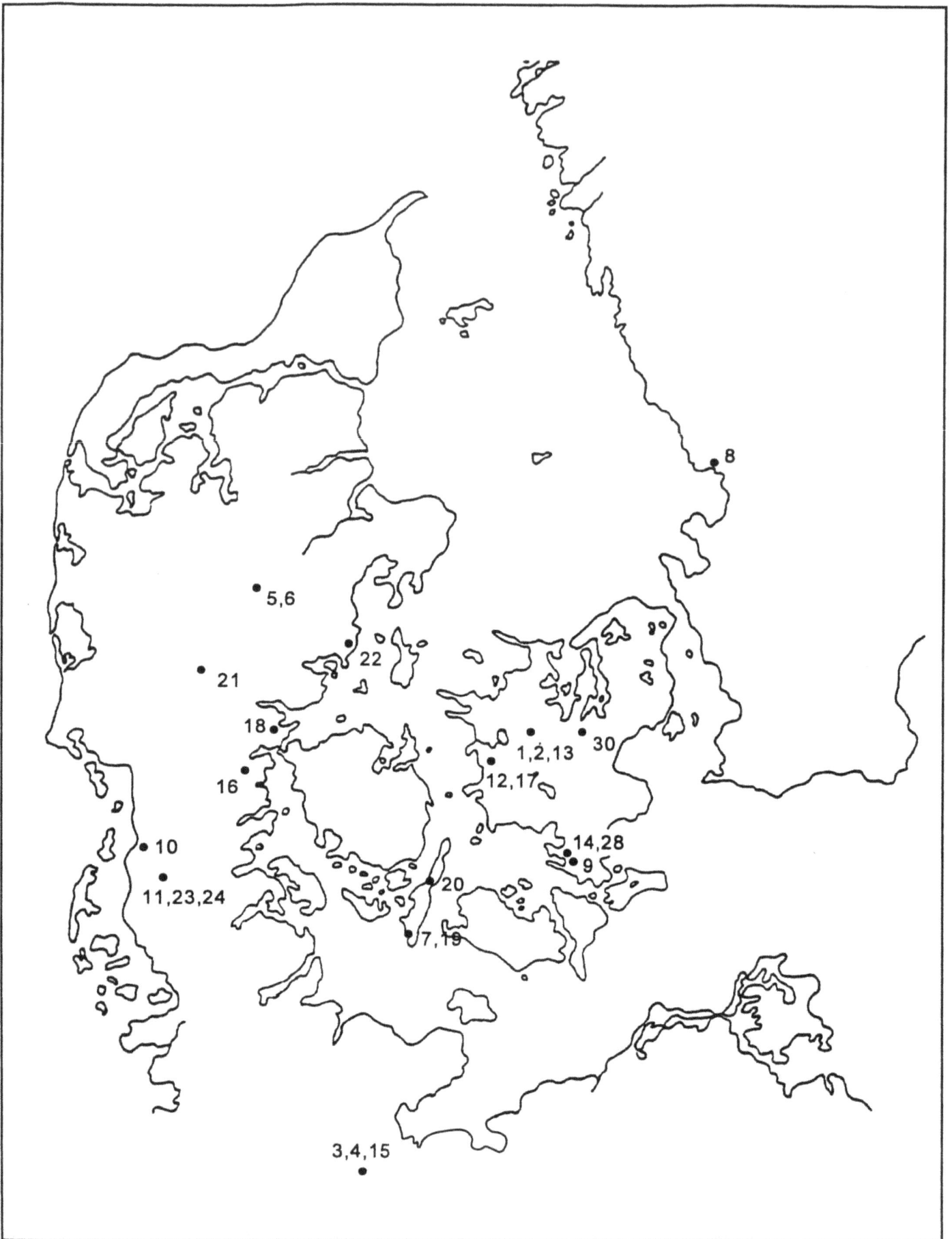

*Map showing the central Maglemosian area with the majority of the sites mentioned in the text. The numbers refer to the catalogue numbers: 1,2,13:Ulkestrup; 3,4,15:Duvensee; 5,6:Klosterlund; 7,19:Magleby Nor; 8:Bare Mosse II; 9:Barmosen I; 10:Hjemsted; 11,23,24:Draved; 12,17:Mullerup; !4,28:Sværdborg II and Hasbjerg II; 16:Svanemosen 28; 18:Stallerupholm; 20:Flaadet; 21:Bøllund; 22:Rude Mark; 30:Lavringe Mose.*

# 1. Introduction

Several basic analytical approaches to distribution patterns have been developed through time. I shall in brief outline the assumptions they are based on, and evaluate how suited they are for the kind of analysis demanded here. Before entering this discussion it is, however, important to discuss three points of importance for the angle of attack: a) that some groups of lithic objects may have very different spatial behaviours during their 'life' on a site and that different distributions of different types of objects thus may reflect their different 'dynamic' patterns rather than the fact that they were used in different areas, b) that there seem to exist some contradictions between morphological and functional typology, and c) that there exist some problems in the use of statistical analysis for interpretation of such distributions.

## 1.1. The sites as dynamic units

Refitting of lithic material from stone age sites clearly demonstrates that some groups of lithic objects may have very different spatial behaviours during their 'life' (e.g. Bodu, Karlin and Ploux 1990; Cziesla 1990a; Löhr 1990; Stapert and Krist 1990). Knives may for instance appear in dumping areas after being discarded, in activity areas representing 'cutting' as well as in other activity areas representing 'production of knives'. Meanwhile, their presence, due to cleaning of the production and cutting areas, may also be restricted to the dumping areas, thus producing a totally misleading picture of where the activities we are interested in, were carried out (Eickhoff 1990). Different object types may on a site have quite different spatial dynamics (eg. Stapert and Krist 1990). And one type of objects may have different dynamic patterns at different sites from the same culture. For instance the cores on some Maglemosian sites seem to follow the walls of the dwellings, whereas they on others appear evenly distributed within the dwelling space (eg. Andersen et.al.1982:21-22,30-31; Johansson 1990:15-17,55).

Of crucial importance for whether artefacts were left in the activity areas they were used in, or whether they were removed, is their size. Different observations all indicate that objects smaller than 4-5 cm are much more infrequently affected by cleaning of the living floors than larger objects (Binford 1978:153; Hayden 1981:142; Johnson 1984:79,92,93; Kroll and Isac 1984:16,24; O'Connel 1987). Thus a study aiming at distinguishing the locations of the activities which precede discarding and dumping should focus on the distributions of items *smaller than approximately 4-5 cm.*

## 1.2. Functional versus morphological types

A necessary but problematic basis for the study of the spatial organisation of the activities on old stone age sites is the traditional morphological typology. Preservation of the lithic surfaces as well as economical factors put serious limitations in the number of cases where a thorough microwear analysis can be applied. Nonetheless the microwear analysis shows for instance that 'scrapers' have been used for boring, 'knives' for scraping etc. (eg. Cahen and Caspar 1984:289-292; Juel Jensen and Brinch Petersen 1985:45-48; Symens 1986:216). This tendency is also obvious from the microwear analysis of the Maglemosian material from the Flaadet site carried out in connection with this study by Nicole Symens and Merete Christensen (report in Langelands Museum LMR j.nr.8321). Consistency between morphological and functional types only seems to exist in very few cases. It is therefore a further and serious methodological constraint that studies of activity organisation should be directed against *morphological types which consistently represent a recognizable function.*

Distributions of objects of organic matter (eg. bone) generally must be regarded as unreliable. The degree of preservation will often vary on the settlement surface. For instance burnt bone from a hearth zone will generally be better preserved than unburnt, thus creating a misleading image of the original distribution.

## 1.3. The use of statistical models

Statistical analysis is used to distinguish non-random patterns on the basis of single observations, each containing a restricted element of randomness.

For instance linear regression is the approximation of a number of points (x,y) by a straight line representing a function. One *precondition* for this operation is that the distribution of the dependent variables y, for given x, is *normal*. This means that the y-values for one x-value, should appear as a normal distribution with a certain mean value and a certain variance. In other words the y-values for one x-value must mainly appear within a certain interval, whereas their exact position within this interval is random, and cannot be predicted. However, if the y values for an x-value are consciously chosen - for instance to form different groups or patterns - the precondition above is not fulfilled. In this case the points (x,y) can be seen only as a number of independent and non-randomly placed points that do not represent a function.

Where statistical analysis is applied to distributions of artefacts it is normally based on the assumption that the positions of the items with a certain restricted element of randomness are the result of functional processes. This makes it possible to discuss whether a scatter of objects is 'random' or not by comparison to models based on for instance Poisson and normal distributions (eg. Blankholm 1991:42; Dacey 1968:172; Johnson 1984:79-80; Newell and Dekin 1978:20; Price 1981:207; Whallon 1974:23). Our interest is to distinguish non-random patterns that deviate from the random ones, because this indicates that they are created by human activity. However, it is a problem that the scatters known to be non-random do not restrict themselves to nice bell-shaped distributions. They may easily assume so complicated shapes, that the construction of suited statistical models for comparison and analysis in practice will be impossible (Binford 1978:340; 1983:153-157; Doran and Hudson 1975: 151; Kroll and Isaac 1984:16; Whallon 1978:33; 1984:275). A more basic problem is that careful conscious ordering on the surface of the lithic objects as Binford observed it in Australia, also seems observable in the archaeological record (Binford 1983:152; Leroi-Gourhan and Brézillon 1972:238). In such cases the objects are consciously placed and thus their position contains no element of randomness. Accordingly the precondition for this kind of statistical analysis is not fulfilled.

## 1.4.1. Multivariant analysis

Multivariant methods - per definition - analyse several different variants (different types of items) together. Their purpose is to distinguish activity areas as zones where several types of items appear in rather constant relative quantitative relations to each other (tool-kits) (eg. Whallon 1973:117). For instance the categories analysed may be: flakes, blades, knives, burins and arrow heads. An activity area may for instance appear as a restricted area where these items appear in relative numbers of approximately 50:10:2:3:1.

A problematic precondition for this kind of analysis in its pure form is, that the positions of all items are seen as the result of one global process - or 'function' (Whallon 1984:245-246). Where the quantitative composition of item types in one area represents overlapping and non-interrelated activities, this is not the case, and the method will produce meaningless results. Actually pure analysis can never reveal if such a precondition is fulfilled.

A further series of more specific problems exist. First, it should be noted that no attention is given to the possible different dynamics of the different classes of objects. They are compared as if they all have similar spatial life-cycles on the settlement surface. Second, all types of items are compared as if they were of the same size and thus were equally exposed to cleaning. Thus an area which was originally used for activities involving flakes, blades, knives, burins and arrow heads in the relation 50:10:2:3:1, in an archaeological context may appear only as a zone with approximately 1 arrow head per square unit due to removal of the larger objects by cleaning. If it is not possible to distinguish the dumping areas by means of archaeological observations, they may easily be taken for zones of intense activity. Third, one will have to rely on morphologically defined types in the majority of cases (Blankholm 1991:38-39). Since only few morphological types seem consistently to correspond to recognizable activities, the results of multivariant analysis may easily be misleading.

Instead of the relative composition of the different categories of objects, Blankholms Presab method registers only their presence or absence (Blankholm 1991:153). This means that the analysis main aim is to distinguish areas where certain types appear together, and not to separate areas where they appear in different relative quantities. In some situations this may cause over and underrepresentation of object categories appearing in extremely small and large numbers.

Many multivariant methods employ statistical analysis to distinguish 'random' and 'non-random' concentrations of objects (eg. Blankholm 1991:61-168). As mentioned above this is based on assumptions that seem, at least in some cases, not to be fulfilled (1.2.3.).

So many problems and unclear points seem imbedded in the multivariant methods that they should rather be avoided. Generally each strategy introduced to eliminate one problem seems to create a series of new ones. Basically the archaeological material seems unable to meet the mathematical and statistical preconditions necessary.

## 1.4.2. Visual inspection

Visual inspection of distributions was the first method of analysis used. Compared to the complexity of multivariant analysis it is theoretically simple. Basically it relies on visual recognition of patterns such as concentrations of items, charac-teristic empty zones, lines of refittings, and linear zones where the concentration seems to drop suddenly ('wall-effect'). Together with the remains of hearths, pits, and dwellings the observed patterns often form the basis of rather subjective interpretations.

Already in the late twenties Krukowski tried to deduct information about economical and social aspects from the shape of flint concentrations (Domanska 1991:55; Krukowski 1929). A typical - and disputed - example of visual inspection are Leroi-Gourhan and Brézillon's interpretations of Pincevent (Binford 1983:148-160; Johnson 1984; Leroi-Gourhan and Brézillon 1966; 1972; Stapert 1989). First they distinguish units consisting of hearths connected to concentrations of material. Thereafter they postulate without any detailed argumentation the outlines of a number of dwelling units (Leroi-Gourhan and Brézillon 1972:215-256). As a matter of fact there are several indications that there has been free passage of objects through the

northern wall of the northwestern unit at section 36 (the refitting lines of debitage, reindeer jaws, and long bones, as well as the distribution of red ochre) (Leroi-Gourhan and Brézillon 1972: 86,108,148,152, 240). There also seems to exist a conflict between the north-eastern postulated dwelling structure and the distribution of faunal remains in this section (Johnson 1984:94).

For visual inspection it is important that the data are given an optimal graphical presentation. However, there is no objective answer to what representation is the best. Cziesla represents a number of systems for visual inspection, where a signature (circle, square etc.) is shown for each square. He has had some success introducing the filled in circle with a range of different diameters expressing the variation in numbers (Cziesla 1989; 1990b). Personally I prefer graphical expressions that do not focus on the intensities in the single squares, but give information on the relation between the concentrations in the different squares. This can be done by interpolation of equidistant contour lines on the basis of the numbers from each square. In natural sciences this would be the normal way to present such data.

Unless remains of dwelling structures are preserved (eg. Møbjerg 1991), it seems difficult to produce convincing interpretations on the basis of pure visual inspection.

## 1.4.3. Analytical strategies based on behavioural models observed ethnographically.

An important element in modern old stone age research is the assumed similarity between prehistoric old stone age cultures and present hunter-gatherers. A logical consequence of this is to try to distinguish general behavioural patterns from the ethnographical material, and thereafter to attempt to distinguish these patterns in the archaeological record.

Binford postulates on the basis of ethnographical observations three general behavioural 'elements' (Binford 1983:156-159):

a) Central hearths located outdoor are generally surrounded by zones of waste (toss and dump-zones). This is not the case with central hearths located indoors.

b) Compared to indoor hearths, outdoor hearths are less structured physically, are less clearly delimited, and have a tendency to move around within a restricted area. The former are generally smaller, encircled by stones, and keep their place in the dwelling space.

c) A person working at an outdoor hearth, will rather build a new fire to his own lee side than move to the lee side of the first hearth if the wind changes.

On the basis of these postulates combined with a very rough visual inspection of the distributions, he interprets the two northwestern hearths at Pincevent 1 as two outdoor hearths used mainly by one person in different wind directions. The south-eastern hearth is interpreted as an indoor hearth (Binford 1983: 156-160).

In principle this approach seems reasonable. However, it is problematic that there exist several exceptions from the postulated general behavioural elements. For instance the Yamana Indians had rather large and apparently rather diffuse hearths inside their dwellings. To increase the sleeping area and to produce a concentration of slowly burning embers the fires were scraped together in the centre of the dwellings for the night (Gusinde 1937:394). Their neighbours, the Selk'nam, had only small fires (approximately 50 cm in diameter) centrally in their dwellings. But here the embers were spread over a larger area when camp was left, to stop them burning (Gusinde 1931:204-206). In an archaeological context such structures undoubtedly would be interpreted as large and diffuse hearths. The Bushmen distinguish between a male and a female side of the central hearth outside their dwellings (Marshall 1959:354). Thus they cannot move deliberately around the fire to avoid the smoke. In spite of this the hearths take up a specific position relative to the entrance, and do not 'move around' (Yellen 1977). With regard to the archaeological material it also seems very unlikely that for instance the hearths found in the central open camp space at Kostienki I should represent indoor activities. The camp consists of an oval arrangement of dugout dwellings with collapsed superstructures constructed from mammoths tusks and large storage pits for meat. The

hearths are located on the central axis of the oval. They are surrounded by numerous stake holes and appear as clearly delimited and well defined physical structures (Praslov 1993; Praslov and Rogachev 1982).

On the basis of Binford's approach, Stapert has developed the so-called 'ring and sector method'. I see a number of problems in the complicated logical structure of this method.

The central hearths of the sites, no matter if they are indoor or outdoor, are regarded as focal points of activity 'defining the global structure of the site'. It is argued that the spatial partition used for analysis should follow this (assumed) original structure. The space is thus separated into concentric rings, and radial sectors with the 'central hearth' as their centre. Due to the change from a square grid coordinate system to a kind of polar coordinate system, the method can only be applied to materials with the locations of the artefacts registered individually. But if the method works only on the basis of the individual coordinates of the artefacts, the argument against registration in a normal grid system falls (Stapert 1989:5-6). On the basis of individual co-ordinates an analysis can easily be formulated which would make a ring and sector analysis possible around any chosen point in a normal grid system. Thus it would be possible to avoid the extremely dangerous process of creating a polar system of spatial separations, which on the one hand focuses the analysis on an assumed 'central hearth' and on the other neglects a similar analysis around other possible central points.

Another dangerous assumption, not explicitly formulated, but underlying and hinted at in the text is that an indoor 'central' hearth will take up a position in the centre of the dwelling space (Stapert 1989: 5,6). In a short discussion of whether hearths might be located in or near entrances, it is stated that: 'It is improbable that people should have placed their hearth in the tent entrance, because this would be rather unpractical' (Stapert 1989:22). It is obvious that the ring and sector method cannot be applied to indoor 'central hearths' located peripherically in the dwelling or open air hearths located immediately outside a dwelling. Its basic idea is that of unrestricted movement around the central hearth. However, the known ethnographic examples of 'central heating sources' placed very close to or immediately beside entrances are innumerable (eg. Birket-Smith 1929:86; Ränk 1951:54; Tanner 1979: 76-79). As we shall see in the following, there are strong indications that the hearths in the Maglemosian dwellings were not placed in the centres either.

Stapert distinguishes two types of distribution patterns around the central hearths. The 'unimodal' distributions show one accumulation of artefacts only, close to the hearth. It is suggested that this pattern reflects activities carried out around an open air hearth, with some artefacts spreading around the centre due to the 'centrifugal effect'. The 'bimodal' distributions show one accumulation of artefacts close to the centre and one peripheral accumulation. It is suggested that they reflect indoor situations, the central one representing the activity centre and the peripheral one material being spread by the centrifugal effect, and stopped by a dwelling wall (Stapert 1989:12-23). Where a 'central hearth' is located asymmetrically inside a dwelling, or outside and immediately adjacent to it, the type of distribution it produces cannot be predicted reasonably. In numerous cases such a location will be impossible to exclude à priori.

An attempt to analyse the Maglemose site Barmosen I (Stapert 1992:143-188), is problematic. Remains of a bark floor were preserved. The cores seem accumulated inside and along the wall of an approximately 4 by 5 metre large, oval dwelling. If this outline is interpreted correctly, then the hearth is located in the eastern half of the dwelling (Johansson 1990:15-17). Thus we are dealing with an asymmetrical situation not suited for ring and sector analysis. In the discussion of analytical principles, it is of minor importance that the analysis is based on misleading data on the distributions, adopted from Blankholm (Grøn 1992a;1994). On this basis the interpretation of the site as an open air site (Stapert 1992:157) must be seriously doubted.

## 1.4.4.a. The present method of analysis - the basic assumption

In ethnography it is regarded as an established fact that the space inside the dwellings of hunter-gatherers (as with all other kinds of primitive cultures) is organized in accordance with a set of rules. Elements of the organizational patterns may differ from one cultural group to the other, whereas they will be consistent within the single group (e.g. Ardener 1981:12; Bernot 1982:41; Faegre 1979:7; Grøn 1989; 1991:100-102; Morice 1909:592-593; Paulson 1952:65; Rapoport 1969:54-55; Ränk 1951: 141; Tanner 1991:26-28).

In the few cases where extremely well preserved neolithic dwellings could be excavated strong indications of such spatial organizational patterns were observed (Childe 1946:28,30,32; Clarke and Sharples 1985:70; Melaart 1967:56-60). With regard to hunter-gatherers the best archaeological examples are from the Arctic due to the good preservation of organic structures here, as well as the widespread use of dug-out dwellings (e.g. Giddings 1952:11-34; Larsen and Rainey 1948: 40,41; Møbjerg 1991:45). On Greenland, Knuth employs the different organizational patterns of the dwelling remains to distinguish between the different prehistoric cultural phases (Knuth 1984: 4,35,39-42,93). Publication of a large number of late palaeolithic sites (tent-rings etc.) from the earlier Soviet area, with important clues to the organizational patterns of such sites, is in preparation.

The ethnographic record shows that the 'rules' of spatial behaviour are generally incorporated into a mythological fabric referring to a multidimensional symbolic space (cosmos) containing the past, the future, the underworld, the 'heaven', etc. of which the dwelling space is often a representation organized as a two or three-dimensional micro-cosmos (e.g. Bernot 1982; Bourdieu 1970:739-758; Doxtater 1991:156-163; Eliade 1976:3,41-43; Fock 1986:61-69; Gracheva 1989; Ohnuki-Tierny 1972:427-457; Parvia 1991:150-152; Tanner 1979:73,88; 1991).

According to social-psychology the use of spatial relations and attitudes between humans is a more important and apparently more ancient means of communicating social relations than spoken messages (Argyle 1976:94,132; Argyle and Dean 1965; Brewer 1968; Canter 1984:215; 1991; Dovido and Ellyson 1982; Exline 1971; Hall 1969; Howells and Becker 1962; Little 1965; Lott and Sommer 1967; Mehrabian 1968; Sommer 1959, 1961,1965, 1968; Steinzor 1950; Strongman and Champness 1968).

This type of behaviour is seen as closely related to what is observed with other primates (Barkow 1976:211; Chance and Jolly 1970:209; Kummer 1969:231).

The basic assumption is thus that space in the habitations of a prehistoric culture (huts, tents, wind screens etc.) was organized in accordance with a fixed set of rules, and that it should therefore be possible to reconstruct parts of their spatial organization (and through this, elements of their social organization) from the distributions of artifacts, waste and structural remains.

One consequence of the existence of such a prescribed spatial organization of the activities in the habitations of a cultural group, should be that the distributions of each of the classes of items found here are not random, but must be regarded as strongly controlled by cultural factors. For instance, the occurrence of skin scrapers might be restricted to what was conceived as the 'female side' of a dwelling, or arrowheads to the positions that by convention were held by the adult males.

Another consequence of the above mentioned restrictions of the activities to certain parts of the dwellings of a specific cultural group - according to the age, sex and social position of the inhabitants involved in them - is that we should expect some patterns of distribution to repeat themselves in a number of cases.

The focus of attention has thus changed from studies of the shape and composition of activity areas on the individual sites, to the observation of distribution patterns that repeat themselves at a number of sites.

## 1.4.4.b. Choice of main object categories for analysis

To reduce the problems of possible redeposition by cleaning, and the confusion concerning the functional aspects, the analysis has been concentrated on the microlithic pieces. The Maglemosian microliths seldomly exceed 4 cm in size and seem only to have served as inserts in arrow or spear heads. The Loshult arrow had lanceolate points as inserts (Petterson 1951:125-127). Aurochs skeletons found in bogs, in

two cases had microliths shot into them (Hartz and Winge 1906; Vang Petersen and Brinch Petersen 1984; Aaris Sørensen 1984). At the site Magleby Nor, where preserved birch tar was found on several pieces of flint, a lanceolate point was found connected to what appeared to be the remains of an arrow shaft (Bechs report in Langelands Museum LMR jnr.11372). Analysis of numerous impacts on microliths confirm this function (Barton and Bergman 1982; Fischer 1984:23; Grøn 1992b), whereas no traces of other activities have been observed in the Maglemosian material analysed. In a few cases traces of cutting, sawing, shaving etc. have been observed on microliths from other cultures (Finlayson 1990). Almost all of these, however, seem to appear on the unworked edges of the original blades, and thus may reflect use prior to the production of the microliths. The low relative number of microliths with damages from use as projectile points, compared to the often very large relative number of microliths with no wear traces at all, most likely reflects that many damaged points were discarded and replaced during the hunt, far from the settlements (Nuzhnyí 1990:114,122).

It should thus be possible on a reasonable basis to assume: a) that the microliths found on the sites represent the intra-site aspect of hunting: production and maintenance of hunting weapons, removal of projectile remains from meat etc., and b) that their distributions, due to their sizes, often much smaller than 4 centimetre, have been minimally affected by cleaning.

However the fact that repeated patterns are found in the distributions of small objects is no guarantee in itself that they are not redeposited. It is important to present further arguments in each case. Systematic 'tossing' or 'dumping' of microlithic items can for instance be observed at the Ulkestrup I. Here we find that nearly all micro burins are found outside the dwelling area (marked by the preserved floor) with the major part found in the 'waste layer', whereas the main body of the other microlithic pieces are found on the bark floor (3.1.6.). A cultural discrimination between micro burins and other microlithic pieces seems quite understandable since the former represent the waste product from the manufacturing of the latter.

Another feature given much attention in the analysis is the position of hearths. An important point is that flint in hearths, and only there, is exposed to so strong a heat that it breaks into a large number of small pieces (Fischer et.al. 1979:23,25-26) rather resistant to cleaning processes. Thus the number of pieces of burnt flint may be a useful indicator of the positions of hearths (3.1.5.), whereas the weight of burnt flint per m² may be misleading, since larger burnt pieces are more easily cleared out from the central hearth area than the small fragments.

The distributions of lithic waste are given some attention as indicators of the locations of dwelling areas and waste layers. This, however, is based on their distribution on known dwelling floors. Due to their size and to the fact that some types of lithic waste at least in one case seem to have been cleaned out selectively (2.1.5. and 2.1.6.), they are not seen as indicators of the locations of activity areas.

Preserved Structural remains of dwellings such as bark floors and dwelling pits, are of course important elements in the analysis.

## 1.4.4.c. Method of graphical presentation

To avoid statistical problems, it has been decided to study and compare the distributions of the individual object categories by graphical representations only. They are presented as equidistant contour lines. Because the distributions of many items have traditionally been registered only in m²-squares, this unit has been chosen as the basis for the interpolation. In a few cases where it was possible, supplementary interpolation on the basis of ¼-m² squares has been used to get a more detailed picture. In general the m²-square unit seems to be a useful unit. From an analytical point of view, however, the possibility for success would be considerably improved if the ¼-m² unit in future excavations was used as the maximum registration unit.

To employ a 100% automatic procedure, producing immediately comparable graphical expressions, all contour maps are produced by the program SURFER 4.1, from Golden Software. The amount of items found in a m²-square is related to the centre of the

square. The distance between the centres of two squares side-by-side is set to 1 data unit, so that the interpolation grid fits the m²-structure. For search for data points, search radius is set to 1.2 data units and the number of nearest points is set to 4. Smoothing of the curves by the factor of 10 has been used to make them easier to read.

The levels interpolated are typically 10%, 20% .. etc. of the maximum value, with an intensity of 0.4 items per m² as the minimum. The curve values used are equidistant (marking intensities of 1X, 2X, 3X etc.) instead of logarithmic, exponential and other curve values (e.g. 0.125K, 0.25K, 0.5K, K, 2K, 4K, 8K, where K, for instance, is the average value). Interpolation with non-equidistant curves will emphasize some elements of the distribution patterns and suppress others.

The appearance of intensity curves with values smaller than 1, such as for instance 0.4 items per m², does not mean that any specific square contains 0.4 scraper, but, that the curve marks the border between areas with intensities below and above 0.4 items per m². The items of course appear in whole numbers in the squares. The purpose of the curves is exclusively to express the actual distributions graphically in a visually, easily understandable way.

In spite of the mechanical production of the graphical pictures, it must be stressed that visual inspection and comparison of distribution patterns expressed by equidistant contour lines, like interpretation of micro wear traces, X-ray pictures, the graphical output from geological equipment such as geo-radars and sediment echo sounders etc., is not an objective procedure. That is, the distinction between important features and unimportant features is a process influenced by such a subjective thing as experience.

A basic experience is that only clear structures should be given attention. 'Weaker' structures will in general - no matter how much energy is put into a refined analysis of them - only give ambiguous and blurred results.

Any attempt to estimate the 'significance' of the observed features statistically will be contradictory to the basic assumption that the distributions of at least some of the objects reflect conscious cultural manipulation. Their repeatability, however, may give an idea of their value as behaviourally 'meaningful units' (Johnson 1984:80).

## 1.5. The material

The available Maglemosian material from the North European Lowland, that is southern Scandinavia, south-eastern Britain and northern Germany, has been used as a basis for the analysis.

The choice of the Maglemose Culture for the analysis is due to a number of factors:

a) Many of the sites contain a large number of artifacts per m². This is important since basic distributional patterns can be distinguished only on the basis of intensities larger than 1, 2 or 3 items per m².

b) Many of the sites contain a large number of artifacts smaller than 4-5 cm, which ought thus to be less exposed to secondary deposition through cleaning of the living surface, than larger items.

c) Many of the sites appear as restricted concentrations of only 5-10 metres in diameter, and typologically as chronologically pure units. This improves the chances that the units analysed represent dwelling units used within a very restricted time interval.

d) In some cases dwelling remains are preserved such as floors made up of branches and bark with hearths on them, shallow dwelling pits, tent rings and in a couple of cases even what appears to be the lower part of the wall stakes. This makes it possible, to establish a relation between the distribution patterns and the dwelling structures.

It shall here be emphasized that by dwelling is meant any kind of hut, tent, windscreen or other structure that has given protection to the central living areas on the sites. To the present study of spatial organization, the types of physical superstructures connected to the different dwelling areas are regarded as irrelevant. The point is that the dwelling space is organized in accordance with a specific set of rules independent of its physical frames.

From ethnography we have examples of situations where the dwellings have no superstructure at all and the spatial rules are still observed. Elisabeth M. Thomas for instance notes a case from the Bushmen: 'The women had not built huts, but had scooped little hollows for themselves and their husbands, which they had lined with soft grass bedding, and had put up two arching sticks at each of these hollows to mark the place where the door would be if a scherm had been there, for the Kung as well as the Gikwe need a sense of place. In fact, the Kung need it even more, for without their grass and marking sticks the Kung feel homeless' (Thomas 1969:191).

## 1.6. Strategy

In chapter 2, we shall first deal with the Ulkestrup Huts, to discuss their character as huts, the fact that flint seems to be present inside the dwelling structures, wall effect, the rather complex dumping strategy that can be observed at Hut I, and a number of other questions. By virtue of their unique preservation and the extremely detailed and well documented excavation of Hut I, they will serve as the key localities for the further analysis.

Chapter 3 is an analysis of repeated distribution patterns at 30 localities. Chapter 4 presents the interpretation of the sites, the different types, their topographical locations and seasonal relations, whereas chapter 5 contains a discussion and a conclusion concerning the spatial and social organization of the sites.

All C14 datings are given as *uncallibrated* values BC.

# 2. The Ulkestrup Huts

The two Ulkestrup Huts were excavated in the bog Åmosen in central Zealand from 1947 to 1950 by Knud Andersen. They both revealed floors consisting of bark and branches, stakes that likely represent the walls of the dwellings, and an enormous number of organic objects such as a paddle, a fishing spear with a part of the shaft still attached, a fragment of a bow, numerous bone points, hazelnut shells, etc. Apart from this both sites yielded large amounts of flint which among other things contained numerous microliths. With regard to excavation technique, the floor of Hut I was excavated in accordance with Troels-Smith's 'systematical method' including exact 3-dimensional measurement of all 'foreign elements' (that is flint, bone, worked wood, charcoal particles and stones). Parts of the waste layer and the major part of Hut II were excavated by a more summary but less time-consuming technique. The finds were here registered in m²-squares, and a systematical registration of charcoal particles etc. was not accomplished. Compared to Hut I, this restricts the usefulness of Hut II, but seen as a whole, the two sites must constitute one of the most important materials for the study of settlement organization in the mesolithic. The following chapter is based on Andersen's publication of the material (Andersen et al. 1982:10-19) and supplemented by information from the excavation report (NM VIII jnr.4058, the Danish National Museum). References in this chapter with side numbers only, refer to the publication. Where I hold other opinions of the material than hitherto published, this is owing to a new detailed analysis of the material, which Knud Andersen has kindly let me have access to.

## 2.1. Hut I

A 0.5 metre broad drainage ditch running east-west revealed in 1947 the floor of Hut I. The measuring system for the excavation was placed so that the ditch took up the southern half of the m²-squares for y=9 south. To make the numbers of items from these squares, of which the one half is missing, comparable to those from the others, they have been multiplied by a factor of 2.

The site is C14 dated to 6050±115 BC (material from the waste layer, K-4998), 6100±115 BC (material from the waste layer, K-4999), 6190±100 BC (hazelnuts from the waste layer, K-2174) and 6420±130 (burnt tree from the waste layer, K-2175). According to Knud Andersen one scalene triangle on the floor is of a style similar to those from Hut II (:27,37). I have argued that this type is really a lanceolate type (Grøn 1987a:309). As such it does not in principle differ from the lanceolates belonging to Hut I. Since the two first C14 datings are of the best quality and the dating of the hazelnut shells has the smallest own-age, it must be concluded that the floor seems to be a chronological unit with a dating to approximately 6100 BC.

### 2.1.1. The floor

The excavation revealed a rectangular floor (fig.1). According to the larger pieces of wood and bark, which made up an apparent frame, the measures were approximately 6 by 4 metres connected to a concentration of lithic waste approximately 4 by 5 metres (fig.7B)(2). In the southern part, the end best preserved, the floor could be seen to consist of a dark upper layer approximately 5 cm thick, almost totally decayed and containing the main part of the flint and the other finds, and a lower part up to 11 cm thick, composed of bundles of branches. The branches were 5 to 6 cm thick, up to 25 cm long, and were mainly from birch, but also hazel and pine were represented. Between them were smaller branches, twigs, petiolates and a few leaves of the bracken *Lastrea thelypteris*. The frame as well as the lower part of the structure rested directly on the peat. The northern end of the floor was less well preserved. Here the dark upper layer rested directly on the peat. This is most likely due to a raising of the northern part of the hut (see 2.1.2) during a period with a higher water level, when it developed into a floating island. In periods with a relatively low water level the raised northern part has been much more exposed to decay than the lower southern one.

A north-south section based on the 3-dimensional registrations of the objects shows the situation in the northern part of the floor (fig.2). Clearly the northern ½ metre of the northernmost corner of the floating island together with the floor was at some time

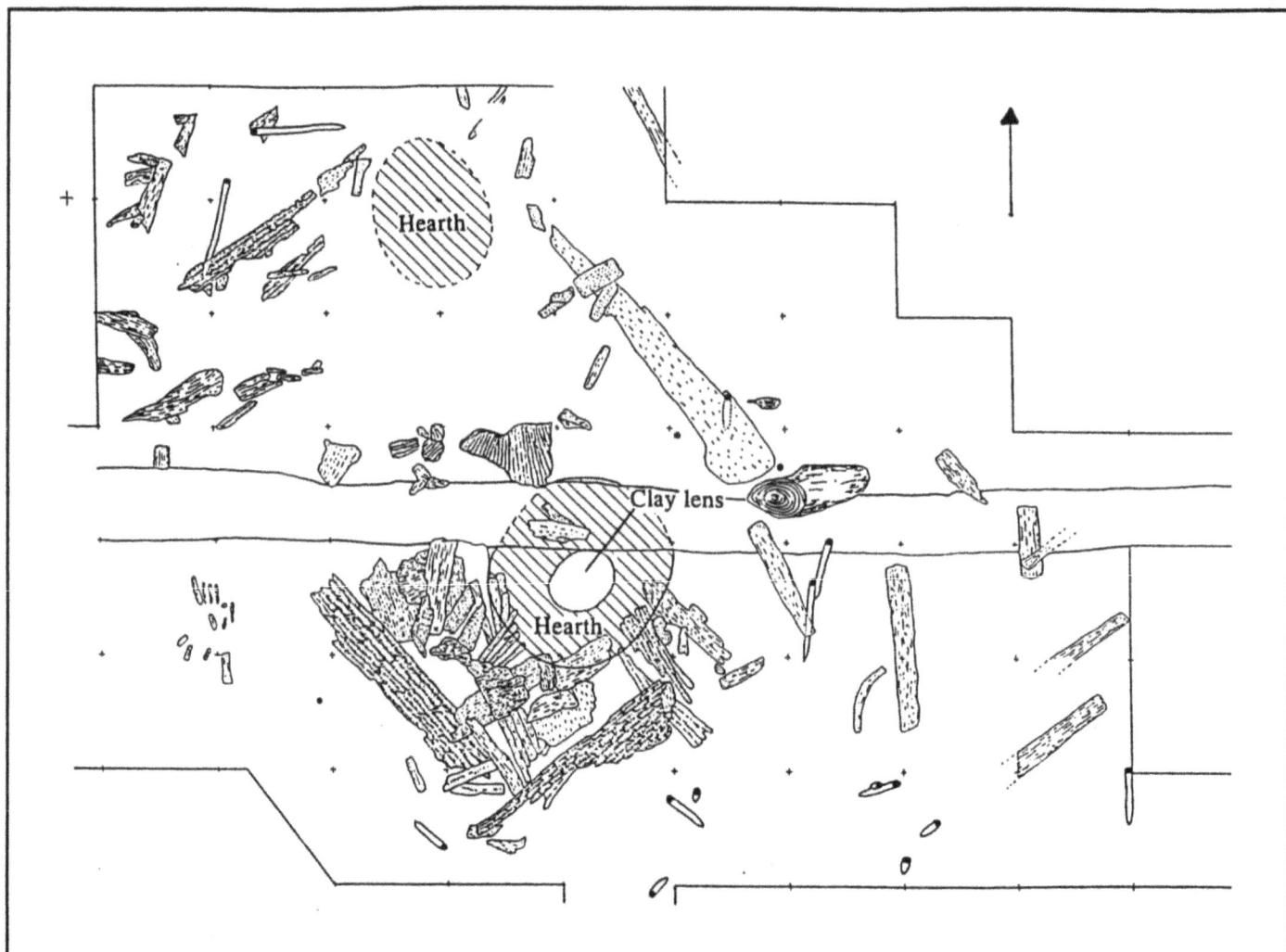

*Fig.1. The floor of Ulkestrup I, with stakes (the upper ends shown as black dots), hearths (hatched areas) and bark pieces.*

forced upwards, so that a break was formed in the peat of the floating island. The minimal change in its horizontal position most likely reflects that the floor and the vegetation held the island together. Some bones, stones and human flint seem to have slipped through the break from the inclining surface of the floor, and are found among the charcoal particles which appear everywhere under the floating island.

## 2.1.2. Hearths

According to the excavator, the only hearth observed was located centrally in the southern end of the rectangular floor. According to the report it consisted of 'sand in several layers, separated by layers of charcoal, everything is black and sticky!'. The sand contained 'some fire damaged flint, some bones and many hazelnuts'. The large, rather diffusely confined sand lens had a diameter of approximately 1.5 m, and it is mentioned that its western part was more

than 6 cm thick. In the bottom was a clay lens measuring approximately 70 by 40 cm, 3 cm thick. The hearth was placed on a 3-8 cm thick dark layer with much charcoal and one 10 cm long piece of wood. This again rested directly on the peat. This hearth is apparently closely related to the type from Duvensee W.6 described by Bokelmann (Bokelmann 1981a: 183).

A concentration of charcoal measuring approximately 50 by 40 cm was observed in the northern part of the floor. The report states: 'It lay only 2-3 cm under the harrowed surface, and may have been trodden into the peat, but it did not look as if this was the case'. It contained a couple of sand blotches, each measuring approximately 10 cm in diameter, some flint, hazelnuts, a small amount of wood and a fragment of a bone point (the latter has been identified as find nr. 9564). The excavators' notes are interesting on this point. A concentration of charcoal with no massive appearance of sand or

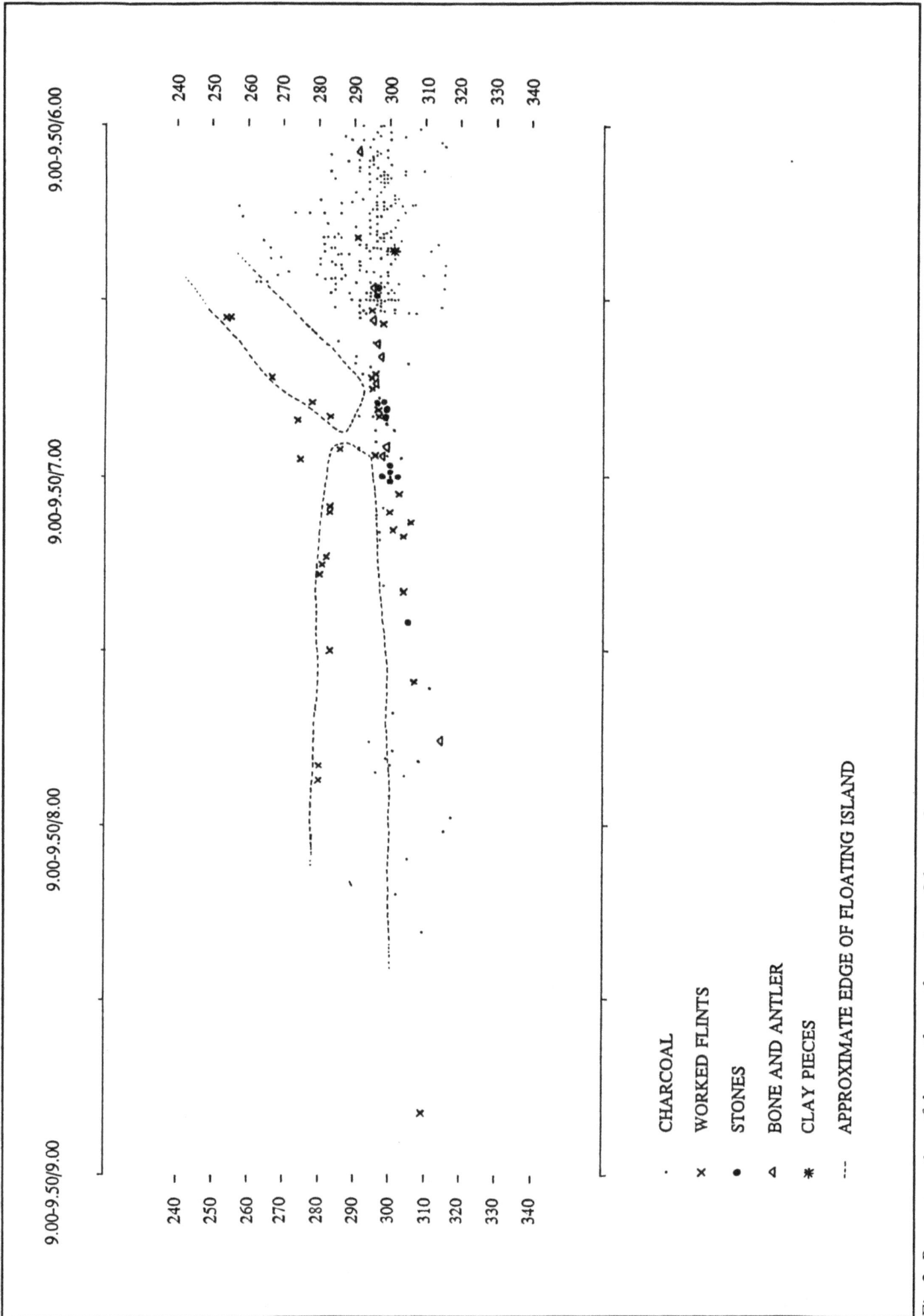

Fig. 2. *Reconstruction of the north-south section of the northern corner of the Ulkestrup II-floor.*

CHARCOAL

WORKED FLINTS

STONES

BONE AND ANTLER

CLAY PIECES

APPROXIMATE EDGE OF FLOATING ISLAND

or other structural elements differs from the hearth structures, as they are found in the peat areas. The notion that it 'might have been trodden into the peat, but this did not seem to be the case' also strongly indicates that we are observing a secondary deposition, and not a regular hearth, in spite of the fact that it was embedded in apparently undisturbed peat.

The excavator regards this feature as not belonging to the find horizon of Hut I. With a top level of 240

The possibilities of transport of material from the floor to a higher level are present since the northern corner, as we saw, at some time bent upwards to a level likely higher than 240 (fig.2). This happened only half a metre to the north of the charcoal concentration observed. Fig.3 shows what may have happened.

The fragment (nr.9564) found in the charcoal concentration is from a flat bone point made out of

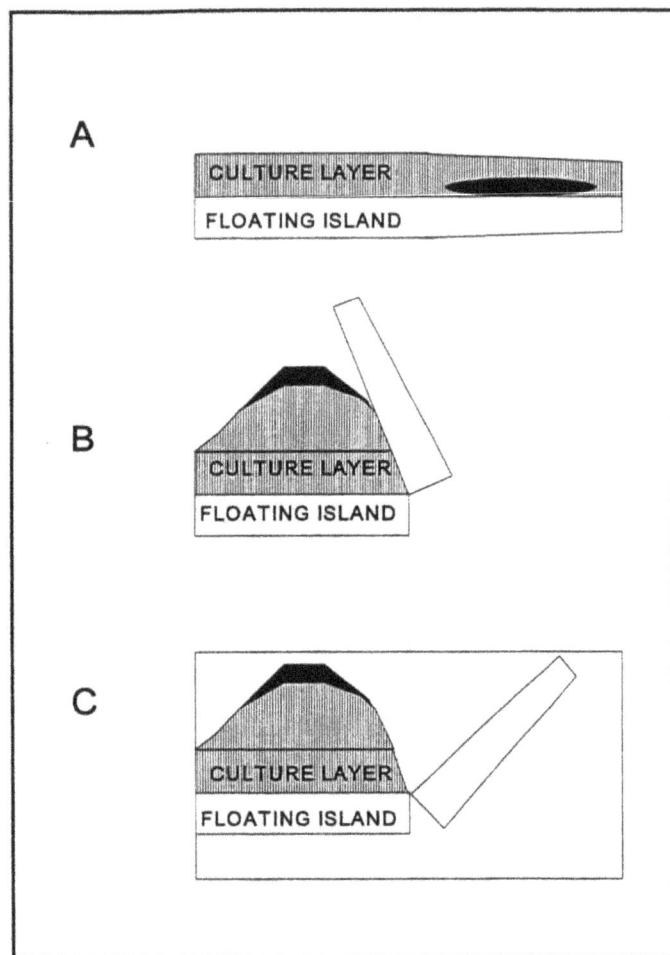

Fig.3. A sketch of how charcoal from the culture layer at Ulkestrup I, may have been elevated.

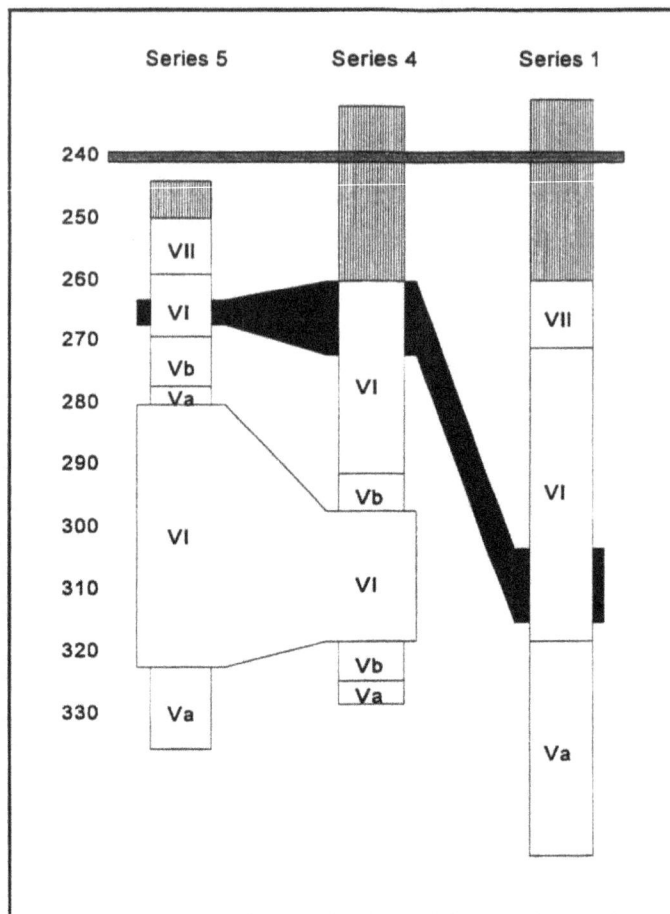

*Fig.4. The pollen series from Ulkestrup I.*

it was approximately 20 cm above the top of the latter, where this, during the excavation, was registered in the profiles, not less than 1 metre from the point of interest. The finds from the elevated concentration of charcoal were not registered three-dimensionally. The bone point fragment was related to the m²-square (8w,7s) and described as 'found at a higher level than the culture layer itself'. The remaining finds were registered as and mixed with the finds collected on the surface. The possibility that the charcoal concentration derives from the hut floor is discussed in the following.

a cloven rib, technically exactly similar to the most normal type found in the culture layer. The use of cloven ribs is characteristic for the Maglemose Culture. In contrast to the later cultures they had access to prey (aurochs and elk) that could provide the broad flat ribs necessary (Mathiassen 1948:36, Brinch Petersen, personal communication). It has unsuccessfully been attempted to refit the fragment with all fragments of bone points from the floor.

The pollen series 4 and 5 are from the area affected by the floating island. The culture layer on this structure is shown in black on fig.4, whereas the disturbance under it is shown as a white block,

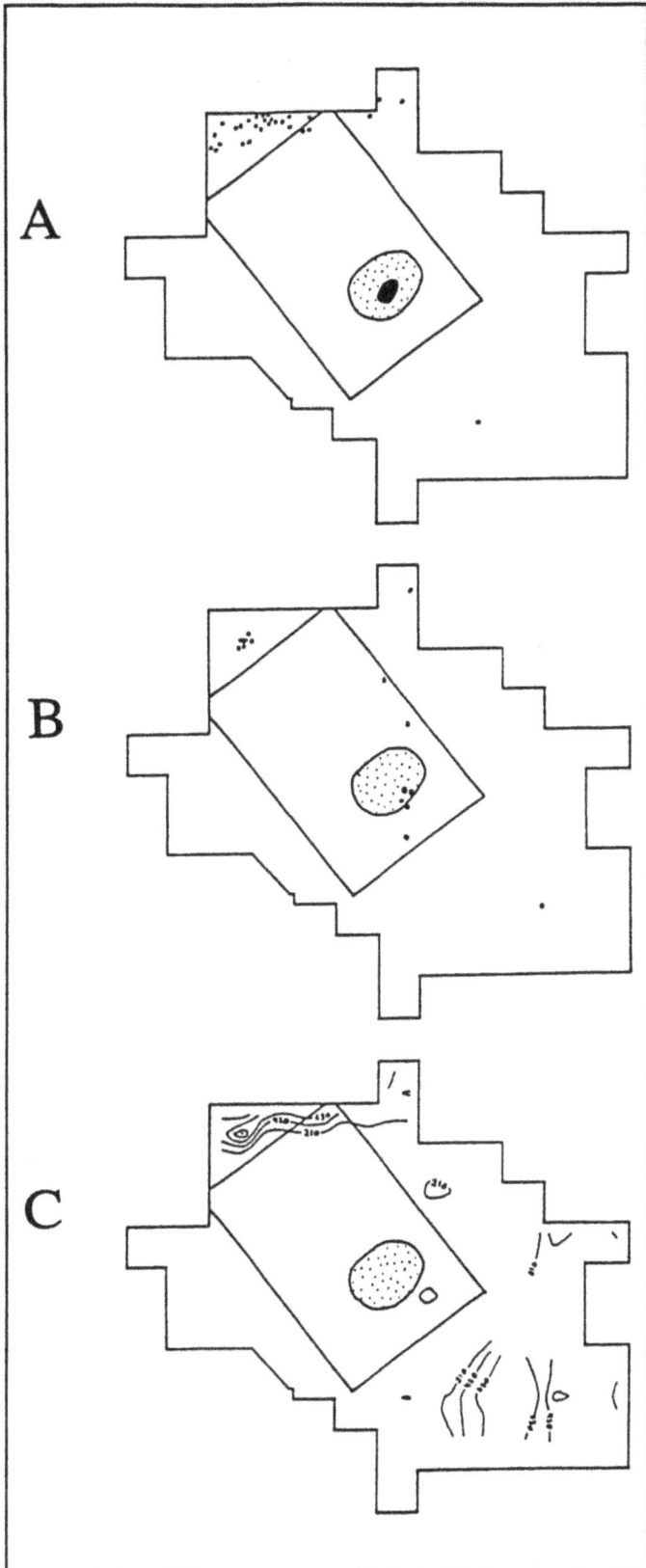

*Fig.5. Ulkestrup I. Distributions of A: clay pieces, B: charcoal 'heaps' and C: charcoal particles (equidistance =210 pieces per square metre).*

Jørgensens zone VII is the Late Atlantic (Ertebølle) (:109-136). The charcoal concentration is found 1 metre to the north of series 4, at level 240, in the area affected by the floating island. If the development of the local topography on this structure was as level as the top of the culture layer and the later topography indicates, then a Late Atlantic age is indicated for the charcoal concentration with the Maglemosian bone point fragment.

According to Knud Andersen, Hut I was localized *before* the drainage ditch intersected it, by the finds of flint, hazelnuts, bark and typical Maglemosian microliths on the surface. This happened during the harrowing of the area in 1947 (:8), and strongly indicates that the top of the culture layer of Hut I was affected by the harrowing. An upper, un-observed, Maglemosian horizon should, according to the palynological results (fig.4), appear in a milieu dated to the Late Atlantic, or later.

According to the excavator's stratigraphical obser-vations, the floor - with a top level of approximately 260 - was in general covered by 15 to 20 cm of undisturbed peat. Thus, we must assume that material from the floor, within a restricted area, was elevated to a higher level by the deformation of the northern corner.

It seems that a large amount of charcoal was present on the northern corner of the floor. The presence of the maximum intensity of charcoal pieces registered in the culture layer - 263 in one m²-square - was found just outside this corner. To obtain a more detailed picture of this distribution, an interpolation has been made on the basis of the intensities in ¼ m² squares (fig.5C). Some areas in the eastern part of the excavation are left blank, as the registration of charcoal particles here during the excavation was not sufficient. Five smaller 'heaps' of charcoal, not registered as 'charcoal particles' were also found in the square (11/6) with the maximum concentration (fig.5B). Only in the eastern part of the southern hearth was there found a similar concentration of 'heaps', four of them in square 7/10, and one in 7/11. Single 'heaps' were registered in - the squares 7/5, 7/7, 7/8 and 4/13.

In the squares 8-11/6 and 7/5, to the east and west of the north corner of the floor, was found a noticeable concentration of small clay pieces (a few centimet-

marked zone VI. Series 1 is taken to the north of the floating island. The culture layer is pollen-dated to early zone VI in Jørgensen's terminology, in accordance with the C14 dating to about 6100 BC.

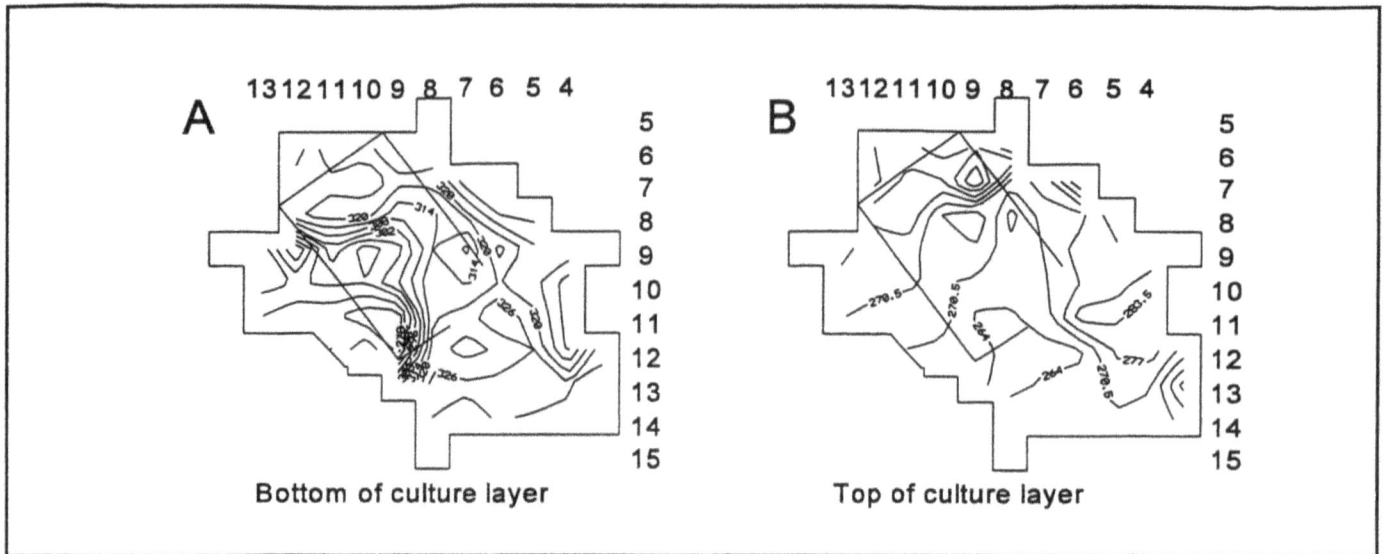

*Fig.6. Ulkestrup I. Bottom and top of culture layer. Equidistance: A: 6.0 cm, B: 6.5 cm.*

res in diameter or less). According to their distribution similar to that of the charcoal, they seem to have fallen off from the floor during its deformation (fig.5A). They may represent some larger piece of clay originally located on the northern corner. Clay on Maglemosian peat sites must be regarded as strongly related to hearth structures (the southern hearth of Hut I; the eastern hearth of Hut II) (Bokelmann 1971:11; Bille Henriksen 1980:57; Johansson 1990:13-14; Schwantes 1925:175).

In all, the charcoal blotch at level 240 seems to originate from the regular culture layer of Hut I. The latter layer actually contains independent indicators of the presence of a second northern hearth on the floor. Thus this floor seems to have been equipped with two hearths (fig.21A).

## 2.1.3. Superstructure

12 stakes stuck deep into the peat (fig.1), preserved in lengths between 30 and 175 cm, surrounded the floor in a way strongly suggesting the existence of a superstructure. The relatively large number of stakes connected to the western corner may have served to stabilize a structure surrounding an entrance. The position of the pieces of the frame and of a possible compressed walking path indicate that an opening may well have been located here (:16-17).

## 2.1.4. The coast line

According to Knud Andersen and Svend Jørgensen, the formation of the floating island took place after Hut I was abandoned (:17,135,136). Nonetheless Knud Andersen still seems to regard the edge of the floating island as an equivalent of the shore-line contemporaneous with the settlement and thereby to accept as a matter of fact that the water did reach the eastern corner, the north-eastern side and part of the northwestern gable during the habitation (:17).

The percentage of flint pieces with desilification of the surface (seen as bluish white to white colouring) might give an indication of the course of the contemporaneous coast line. In the Åmose basin generally only flint exposed to air has reacted chemically (Andersen 1983:17). However, only the flint material of the central part of the floor and to the west of it showed high percentages of de-silification, indicating that the chemical process was active during a - maybe rather long - period when the site was mainly submerged. We must conclude that this feature contains no information on the distribution of dry land and water during the phase of habitation.

Since there was no thorough registration of the top and bottom level of the culture layer, this was for each square estimated from the position of the three-dimensionally registered items.

Concerning the *bottom level* (fig.6A), this approach reveals that finds appear down to a level of 301-332 in all squares in the zone affected by the floating island and to the north, north-east and east of it. In the south-western part, where the floating island phenomenon was not present, they are found only down to the levels between 272 and 294. This must reflect an original bias in the level of the activity surface. In spite of the fact that the floating island blurs the original horizontal transition zone from the one to the other (the lower one clearly is over-represented) we must conclude that there has been a relatively high activity surface to the southwest, originally including the floor in a rather level state, and a lower one to the north-east. Connected to the lower zone is the 'waste layer'. It shows a far better preservation of organic materials such as for instance leaves and twigs (:16). The most reasonable explanation of the bias is that the latter zone re-presents the shore or the bottom of the lake just outside the site, not necessarily with an essentially lower top level than the land surface, but with the objects trodden deeper into it due to its sogginess.

Concerning the *top level* of the find yielding layer (fig.6B), a similar bias in two levels of the activity surface is indicated: a raised zone in the central and southern parts of the excavation and a lower one to the north and north-east. In spite of the fact that the raised zone comprises the area affected by the floating island, the border between the two zones appears to behave independently of its edge, and thus to give an impression of the topography prior to its formation. Therefore, a line running NW-SE close to the edge of the north-easternmost part of the exca-vated area, at least 1.5 metre from the floor, seems to represent a more logical border between land and water (fig.21A). A little but pronounced southwest orientated 'inlet' a few metres broad and long, just south of the floor, represents an area where the top of the culture layer is extremely low, as if the material had been worn away by some mechanical process. Since the structure is found at a right angle to the edge of, and mainly outside, the zone disturbed by the floating island, it cannot be explained as a consequence of this. Probably it represents an origi-nally water filled surface feature that may have been used for landing of light boats. This is sup-ported by the find of a paddle in its southernmost part (:82).

The method employed for the eastern part of the excavation was summary, and therefore it has been impossible to elucidate the course of the coast fur-ther on the basis of finer observations made here.

## 2.1.5. Deposition of waste outside the floor

The excavator, because of the good preservation, interprets 'the waste layer', south-east of Hut I (fig.7A - concentration A; fig.7B), as an underwater deposit contemporaneous with the habitation (:16). According to the course of the coast line supposed above, the layer was more likely deposited in the moist shore zone of the inlet. This may as well explain its good state of preservation.

Knud Andersen supports his point of view, that the waste layer consisted of material thrown out from dry land into the water, by noting that the largest and heaviest pieces of flint were found at the greatest distance from land (:16). Most likely some of the material was 'thrown' out, but a detailed analysis of the material points to more complex behaviour.

To achieve a better understanding of the deposition of waste on the site, the lithic waste has been separated into four categories: 'blades', 'micro blades', 'flakes' and 'irregular pieces' (pieces not fitting into the definitions of the three former cate-gories).

## 2.1.5.a. The 'waste layer' - waste concen-tration A

An analysis of the concentration A (fig.7A), tra-ditionally conceived of as 'the waste layer' shows that the different categories of waste take up dif-ferent positions in it. The bone waste is confined to the two squares (4-5w,13s) (fig.8F). The same ten-dency is valid for a number of smaller stones (1-10 cm in size)(fig.8H). Irregular pieces, flakes and burnt flints (fig.7E-G respectively) show a marked concen-tration in square (5w,12s), and is for the most confi-ned to this. Micro blades and blades (fig.7C,D) show a complementary concentration in square (5w,11s) with only a slight representation in square (5w,12s). Cores (fig.7H) show a marked concentration in square (5w,13s), and a somewhat smaller one in square (5w,11s). Bone points and their fragments (fig.8G) concentrate in the squares (4-5w,11-13s) and the bone and antler (fig.8F) show a concentration in the squares (4-5w,13s), and behave apparently complementary to the irregular pieces, flakes, blades, micro blades, and the burnt flints (fig.7C-G). Microlithic pieces as well as micro burins (fig.8A,E) concentrate in square (5w,11s), and have a somewhat weaker representation in (4w,11s). 'Square-knives' (fig.9B) concentrate in the square (5w,12s).

The remaining artifact types are not represented within this area in amounts that allow a reasonable analysis of their distributions. The charcoal particles registered in connection with this concentration reach intensities larger than 1000 per m² (fig.5C). It is impossible to make an exact comparison with their distribution in the western squares here since they are not registered in some of these.

The squares (5w,11-13s),(4w,10-13s) and (3w,11s) thus contain a deposit of highly spatially structured waste. This must imply that the material was placed deliberately in a more or less moist coastal zone. One gets the impression of a short term deposition with the material more or less gathered in heaps. Such a spatial structure would probably appear much more blurred if it had been deposited through a longer time interval and, even more so, if it had been deposited through several habitations.

## 2.1.5.b. The northern concentration of waste - B

In the squares (12w,7s) and (10-11w,6s) immediately north of the central part of the north-western end of the floor is concentration B, another pronounced concentration of waste, already mentioned in connection with the possible northern hearth. It consists of charcoal with concentrations of up to 1020 pieces per m², a number of charcoal concentrations or 'heaps', a large number of clay particles up to 2 cm in diameter (fig.5A-C), and up to 48 stones (measuring from 1 to more than 10 cm in diameter) per m² (fig.8H). A smaller concentration of bone material with up to 8 pieces per m² is also found there (fig.8F).

The distribution of the items that have been registered 3-dimensionally, shows that this waste concentration is confined to a 0.5 metre narrow brim adjacent to the end of the floor. Its western end appears inside the excavated area, whereas its eastern limit has not been uncovered. According to the sections 11.75-12.00 west, 6.00-8.50 south, 11.00-11.25 west, 6.00-8.80 south (:15) and 9.00-9.50 west, 6.00-9.00 south (fig.2) it is obvious that this concentration has been affected by the upheaval of the floating island. Whereas the charcoal particles seem to have been exposed to a considerable secondary redeposition (they are found in large numbers in the fluviatile deposits under the floating island), the heavier items such as worked flint, and other stone objects have been much more resistant to secondary dislocation, and to a large extent seem to have kept their positions on the floor - even on the northern corner when it tipped to a nearly vertical position.

One of the sections (:15) shows how some stones and charcoal particles were found on top of the floating island to the north of the floor, but still inside the area marked by the stakes. The shape of the concentration seems to support the idea that its extension to the north was restricted by a physical barrier - possibly a hut wall (fig.7A,B). In connection with the upheaval of the floating island much of the material has fallen to the lower level, most likely only with a slight horizontal displacement. The location of the stones, up to 30 in some of the ¼-m²-squares, does not fit Knud Andersen's idea of a serious dislocation of the material from the northernmost part of the floor (:17) caused by rather heavy waves. If such were the situation, it should have produced a much more dispersed pattern.

The conclusion is that the waste concentration B represents an original deposition of charcoal, stones and some bone material originally located inside and along the north-western border of the supposed superstructure. The contents, as already mentioned, support the idea of a hearth in the adjacent area.

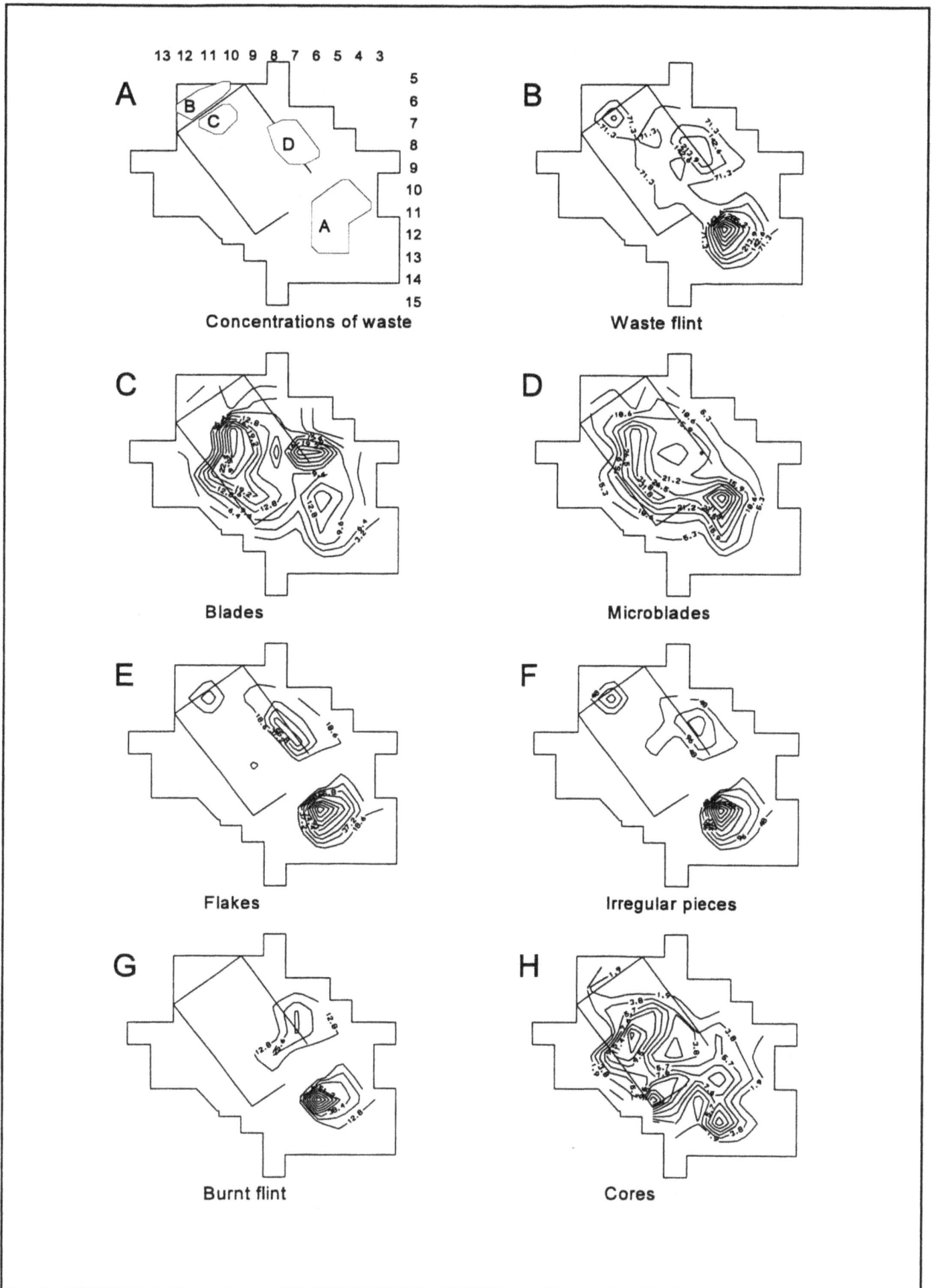

Fig.7. Ulkestrup I. Distributions. Equidistances B: 71,3; C: 3.2; D: 5.3; E: 18.6; F: 48.0; G: 12.8; H: 1.9.

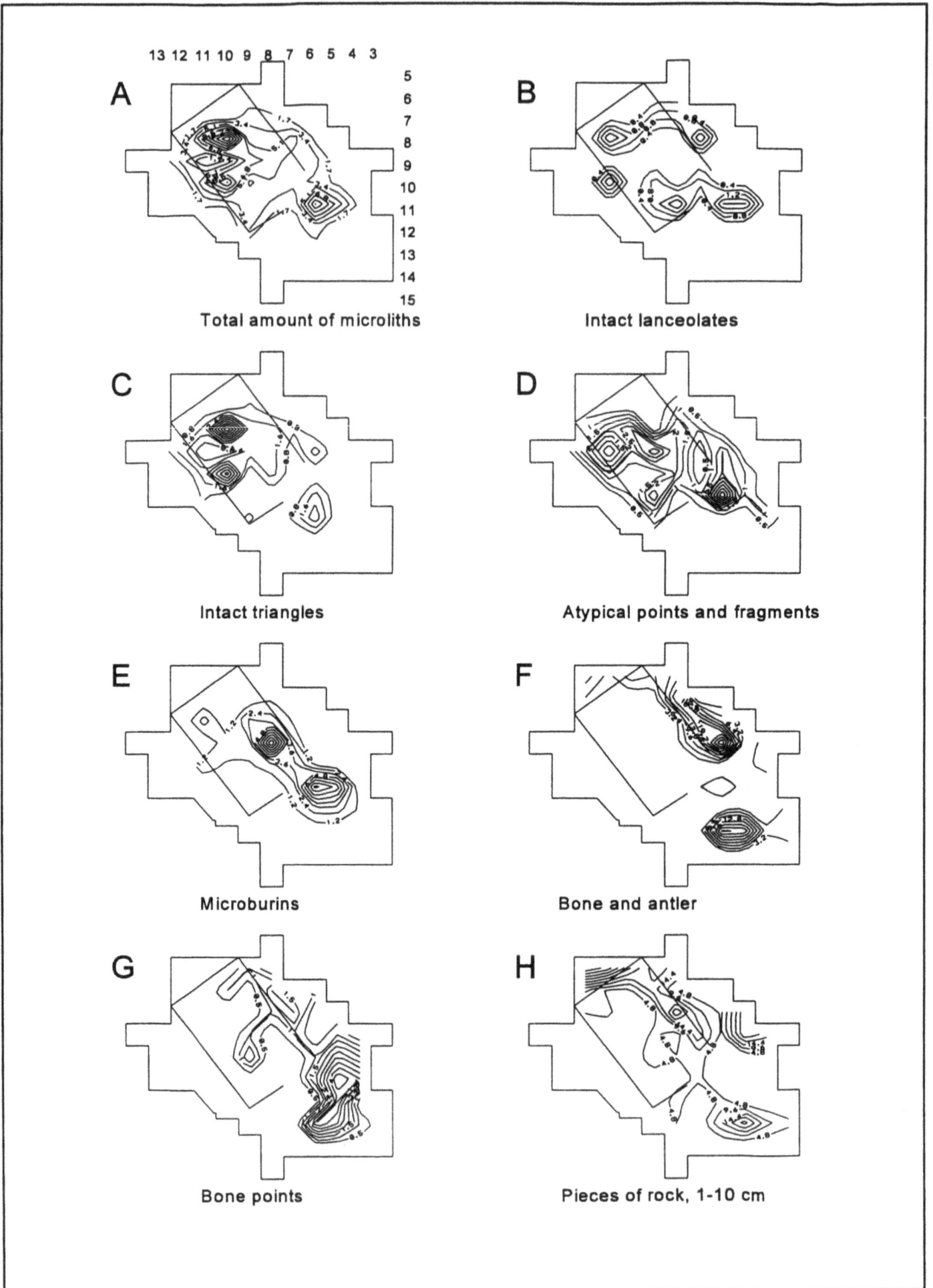

Fig.8. Ulkestrup I. Distributions. Equidistances A: 1.7; B: 0.4; C: 0.8; D: 0.5; E: 1.2; F: 3.2; G: 0.5; H: 4.8.

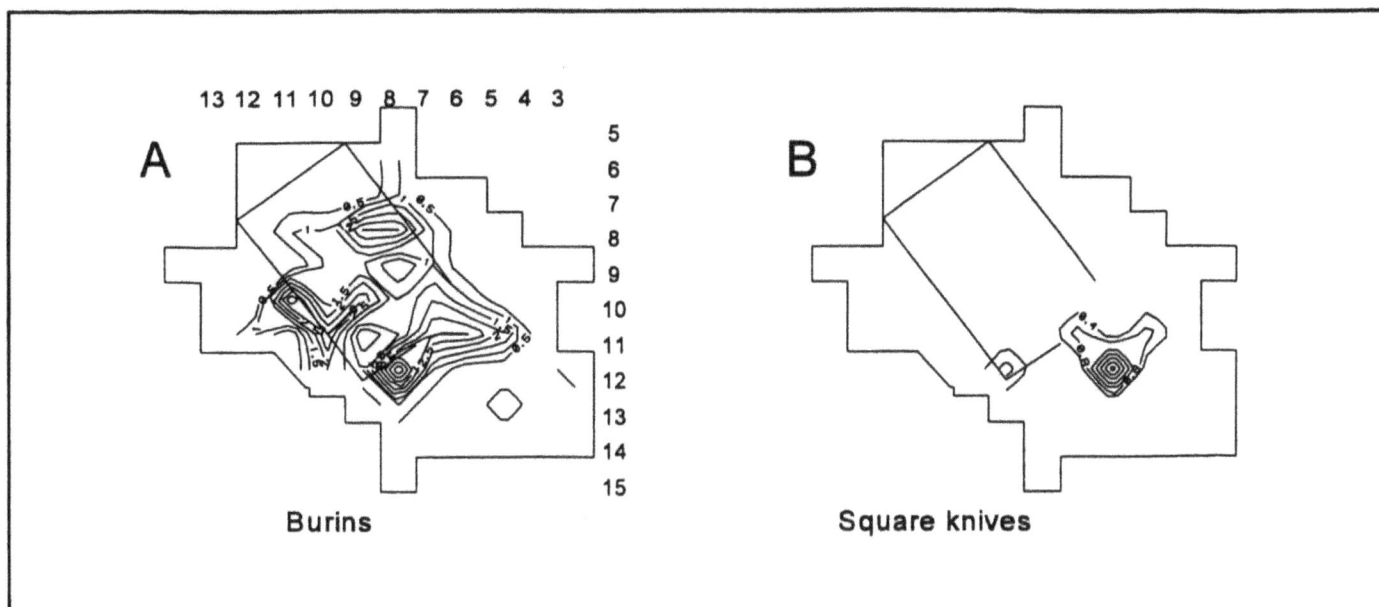

*Fig.9. Ulkestrup I. Distributions. Equidistances A: 0.5; B: 0.4*

## 2.1.6. Deposition of waste on the floor – the concentrations C and D

Interestingly enough, the floor has only extremely low concentrations of irregular pieces and flakes, except for two smaller concentrations. One is located centrally in the northern end (concentration C) (fig.7A) and consist of flakes and irregular pieces (fig.7E; fig.7F).

Another oblong concentration orientated NW-SE (concentration D)(fig.7A) runs parallel to and on the north-eastern edge of the floor. It consists of blades (restricted to its southern part)(fig.7C), flakes (fig.7E), irregular pieces (fig.7F), burnt flints (fig.7G), stones (fig.8H), bone and antler (fig.8F) and a low concentration of bone points (fig.8G) - but no concentration of micro blades at all (fig.7D).

The section 5.00-8.00 west, 9.00-9.50 south, through concentration D, at a right angle to the edge of the floating island (fig.10), shows a situation nearly identical to the one from the northern waste con-centrations (B and C) (fig.2). The edge of the floating island probably touches the stakes 8 and 9. The concentration is seen on the outermost part of the floor to the west of - and 'inside' - the two stakes 8 and 9. The material to the east of it, in square (5w,9s), contains a rather high percentage of bone waste. This has probably been washed down from the floor, thereby allowing good preservation of the bone under wet conditions (on the floor mainly burnt

bone pieces are preserved). Since the larger part of the flint and the stones have remained on the floor, the dislocating effect of the natural forces seems restricted. Probably this is another concentration of waste along the edge of the floor and inside the assumed superstructure, similar to the one consisting of B and C together.

Whereas the floor area, apart from the concentrations already discussed, contains flakes and irregular pieces only in extremely restricted relative numbers, there is no shortage of blades, micro blades and cores! It seems as if someone has removed the two former types from the floor and placed them outside in square (5w,12s) or swept them to its periphery together with the stones. It seems unlikely that a production of blades and micro blades should have taken place on the floor without leaving more flakes and irregular pieces than those found on it. The micro blades, blades and cores make up an oblong concentration in the central and southern part of the floor (fig.7C,D,H). The cores divide into two mark-ed concentrations, a central and a southern one.

A couple of burnt bone point fragments are pre-served at the location of the hearth (fig.8G). This is certainly due to the fact that burnt bone is better preserved than unburnt. It is very unlikely that it indicates a representative distribution pattern for this type.

The burins (fig.9A) show two concentrations inside

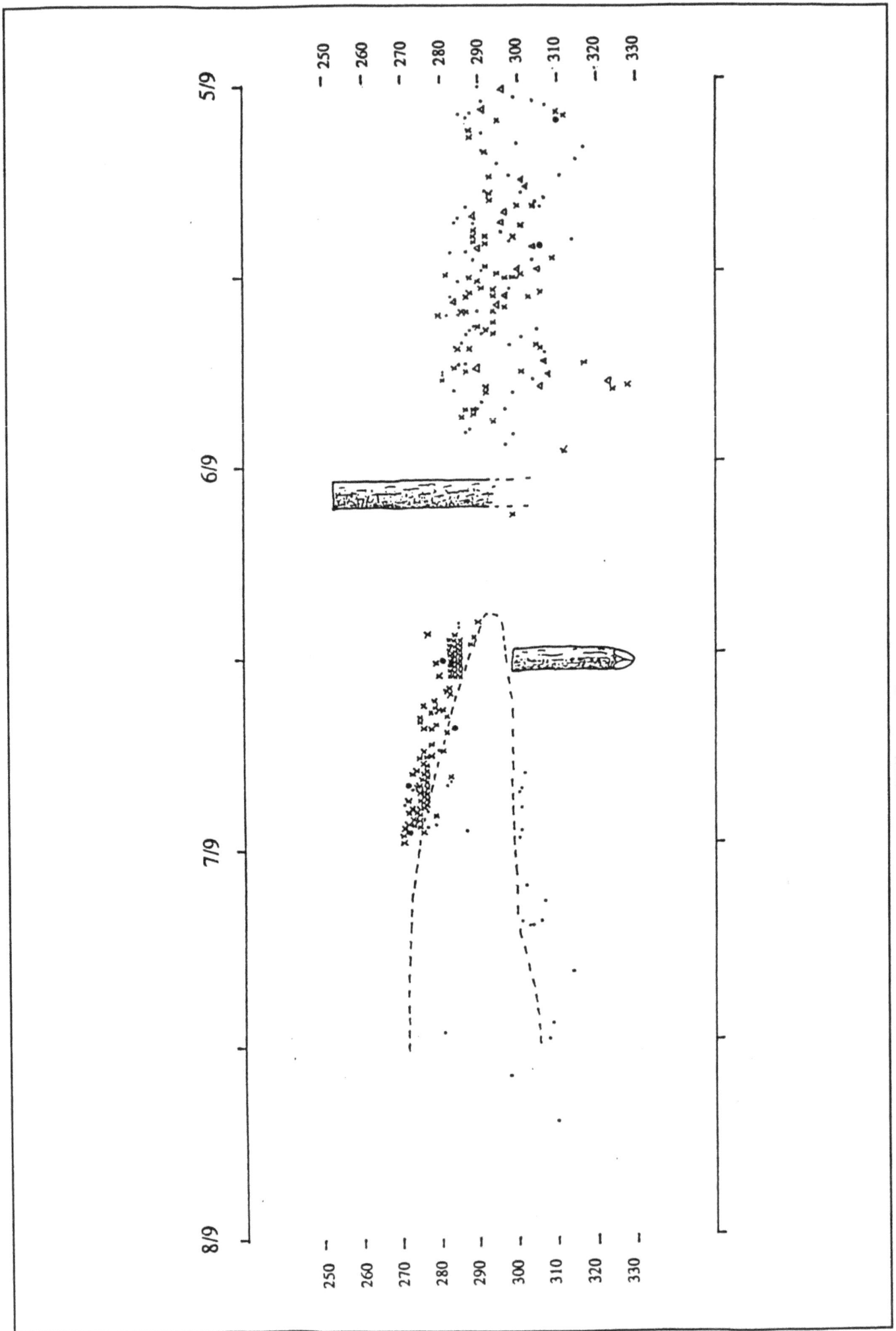

Fig. 10. The reconstructed section through the eastern corner of Ulkestrup I.

the floor, centrally located on each of its two sides. A third one is located outside the floor between its south-western corner and the stake structure to the south of it.

The distribution of burnt flint (fig.7G) shows a small concentration starting around the hearth and proceeding to concentration D on the eastern edge of the floor. A noticeable concentration is found outside the floor in square (5w,12s), together with the flakes and irregular pieces. The presence of a northern hearth is not reflected in this distribution. The flint pieces found with it were, as already mentioned, registered with the surface finds, and thus cannot be related to a specific square. A registration of these might have increased the percentage of burnt pieces there.

The general picture we have thus obtained is one of a rather well preserved and undisturbed unit. The significant absence of the two most numerous categories of lithic waste from the major part of the floor must be caused by cleaning. The general absence of bone on the floor must at least in part be due to bad preservation during one or more phases of low water level. Whether cleaning is a further reason is impossible to say. A dislocation of the lithic pieces left on the floor by wave activity seems unlikely, since they appear to have discrete and characteristic distributions. If the lack of blades and micro blades in the north-eastern part is due to such natural forces, then the cores, burins and the lithic waste on and close to the northern and eastern edge of the floating island should be lacking there as well. The largest amount of burnt flint inside the floor is found in connection with the well preserved hearth zone as should be expected. This is also the case with the few fragments of burnt bone points.

The coincidence between the edge of the floor, the location of the stakes and the northern and north-eastern edge of the floating island is probably not accidental. After the site was abandoned the floor must have developed into an at least 16 cm thick coherent mat of wooden pieces, bark and branches, covered by and held together by the vegetation and held in position by the stakes around it. During a rise of the water level, such a unit must not only have been extremely resistant, but also have given good protection against serious dislocation of the objects in it.

## 2.1.7. Distribution of microlithic waste

The microliths (intact pieces and fragments) (fig.8A) inside the floor area show a characteristic pattern consisting of two small concentrations, the northern one with up to 17 pieces per m², the southern one with up to 12 per m². They are separated by a zone with less than 8 pieces per m². The real numbers here are 4 items per m² and below, but as already mentioned (2.1.), they have been multiplied by a factor of 2 to compensate for the material removed by the ditch. The two concentrations occupy the western half of the floor.

Inside the two main concentrations of microlithic types, the distributions of the microlithic subcategories show a systematical difference in their distributions (3.1.6.). This strongly indicates that they represent different aspects of the main activities bound to different areas inside each of the two microlithic main concentrations and that the latter are not deliberately dumped material, where all the pieces would have been handled together as one category.

The micro burins (fig.8E) show quite another pattern. On the floor they have an extremely noticeable concentration in its eastern half in square (7w,9s). Outside the floor they concentrate in the squares (4-5w,11s) like the other microlithic pieces.

## 2.1.8. The hut and its organization

The floor coincides more or less exactly with the stakes. The eastern and the north-western oblong concentrations of waste (D and B+C respectively) appear to represent material originally located on the floor and with a distribution stopped by a physical structure coinciding with the stakes. Outside the floor, lithic waste is only found in larger amounts in concentration A close to the eastern corner. Everything indicates that we are concerned with the remains of a dwelling structure, a hut, and that its floor contained quite a number of sharp blades, micro blades and cores as well as of microlithic pieces. The indications of a systematical clearing out of material from the floor into a spatially structured waste area outside it is a suitable notion.

On the floor the microliths are distributed in two

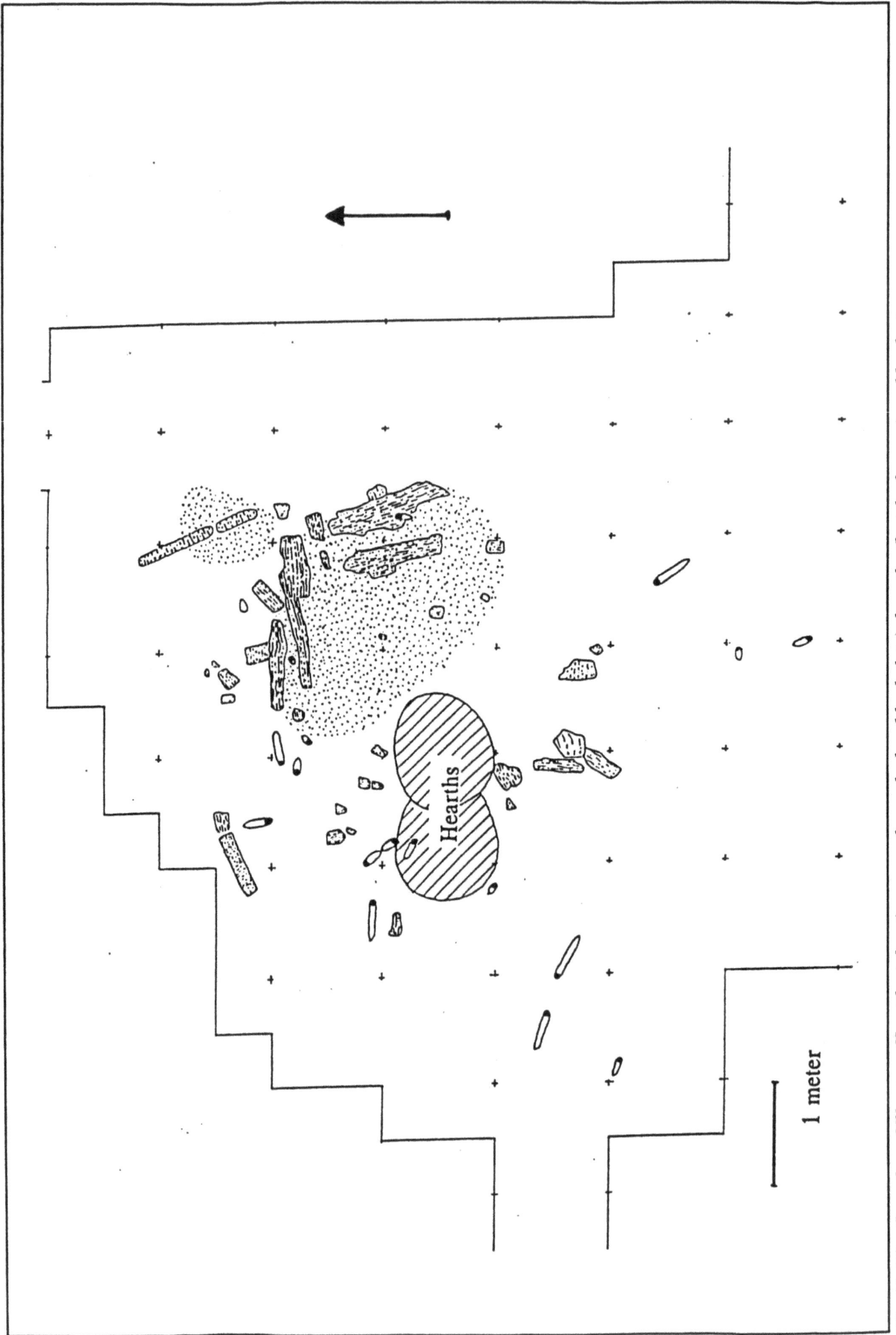

Fig. 11. The floor from Ulkestrup II, with stakes (upper ends marked as black dots), hearths (hatched areas) and bark pieces.

1 meter

similar concentrations, which according to their similar internal structuring are unlikely to represent tossing or dumping, but instead a conscious handling of microlithic material (3.1.6.). As microliths, due to their size, are rather resistant to cleaning, we may assume that we are dealing with primarily deposited microlithic pieces representing two congruent activity areas and their spatial locations. The two concentrations of cores on the floor correspond spatially to these. If we furthermore assume the existence of a second northern hearth contemporaneous with the floor, we have indications of two spatially separate activity zones containing a repeated set of elements each with a similar spatial organization (fig.21A).

### 2.1.9. Chronological unity of the material

From a typological point of view the Hut I seems to constitute a single chronological unit (Andersen et al. 1982:78,79; Brinch Petersen 1972:72). On such a basis it is of course impossible to say whether the material constitutes one or more habitations through a period of a few years. However, it must be noted that all triangles from Hut I are 'left-orientated', and that there are thus no indications of different habitation phases as with Hut II (:26,27,61)(2.2.7.).

A good argument that the material only represents one habitation phase is that delicate spatial patterns such as the internal organization of the microlith concentrations and the different types of waste in the 'waste layer' are not blurred.

### 2.2. Hut II

In centre to centre distance Hut II was located 28 metres southwest of Hut I. Due to the more severe damage on the floating island here, and to the less detailed excavation technique employed, the collected data are a bit more complicated to interpret. This unit is C14 dated to 6030±115 BC (material from the waste layer, K-4997), 6230±100 BC (birch trunk from the destroyed floor, K-2176), 6220±120 BC (two birch-bark rolls from the floor, K-1507), 6080±140 BC (burnt pine tree from the waste layer, K-1508) and 6100±140 (tinder fungus from the waste layer, K-1509) and thus approximately to 6100

BC (Andersen et.al. 1982:77; Andersen, personal communication).

In terms of normal typology the site must be regarded as a single chronological unit (Grøn 1987a: 309). On the basis of the microliths Andersen distinguishes between one phase of habitation with microliths similar to those from Hut I, and another with microliths of another style (:37,61). This distinction will be discussed in the following paragraphs (2.2.7. and 2.3.)

### 2.2.1. The floor

The floor (fig.11) was far less well preserved than that of Hut I. Apart from a few pieces of bark and the remains of a few branches, the main part is described as 'a totally dissolved floor layer'. The floor and the area south of it were full of cracks which had split the underlying swamp peat into blocks. Flint and sand had fallen into the cracks (:18).

### 2.2.2. Hearths

According to the stratigraphic observations there were two hearths, the western one partially overlapping the eastern. The 'upper' one, mainly restricted to square (25w,29s), was represented by a sand layer covering the remains of a badly preserved clay lens similar to the one found in Hut I. Separated from this by a layer of dark culture soil, the other one was observed as a lower sandy layer, mainly confined to square (26w,29s) (:18,19). Most likely both hearths had a larger extension than indicated by the ob-servations. The presence of two stratigraphically separated hearth structures indicates two habitation phases on the site. The situation may in principle not differ from that which Schwantes observed in Duvensee (see 2.2.7.).

### 2.2.3. Superstructure

16 stakes make up a regular 'trapezoid' U-shape 4 metres broad and 4.5 metres deep. As positions for the stakes the top-coordinates have been used. Their bottom-coordinates may differ substantially from these, among other things due to the possible

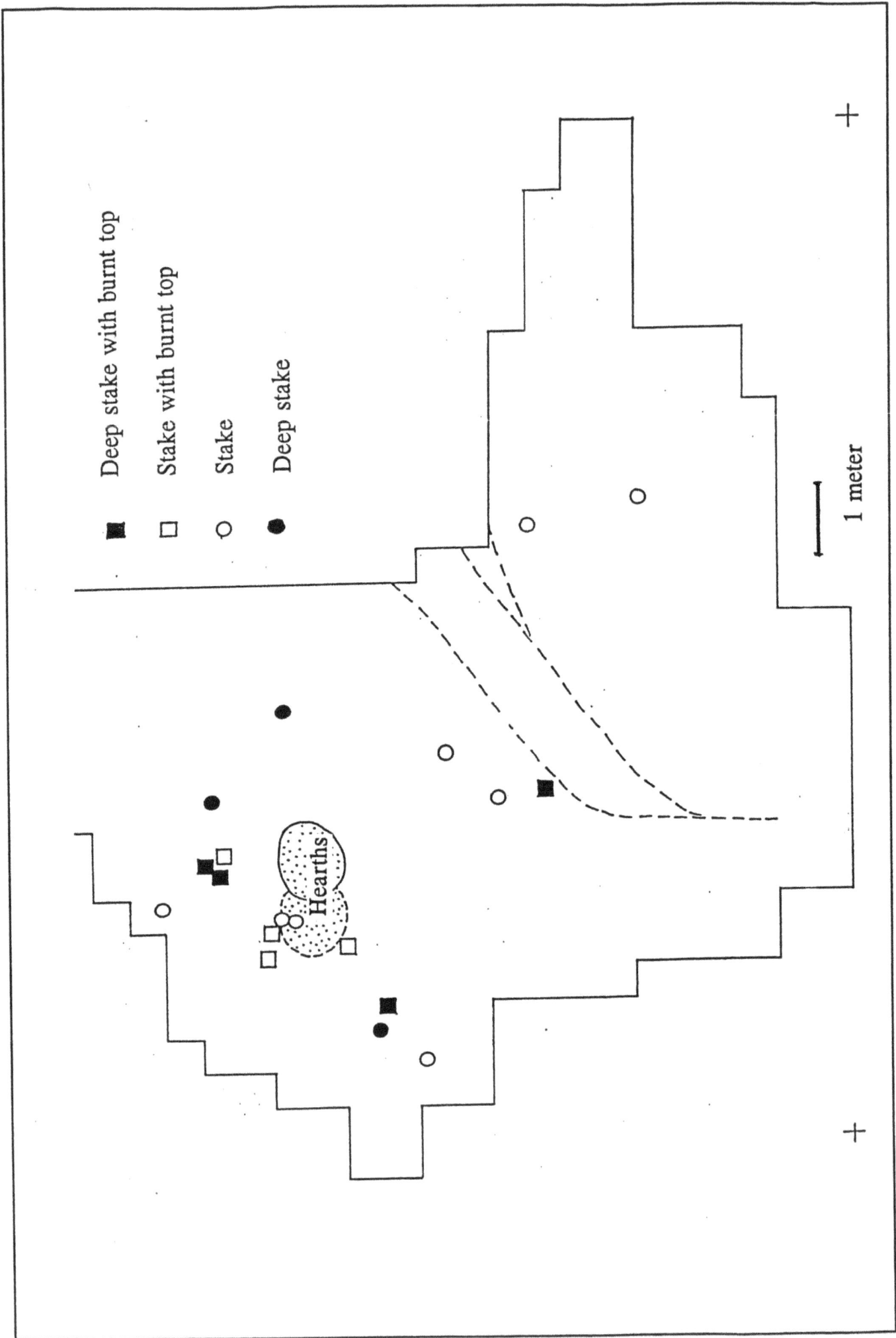

Fig 12. The stakes and the edge of the floating island at Ulkestrup II.

**Legend:**
- ■ Deep stake with burnt top
- □ Stake with burnt top
- ○ Stake
- ● Deep stake

Hearths

1 meter

secondary horizontal movement of the floating island. The top-coordinates must be most directly related to the original settlement surface and its features (Knud Andersen has used the bottom-coordinates). According to the distribution of the remains of the floor, the stakes seem to mark its border. 7 stakes reach a level equal to or deeper than 310, 2 reach level 305 and 8 do not go deeper than level 294. The top level of the surface is around 275. Six out of the seven deepest ones make up the corners: 2 the western, 2 the northern, 1 the eastern and 1 the southern one. The last one is placed centrally in the north-eastern wall (fig.12).

The southernmost stake in the south-eastern wall is burnt at the top, whereas this is the case with seven of those related to the north-western wall. To speak of one burnt and one unburnt line of poles in the north-western wall, as the excavator does (:19), is not consistent with the data. The main part of the burnt stakes are found relatively close to the hearth zone. Cinders hidden in the sand used in and around the hearths used for roasting etc. (see Bokelmann 1981a:183 for detailed description of the use of such a hearth or 'röststelle') may have scorched the stakes at surface level without causing a regular fire. However, the two deep stakes at each corner of the north-western wall may indicate that this was renewed/strengthened at some time, possibly in connection with a second phase of habitation.

## 2.2.4. The coast line

The exact course of the coastline contemporaneous with the habitation of the hut is impossible to reconstruct. Most likely it was to the south-east of the edge of the floating island, as Knud Andersen is also inclined to think (:19). Thus the 'waste layer' should have been deposited in a moist coast zone or on dry land. At least the water cannot have been too far away toward the south-east.

## 2.2.5. The distribution of waste

The distribution of lithic waste (fig.13A) is different from what we saw at Hut I. There are slight differences in where the different categories have their main concentrations *outside* the hut area, but generally the waste concentration south-east of the hut is far less structured spatially than the one at Hut I. Micro blades, flakes and irregular pieces (fig.13C, D and E respectively) occur with only relatively low concentrations in the squares (22w,32-33s),(23w,31-33s) and (24w,32s), outside the hut, whereas blades (fig.13B) appear in relatively large and noticeable concentrations in the squares (24w,33s), (23w,35s) and together with a concentration of cores (fig.13G) in (22w,32-33s).

The main concentration of lithic waste in this case is found in the north-eastern half of the hut area with quite similar distribution patterns for blades, flakes, irregular pieces and burnt flints. Micro blades (fig.13C) show a slight, but not very noticeable, preference for square (24w,30s), whereas cores (fig. 13G) clearly are concentrated in the two northern corners (23w,29s) and (26w,28s).

The burnt flint (fig.12,13F,20A) is concentrated inside the hut area, in a zone to the north and east of and partly overlapping the hearth zone. Outside, smaller concentrations are found immediately south of the hut area in square (26w,32s) and also in square (23w,33s).

The distributions of charcoal and bone are not representative due to their unsystematical registration.

Burins (fig.14D) show a noticeable concentration in the squares (22w,33-34s) outside the hut area and inside it, in its eastern corner (24-25w,29-30s).

Scrapers (fig.13H) make up an oblong concentration south of the southern corner (24w,32s),(23w,33s). A concentration to the north of the northern corner (26w,27s) must most likely be connected to the area outside the hut, whereas the concentration in square (27w,29s) probably belongs to the inside.

Knives and square-knives (fig.14E) both show noticeable concentrations inside the northern corner in the squares (26w,28s) and (25w,29s).

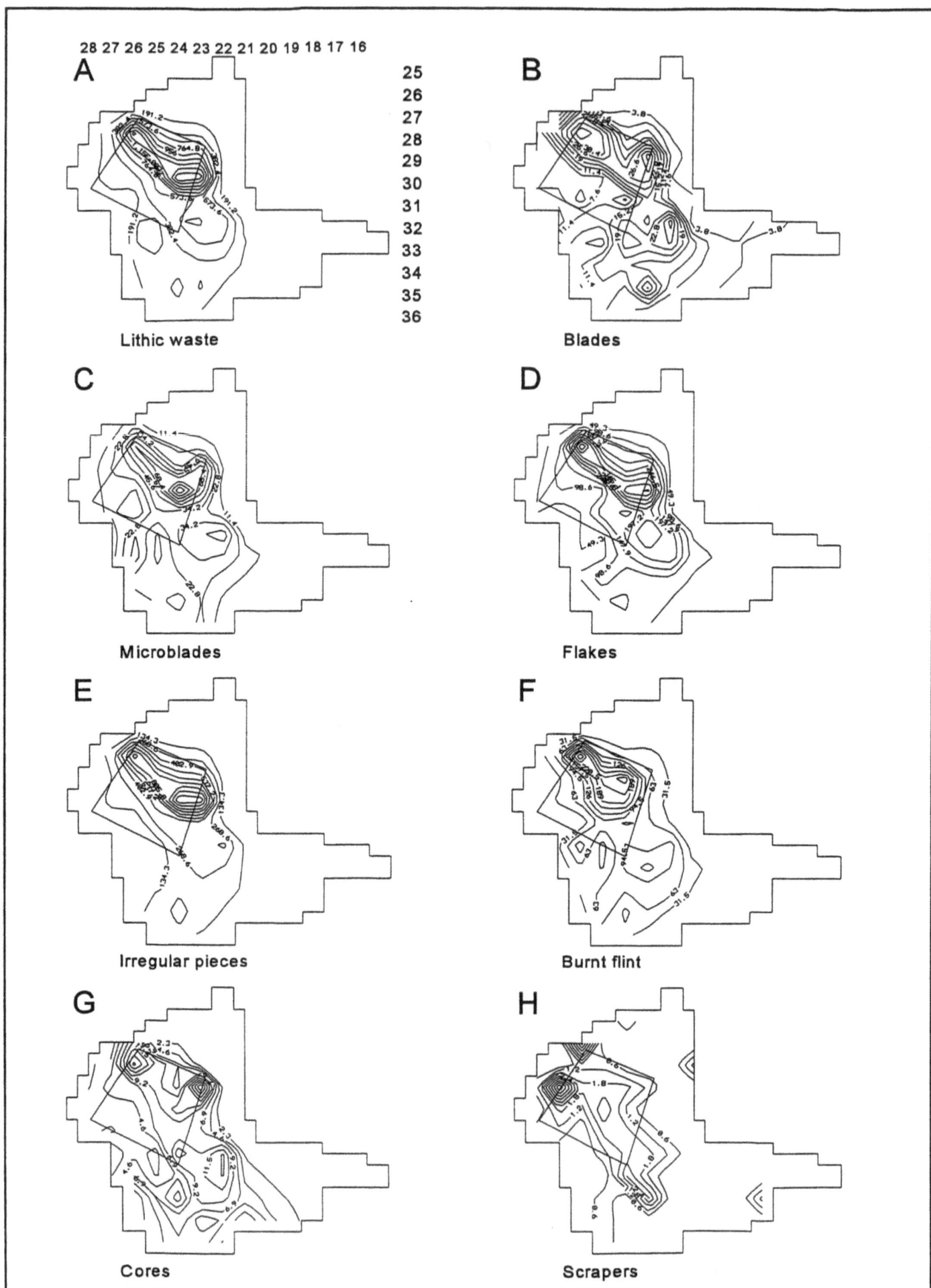

Fig.13. Ulkestrup II. Distributions. Equidistances  A: 191.2;  B: 3.8;  C: 11.4;  D: 49.3;  E: 134,3;
F: 31.5;  G: 2.3;  H: 0.6

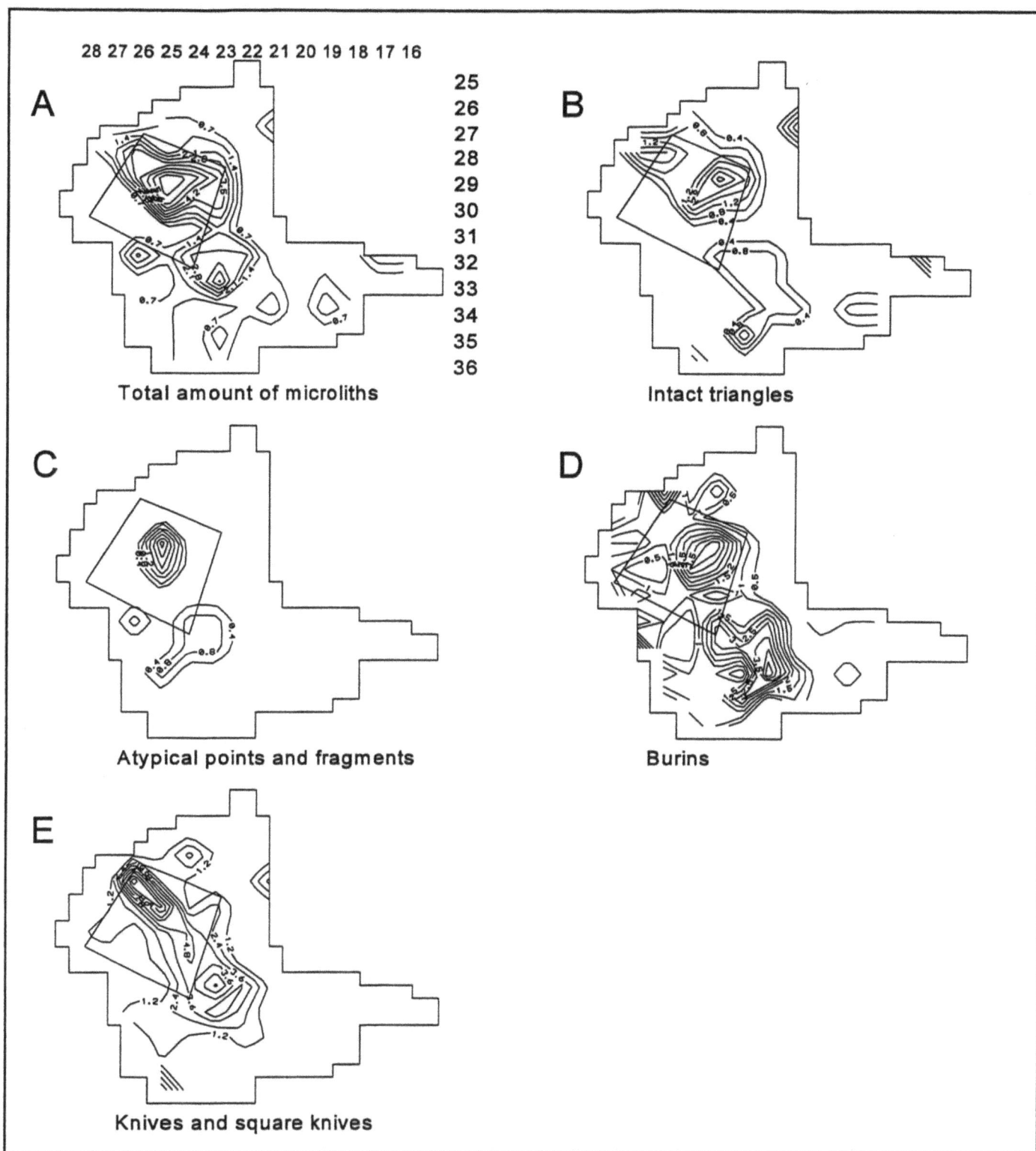

Fig.14. Ulkestrup II. Distributions. Equidistances  A: 0.7;  B: 0.4;  C: 0.4;  D: 0.5;  E: 1.2

## 2.2.6. Distribution of microlithic waste

The microlithic pieces (fig.14A) are confined to the north-eastern half inside the hut, with the main concentration in square (25w,29s). The intact triangles (fig.14B) have their main concentration in square (24w,29s) just to the east of the hearths, whereas indeterminable microlithic pieces and fragments (fig.14C) are strictly concentrated in square (25w,29s). The high degree of fragmentation and fire damage here may be due to the activities related to the hearth zone. Due to the small numbers of lanceolate points and other sub-types, a more detailed analysis of their relative distributions is irrelevant.

31

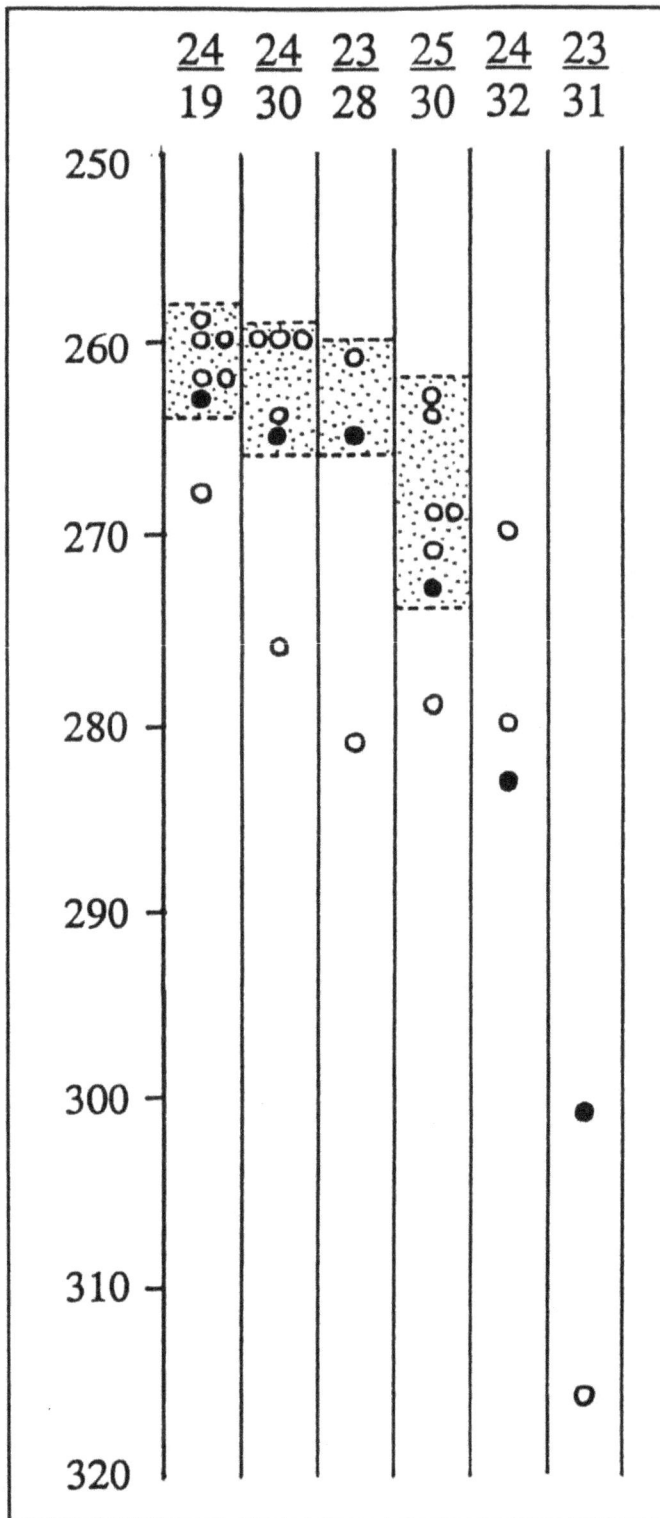

*Fig.15. The stratigraphical positions of the right-orientated triangles (circles) and the left-orientated triangles (dots), relative to the culture layer (shaded area).*

of the culture layer, deeper than the other microlithic pieces. 17 microlithic pieces appear at a higher level than the left-orientated triangles, whereas only 5 appear below them (fig.15). From the levelling at least three of the latter 5 appear to be out of context with the culture layer, probably because they have fallen into cracks in the peat (2.2.). It thus seems likely that the left-orientated triangles are connected with the lower hearth with its centre in square (26w,29s). They are found to the east of the hearth zone, like the main concentration of the remaining microlithic types.

Outside the floor the microliths appear with the same large relative concentration south-east of the hut as did the lithic waste.

## 2.2.7. The hut, its organization and chronological factors

The line indicated by the stakes serves as a border for most of the distributions studied. It seems to have served as some kind of physical screen, and Knud Andersen's assumption, that we are dealing with a hut, appears correct. The major part of the lithic waste in this case occurs inside the dwelling area, originally on (or in) the floor.

The location of an outer waste concentration adjacent to the southern corner, and the fact that many of the distribution patterns 'pass through' the border of the hut area here, indicates that this is the probable position of an entrance, possibly connected with the two extra stakes here.

Everything seems to suggest that Hut II was inhabited twice. The double corner stakes in the northwestern wall may imply repair during a phase of reuse of the hut. It is important to note that the hearths, and, as far as we can see, also the two concentrations of microliths took up approximately the same positions in the dwelling space. *Thus, the presence of two phases of habitation in the dwelling does not seem to disturb our analysis of its spatial organization.* Actually the situation seems similar to the one Schwantes observed in Duvensee where several bark floors were found the one on top of the other: 'Vielfach in bestimmter Regionen übereinander liegende mit Sand oder Ton abgedichtete

Knud Andersen distinguishes between left and right-orientated triangles in the material from hut II, suggesting that this difference in orientation reflects the working habits of different persons (:26,27). In the 6 squares where both left and right-orientated triangles appear, the former are found in the bottom

Aschenschichten deuten darauf, daß der Herd bereits einen festen Platz im Wohnraum hatte' (Schwantes 1925:175).

The spatial structuring of the waste layer with more or less congruent distributions for all the different types is what one ought to expect at a site with more than one habitation phase.

## 2.3. Conclusion and a postulate

The distributions of items that show no characteristic patterns or appear in so small numbers that they cannot be regarded as reliable have been omitted from the discussion.

We have seen what must be conceived of as two dwellings containing large concentrations of lithic waste as well as two different patterns of spatial organization inside them. Hut I has two 'congruent' concentrations of microliths and one, more likely two, hearths, whereas each of the two phases of Hut II appears to have only one concentration of micro-liths and one hearth. Hut I seems to have been inhabited only once, whereas three independent observations indicate that the latter was inhabited twice, each time with an identical organization of the dwelling space. The first phase may well be con-temporaneous with Hut I and the second, due to the repair not very much later.

The postulate is now that Maglemosian dwelling spaces in general (wind screens, tents, huts, houses etc.) were organized in accordance with one of the two patterns observed here (fig.20-23).

We may expect that a number of different dwelling types and constructions were in use at that time, but as Tanner writes about the Mistassini Cree: 'Whether it was a small oblong wall tent, a large dome tent, a wooden framed, canvas covered tent or a log cabin, the standardized internal arrangement is such that the dwelling seems to always occupy the same place' (Tanner 1979:73).

The internal arrangements of the two Ulkestrup Huts with their wall stakes preserved are thus used as models for the remaining sites. In the following chapters we shall try out this hypothesis by analy-sing the remaining sites suited for analysis.

# 3. Analysis of general distribution patterns

## 3.1. Introduction

In the search for repeated distribution patterns on the Maglemosian sites, all accessible distributions have been analysed and compared. The present analysis is restricted to these distributions, that seem related to such repeated patterns. As already mentioned (1.2.2.a.), only the object types smaller than 5 cm (eg. the microlithic pieces) show such clear, characteristic and repeated patterns. Inside the main concentrations of material, concentrations of burnt flint, mainly consisting of small burnt fragments (1.2.2.a. and 3.1.5.), seem to give a reasonable idea of the locations of hearths not preserved. The distributions of the lithic waste, including flakes, micro blades and blades, appear as the large, not too clearly confined main concentrations that seem to coincide with the dwelling areas (3.1.4.), in most cases connected to a lower lying tongue of waste, the 'waste layer'.

The remaining item types, possibly due to their restricted numbers and larger size, show no consistent and repeated patterns. Some of their distributions are shown in the catalogue. If it is possible at all to distinguish general distributional traits with these items, a much larger number of excavated sites than the one available today will be necessary.

A number of excavations not of prime quality have been included in the analysis because it is regarded as important not only to demonstrate that *some* sites fit the patterns postulated, but also that the reliable patterns observed at the excavations of a lower quality do *not* contradict the regularities postulated.

To improve the comprehensibility of this work, the basic data of the sites are represented in table 1. A concise description of each of the sites with distribution plans, references to publications, reports, datings and personal communication with the excavators is found in the catalogue. The site numbers in the table refer to their numbers in the catalogue. Table 1 yields information on a number of factors discussed further below. The sites have been separated into three groups: one with close affinities to Ulkestrup II, one with close affinities to Ulkestrup

I and a group of problematic sites from which only little reliable data of relevance for this analysis can be extracted. This group also comprises the two so-called Maglemose dwellings Tingby and Lavringe Mose. In the catalogue are presented arguments that these are probably not dwellings.

The figures 20-23 are iconographic representations of the concentrations of flint, microliths and burnt flint/hearths on the sites. They also show the course of the shore-line or, if it is distant, the direction to it. The numbers here also refer to the catalogue numbers of the sites.

## 3.1.1. References to the catalogue (column 1)

In table 1 the sites are represented by their name and the number they are given in the catalogue (6.). The first column contains their names and numbers. Round brackets ( ) around a name show that some of the information related to this site must be taken with some precaution. Square brackets [ ] around a name show that some or all data related to this site are directly unreliable.

The single values in the table that must be taken as reliable with some precaution are given in round brackets. Values that seem likely, but not more, are marked by square brackets. Values it is impossible to give a reasonable estimation of are marked by one or two question marks, marking decreasing reliability.

## 3.1.2. Distances and directions to the prehistoric shore-line (columns 2 and 3)

The changing water levels of the prehistoric inland water systems do not allow simplistic assumptions about the course of their prehistoric shore-lines. However, in many cases it is obvious from the preservation of the settlement material that some parts of it must have been deposited under anaerobe conditions - that is under water or trampled into the mud of a moist shore zone - whereas other parts are less well preserved due to their exposure to oxygen on the settlement surface. Differences in patination due to different conditions for desilification may also be a good indicator of flint deposited under dry and

| Locality | distance to water | direction to water | structural remains bark floor/sand lens | Area in m² | Hearths: nr./angle/distance | Microlith conentrations: nr./angle/distance | Angle of hearth-microlith axis | Dating in C-14 years B.C. | Comments |
|---|---|---|---|---|---|---|---|---|---|
| **Ulkestrup II units:** | | | | | | | | | |
| 1. Ulkestrup II-upper | ≤5 | SE | X - | 17 | - | - | 50° | 6100 | The upper floor |
| 2. Ulkestrup II-lower | ≤5 | SE | X - | 17 | - | (1) | 45° | 6100 | The lower floor |
| 3. Duvensee W.8 | ≤5 | E | X - | 9 | - | - | 15° | 7580 | |
| 4. Duvensee W.13 | ≤5 | S(-E) | X - | 12 | - | - | 0°(-35°) | 6850 | |
| 5. Klosterlund 1E | ≤5 | S | - - | 18 | (1) | - | 10° | 7250 | |
| 6. Klosterlund 1W | ≤5 | S | - X (41cm) | 16 | (1) | - | 35° | 7250 | |
| 7. Magleby Nor A | (≤5) | N(-W) | - - | 14 | - | - | 0°(-45°) | 7000 | |
| 8. Bare Mosse II | ≤5 | (NE) | - - | 15 | (1) | - | (45°) | 7110 | |
| 9. (Barmosen I) | [≤5?] | [E??] | X - | 12 | - | - | ? | 7500 | |
| 10. (Hjemsted) | ≤5 | E | - X (17cm) | 8 | (1) | 0 | - | 7100 | Tent ring of stones |
| 11. (Draved 35) | ? | ? | - - | 16 | (1) | - | 0°(-45°) | 7450 | |
| 12. (Mullerup 1915) | ? | ? | X - | 12 | - | ? | - | ? | |
| **Ulkestrup I units** | | | | | | | | | |
| 13. Ulkestrup I | ≤5 | NE | X - | 24 | (2) - 40° - 2m | 2 - 20° - 3.5m | 60°,80° | 6100 | |
| 14. Sværdborg II | ≤5 | SW | - - | 24 | (1) | 2 - 0° - 3m | - - | 6200 | |
| 15. Duvensee W.6 | ≤5 | SE | X - | 21 | 2 - 0° - 3m | 2 - 5° - 2.5m | 50°,70° | 7000 | |
| 16. Svanemosen 28 | ≤5 | N | - X (30cm) | 24 | 2 - 5° - 2m | 2 - 5° - 2.5m | 60°,90° | 6000 | |
| 17. (Mullerup 1900) | [5?] | SW | - - | 24 | (2) - (0°)-(2.5m) | ? | - - | 6600 | |
| 18. (Stallerupholm) | [5??] | (NE) | - X (45cm) | [24?] | [2??]-[0°]-[4m??] | [2?]-[10°?]-[2.5m] | - - | 6370 | |
| 19. (Magleby Nor B) | (≤5) | N(-NW) | - - | (22) | [??] | (2) - (15°) - (3.5m) | - - | 7000 | |
| 20. Flaadet | 20 | N | - - | 56 | (2) - 5° - 2m | 2 - 10° - 2.5m | 85°,90° | 7000 | |
| 21. Bøllund | 150 | W | - - | 56 | (2) - 80° - 2.5m | 2 - 70° - 2m | 10°,45° | 6800 | |
| 22. (Rude Mark) | 200 | N | - X (20cm) | 54 | (2) - 85° - 4m | 2 - 80° - 3.5m | (30°,45°) | 6200 | |
| **Problematic sites** | | | | | | | | | |
| 23. [Draved 31] | - | - | - - | - | - | - | | - | |
| 24. [Draved 32] | - | - | - - | - | - | - | | - | |
| 25. [Star Carr 1] | (≤5) | S | - - | (22) | - | [2] - 15° - 2m | | 7550 | |
| 26. [Star Carr 2] | (≤5) | S | - - | (13) | - | [1] | | 7550 | |
| 27. [Star Carr 3] | [≤5] | V | - - | (12) | - | [1] | | 7550 | |
| 28. [Hasbjerg II] | - | - | - - | 24 | (1) | (1) | | 7500 | |
| 29. [Tingby] | - | - | - - | - | - | - | | - | No dwelling ? |
| 30. [Lavringe Mose] | - | - | - - | - | - | - | | 6900 | No dwelling ? |

*Table 1. The basic values and informations for the analysis. The expressions connected to the columns are explained in the text. The numbers of the sites refer to their numbers in the catalogue.*

wet conditions (Andersen 1983:16,17). Thus, in a number of cases, it is possible to distinguish the course of the waterline reasonably exactly. With a large number of sites the distance to the water or to a muddy shore zone (column 2) has been in the magnitude of 1-5 metres. Instead of entering into an obviously hopeless discussion of whether each site was 1, 2, 3, etc. metres from the moist ground or water, they have been grouped as sites with a distance of ≤5 m (5 metres or less) to the shore.

Where the distance to the water cannot be judged exactly, estimates based on different factors are used. Such estimates are presented in brackets according to their assumed reliability.

Direction to the water (column 3) is the direction from the centre of the main concentration to the nearest water.

## 3.1.3. Structural remains of the dwellings (column 4)

### 3.1.3.a. Bark floors

Out of the main concentrations located in peat, 8 coincided with the remains of bark floors. From the Duvensee sites W.1,W.2 and W.5, seven further small main concentrations on such bark floors are known, unfortunately with no exact registration of the locations of the artifacts and waste. They contained one hearth each (Bokelmann 1971:11; 1986:161; Schwantes 1925:175). In 1944, on the site Holmegård IV, Becker found 2 floors with only little flint and little bone but enormous concentrations of hazelnut shells on them. The most well preserved floor contained a hearth (Becker 1945:63). Sernander and Almgren in 1908 excavated three similar bark-floors with concentrations of flints, hazelnuts, charcoal etc. restricted to the floors (Welinder 1971:50,62; Althin 1954:48). Only at Ulkestrup I and II, have reliable traces of super-structures been found, consisting of thin stakes surrounding the floors.

### 3.1.3.b. Grey sand lenses

Of the sites located on solid ground the main concentrations of five of these coincide with homogeneous, lenticular greyish sand layers. Since ploughing must be expected to have reduced their observable thickness, the values for their thickness given in table 1 are minimum values. In some of the remaining cases ploughing may have made such structures impossible to observe, if they were present originally. A tradition for insufficient observation of the sediments connected to culture layers of sites on solid ground may also partly explain why such lenses have not been observed more often. Three further concentrations of material in small, grey sand lenses were found at Tobisborg in Scania in connection with rather old Maglemosian material (Strömberg 1976:14-17), and similar structures were observed by Becker on Bornholm (Becker 1952: 99,104,108).

Since these lenses, like the bark floors of the peat sites, coincide with the main concentrations of material, it seems likely that they represent some kind of structures connected to the dwellings, for instance shallow pits excavated before they were erected. If such pits were filled with flooring material of the same type as the peat sites, the sand carried into them by the general movement would slowly fill the pits, mixed with organic matter and charcoal from activities on the floor. In time, as the organic flooring material decayed, a homogeneous lens like the ones observed (4.2.) would develop.

Similar lenticular culture layers containing main concentrations of mesolithic material and apparently conjoining with dwelling structures have been observed at Oerlinghausen (Teutoburger wald, Germany) surrounded by stake holes (Dieckmann 1931), at the site Friesheim 2 (near Regensburg, Germany) surrounded by a shallow wall ditch (Schönweiss and Werner 1977:63-65), at site no.11 at Saxtorp (western Scania, Sweden) in an apparently dugout pit (Larsson 1975:9), at Ageröd I:H (central Scania, Sweden) partly surrounded by stake holes (Larsson 1975:13; 1978:198), at construction 10 at Skateholm (southern Scania, Sweden) in an apparently dugout pit with several post and stake holes (Larsson 1985:199-205), at Deepcar (Yorkshire, England) in a shallow dugout pit surrounded by a 'stone ring'

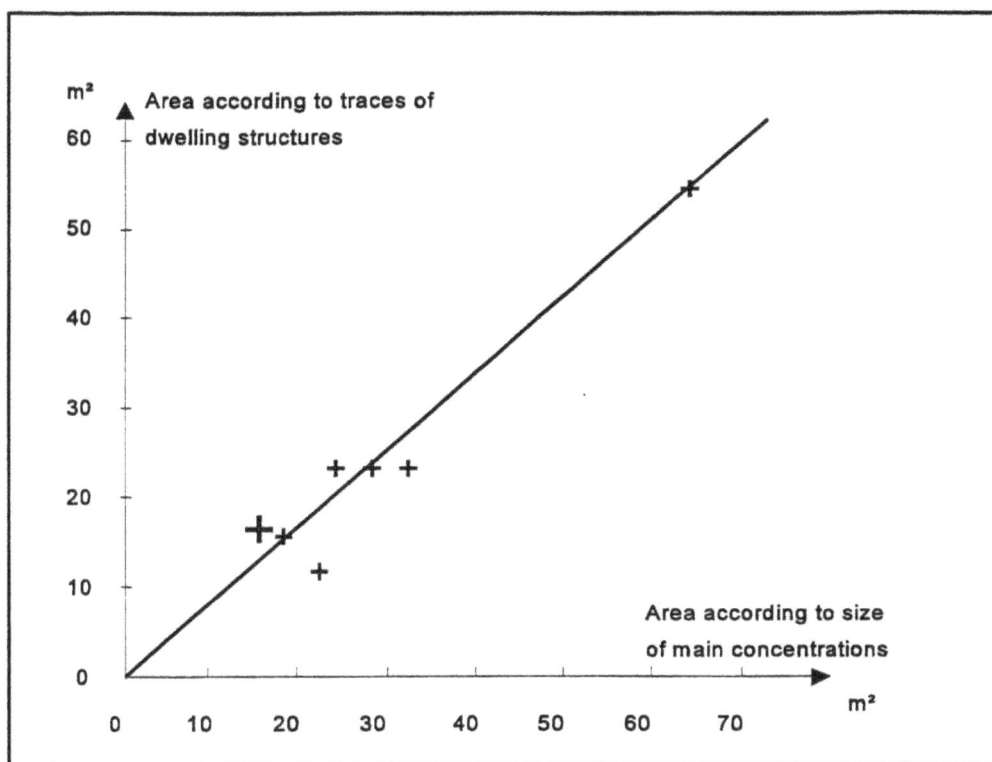

*Fig.16. The relation between the estimated sizes of the main concentrations and the sizes of their related dwellings as indicated by the preserved physical remains. The large cross represents two coinciding values.*

### 3.1.3.c. Other structural features

From two sites (Svanemosen 28 and Flaadet) we have indications of shallow holes for central posts supporting some kind of asymmetrical saddle roof with the ridge drawn approximately 50 cm from the central line in a direction away from the shoreline. Since the central post holes are not very deep (at Svanemosen 28 the posts only seem to have rested on the bottom of the grey sand lens found there), the sidewards stability must have come from the walls. Structures like the tent-shaped 'kotes' of the Sames may not have been foreign to the Maglemose culture.

From three sites on solid ground we have indications of 'tent rings' surrounding the main concentration. Apart from Hjemsted these are the little rather irregular, D-shaped stone structure close to Glamsbjerg, Funen, 4 metres in diameter, surrounding a little concentration of Maglemose flint, typologically dated to around 6200 BC (Bech 1966:167) and the 4.5 by 6 metres large oval to rectangular stone structure at Wierzchowo 6, confining a concentration of late Maglemosian material (Bagniewski 1990: 347-350).

### 3.1.4. Area of the structures (column 5)

For the sites with remains of dwelling structures, both the size of the main concentration and that of the structure connected to it has been estimated. It seems impossible to develop an automatic procedure for 'exact' estimation of the 'size' of concentrations of material. Therefore these data have been obtained by subjective inspection with a ruler. From the data it appears that the size of the concentrations is generally estimated 10 % larger than the traces or remains of physical structures. In 2 out of 8 cases the

(Radley and Mellars 1964) and at Mount Sandel (Ireland) where at least seven more or less undisturbed dugout dwelling-pits surrounded by post hole alignments were found (Woodman 1985:10-15,172).

The possibility that the coloured lenses represent material trodden into the sand, can be excluded. Uncovered loose sand is not a very practical flooring material in a dwelling. Furthermore, walking on a surface - even one consisting of loose sand - cannot produce a homogeneous colouring 30-45 cm deep. Experimental heavy trampling of flints into loose sand shows that the main part of the pieces under such extreme circumstances do not go deeper than 7 cm, and the deepest pieces not more than 12 cm (Gonzalez et.al. 1985), apparently indicating the maximum depth one can trample. The main part of finds from the central part of the 30 cm thick grey sand lens at Svanemosen 28 was found in its upper half, and thus indicates here the existence of an unpreserved floor. This seems parallel to the situation observed with the southern end of the bark floor at Ulkestrup I, were the upper 5 cm thick part contained the main part of the flint and an up to 11 cm thick lower part mainly contained bundles of branches (2.1.1.) (Andersen et al. 1982:11,12).

former are a bit smaller than the latter, in 5 cases they are 2-10 m² larger (fig.16).

The size of preserved dwelling structures (bark floors or sand lenses) is of course regarded as the most important data. Where these are not available or sufficiently informative, the estimated size of the concentration is employed. Its possible deviation from the 'real' size of a physical structure is not regarded as a serious problem.

## 3.1.5. Hearths (column 6)

The hearths in the main concentrations are often in such a bad state of preservation that their locations can only be deduced from such secondary phenomena as the distribution of burnt flint (eg. Brinch Petersen 1972:48). The numbers of indirectly observed hearths are in brackets, the problematic ones in square brackets. The question is if the general assumption is correct, that inside a dwelling a hearth will produce a noticeable concentration of burnt flint on its location.

From some Maglemosian sites we have information on the distribution of both lithic waste and burnt flint in relation to preserved bark floors and hearths: Ulkestrup I and II, Svanemosen 28, Magleby Nor A and Barmosen I. From Rude Mark we also have information on the distribution of burnt flint in relation to a large hearth structure.

At Ulkestrup I the lithic waste found with the postulated northern hearth was not registered separately due to its high position in relation to the culture layer, as mentioned before. Thus we must confine ourselves to the southern hearth to gather information on this aspect. From fig.7G and fig.21A, it is apparent that the largest concentration of burnt flint inside the floor area coincides with the position of the southern hearth zone.

Fig.13F and fig.20A show the two hearths at Ulkestrup II overlapping in the centre of a rather large concentration of burnt flint. We must bear in mind that the Maglemosian hearths often are large diffuse structures not strictly confined to the shallow pit they were often centred around (eg. Bokelmann 1981a:183; 1985:18-19). The large concentration of burnt flint most likely represents what we may call

'the expanded hearth zone'.

At Svanemosen 28, the two structures interpreted as hearths are found inside the main concentration and the shallow pit which probably represents the dwelling area. Also here they coincide with the large central concentration of burnt flint (3.2.2.; fig.21B; fig.39B).

A concentration of charcoal particles and a diffuse shallow pit-like structure containing charcoal-coloured sand was found inside the main concentration at Magleby Nor A. This indicates a hearth zone measuring several square metres. A small concentration of burnt flint (fig.20C; fig.32B) overlapped the southern part of this zone.

At the site Barmosen I (fig.22B; fig.34B,D), a well-preserved hearth was excavated in the centre of a little bark floor (Johansson 1990:14-17). Some of the central squares measure 2 by 2 metres. Only a part of the burnt flint were registered in m²-units. Nonetheless, it is obvious that the number of the burnt flints is much greater in the hearth zone than anywhere else inside the excavated area (Johansson 1990:17,19).

On Rude Mark a large pit containing reddish and humic sand, charcoal and burnt hazelnut shells was found, centrally in the sand lens and the main concentration. This was interpreted as the remains of a hearth structure. There is an obvious spatial relationship between the main concentration of burnt flint and the proposed hearth zone (Boas 1987:14-17).

The concentrations of burnt flint thus appear in connection with the positions of the hearths, where these are preserved. This allows us a reasonable indication - though not exact - of the positions of unpreserved hearths. Often flints damaged by fire break into so small fragments that they must be expected to be relatively resistant to deliberate removal (1.2.2.1.). On the other hand cleaning may have produced concentrations of larger burnt pieces in areas with no hearths. Hearths indicated by concentrations of burnt flint only are shown in round brackets.

Generally the sites have one or two hearths. For sites with two hearths the angle between the line through their centres and the approximate course of the coast line as well as the approximate distance between their centres has been registered.

## 3.1.6. Microlith concentrations (column 7)

The number of microlith concentrations inside each main concentration has been registered. In the majority of cases there are 1 or 2. In the cases with 2, the angle between the line through their centres and the approximate course of the nearest coast line as well as the approximate distance between their centres has been registered.

With regard to the concentrations of microliths it is important to find out whether they consist of redeposited material. The two best sites for a discussion of this aspect are Svanemosen 28 and Ulkestrup II. The former because 1) it was sifted, so that it can be assumed that nearly all small fragments have been registered and 2) the existence of the grey sandy lens strongly indicates that the main concentration - with its two microlith concentrations and two hearths - belong to a 4 by 6 metres large, slightly dugout dwelling. The latter because its 4 by 6 metres large 'bark' floor was excavated very carefully, and also seems to contain two microlith concentrations and likely two hearths.

The basic argument is that if lanceolate points, triangles and their fragments all represent different aspects of the activities performed inside a smaller activity area devoted to microlith-related activities, then this might result in different distributions of the different microlithic subtypes inside this activity area. For instance the intact microliths may represent a pre-mounting phase, whereas the fragments may well represent a post mounting phase. Production of different types of microliths may produce different patterns of distribution inside such a zone. Production of microliths may also produce other distribution patterns inside the activity zone than would the removal of microlith fragments from shafts and meat for instance. On the other hand, secondarily deposited concentrations of microlithic pieces should not be expected to contain different distribution patterns for the different sub-types. In short: if the microlithic subtypes have different distributions inside a smaller concentration, then we

are probably dealing with a primary deposition.

If two microlith concentrations belonging to one main concentration show the *same* deviant patterns in the distribution of the subtypes, that is if the distributions of the different subtypes differ from each other but those of each single subtype are similarly distributed inside the two concentrations, then this must be a direct reflection of different spatial organizations of different working processes inside a restricted working zone. We are thus most likely regarding primary depositions. A secondary deposition could not produce such a repeated differentiation between different items of the same magnitude.

At Svanemosen 28 it is obvious that the intact lanceolates (fig.17B) and triangles (fig.17C) belonging to the two concentrations show similar distributions, deviating in the same manner. The intact lanceolates have rather large 'smooth' concentrations of approximately 4 m², whereas the intact triangles occur in smaller noticeable concentrations restricted to the southern half of the concentrations of lanceolates. The lanceolate fragments (fig.17A) have distributions similar to that of the intact triangles but complementary to the distribution of triangle fragments (fig.17D). The burnt microlith fragments (fig.17E) are found in two concentrations, centrally and immediately to the south of the two hearths, also conforming to the distributions of the lanceolate fragments.

At Ulkestrup I, the intact lanceolates (fig.18B) and intact triangles (fig.18C) belonging to the two concentrations here are complementary. The lanceolates are positioned to the west, whereas the triangles are positioned to the east. The fragments of triangles and of lanceolates (fig.18A,D) have an eastwardly distribution congruent with the intact triangles.

Thus both at Svanemosen 28 and Ulkestrup I systematic deviations can be observed in the patterns of microlithic subtypes within the two microlith concentrations. This strongly indicates that these microlith concentrations represent primary deposited material. We must therefore assume that the microlith concentrations at other sites, where such obvious differences in their internal organization cannot be observed, also represent primary deposits.

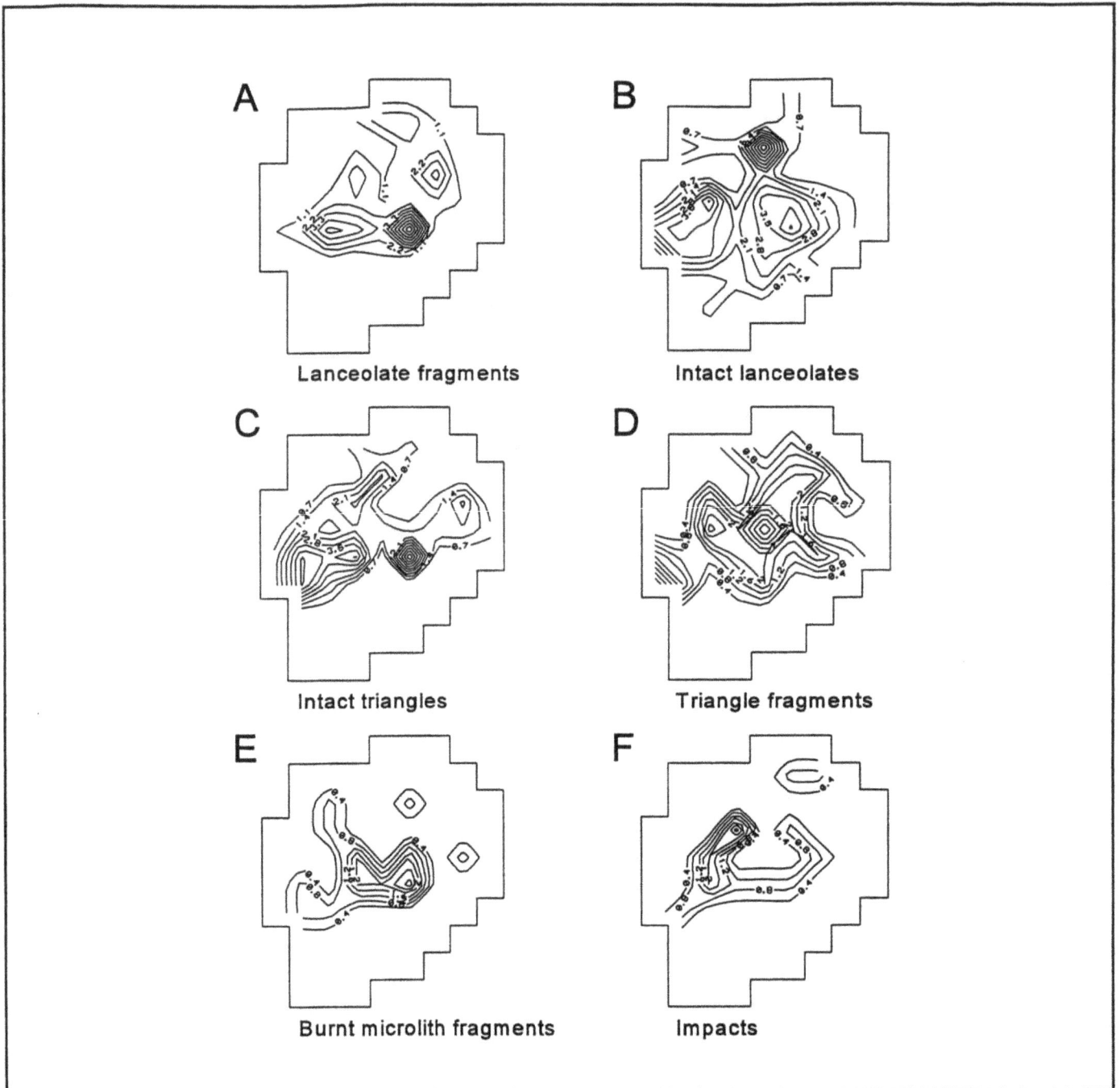

*Fig.17. Svanemosen 28. Distributions. Equidistances A: 1,1; B: 0,7; C: 0,7; D: 0,4; E: 0,4; F: 0,4*

## 3.1.7. Angle between the 'hearth-micro-lith axis' and the shore (column 8)

The 'hearth-microlith axis' is the axis through the centres of a hearth and a microlith concentration immediately adjacent to it. The angles between these axes and the shore are presented in table 1. For sites with only one hearth and one microlith concentration, only one value is given. For sites where two such sets are found, both values are given. Minimum and maximum values are 0° and 90°. Where more than one course of the contemporaneous shore-line is possible, the least likely extreme is presented in brackets to give an impression of the possible interval.

## 3.1.8. Datings (column 9)

For sites with C14 datings these are shown as conventional datings BC TL and OSL datings are also shown in years BC. For sites lacking scientific dating, the chronological positions have been estimated typologically.

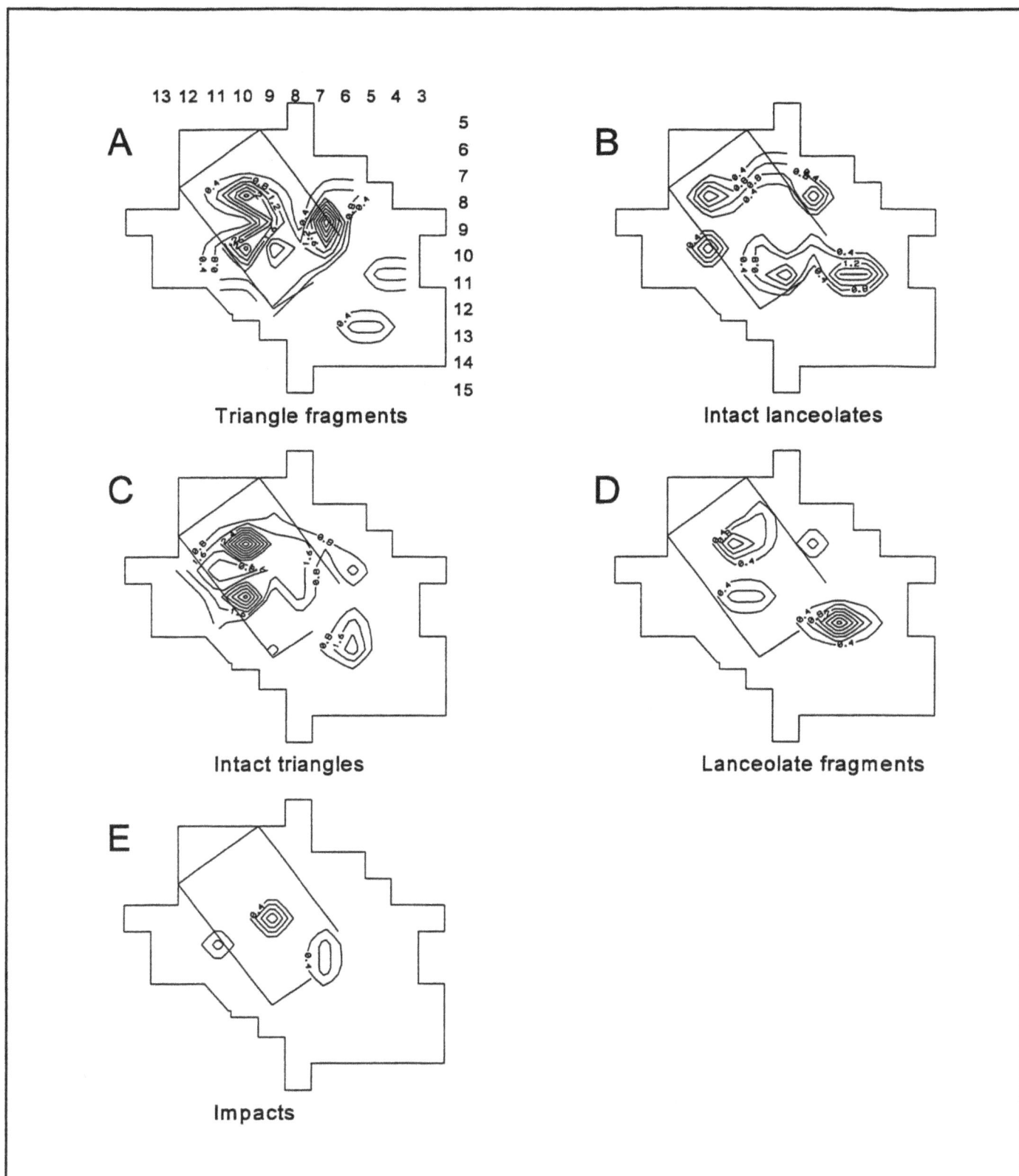

*Fig.18. Ulkestrup I. Distributions. Equidistance A: 0,4; B: 0,4; C: 0,8; D: 0,4; E: 0,4*

## 3.2. Analysis of the sites

The relations between the different sites are analysed on the basis of the data in table 1. It is obvious that concentrations of material with one microlith concentration and one hearth (Ulkestrup II-type), and those containing two microlith concentrations and two hearths (Ulkestrup I-type) constitute two consistently differing groups with only few exceptions (column 6 and 7).

The lack of a microlith concentration at Hjemsted may derive from the very restricted size of the material. Only approximately 100 pieces of lithic waste were found. Statistically one should expect to find only about 1 microlith in a sample of that size.

At Sværdborg II the location of the suggested hearth was indirectly indicated by the central concentration of burnt flint. At Svanemosen 28, where two hearths can be observed, the burnt flint, however, forms one yet larger, central concentration. It cannot be excluded that burnt flint from two possible hearths at Sværdborg II together form the concentration observed there.

## 3.2.1. Area of the units (column 5)

The relation between the Ulkestrup II and the Ulkestrup I sites is very simple. Regarding the area of the main concentrations, the former ones have an area from 8 to 18 m², the latter ones from 20 to 56 m². It is also obvious that the sites of Ulkestrup I-type separate into two subgroups: those with areas between 20 and 24 m² (Ulkestrup IA-type) and those with areas between 54 and 56 m² (Ulkestrup IB-type) (fig.19).

## 3.2.2. Distance to the water (column 2)

This factor is interesting because it supports the division of the sites of Ulkestrup I-type into the two subgroups. The sites of Ulkestrup II and Ulkestrup IA-type all have values ≤5 m, and were apparently located directly on the shoreline. The analysed sites of Ulkestrup IB-type all have values between 20 metres and 200 metres, and are not only located relatively distant from the banks or shores, but are also located in a different topographical position. They are located on the edges of plateaus, where the landscape slopes down to the water (Boas 1987: 14,15; Skaarup 1979:12,plan 1; Vebæk 1940).

## 3.2.3. Angle between the 'hearth-microlith axis' and the shore (column 8)

This factor expresses the approximate angle between the nearby shore-line and the axis through the centres of a set comprising one hearth and one microlith concentration. For the Ulkestrup II sites the values are in the interval 0-50° (mean value=22°, Σ=9), whereas the Ulkestrup IA sites have values from 50-

90° (mean value=68°, Σ=6). The Ulkestrup IB sites have values from 10-90° (mean value=51°, Σ=6).

With the Ulkestrup II-type sites the axis through the centres of the hearth and the microlith concentration is more or less parallel to the nearby shore-line, whereas with the Ulkestrup IA sites, the axes of their two sets are more or less perpendicular to it. Since their range of angle values do not overlap, this is a very important indication that the Ulkestrup IA units *do not* consist of two overlapping Ulkestrup II units. If this had been the case, the axes of the hearth-microlith sets would have been orientated more or less parallel to the shore-line!

Opposite the Ulkestrup IA sites, the Ulkestrup IB sites seem to have no fixed orientation in relation to the nearest water. This is supported by the following paragraph.

## 3.2.4. The orientation of the pairs of hearths and the pairs of microlith concentrations relative to the shore-line, at the Ulkestrup I-type sites (columns 6 and 7).

With the Ulkestrup IA units, an axis through the centres of the two hearths deviates 0-40° (mean value=11°, Σ=4) from the orientation of the nearby shore-line. For the axis through the centres of the two microlith concentrations the deviation observed is 0-20° (mean value=8°, Σ=4). The hearths are generally closer to the shore-line than are the microlith concentrations. Obviously the orientation in relation to the shore-line is important with this type.

For the Ulkestrup IB units the corresponding values are 5-85° (mean value=57°, Σ=3) and 10-80° (mean value=53°, Σ=3), indicating that here the orientation in relation to the nearby water is of no importance.

## 3.2.5. Direction to the nearby water

Regarding the direction to the nearest water, there are also here noticeable differences between the groups (fig.24). Vector addition of the directions, each given the length 1, for the groups Ulkestrup II

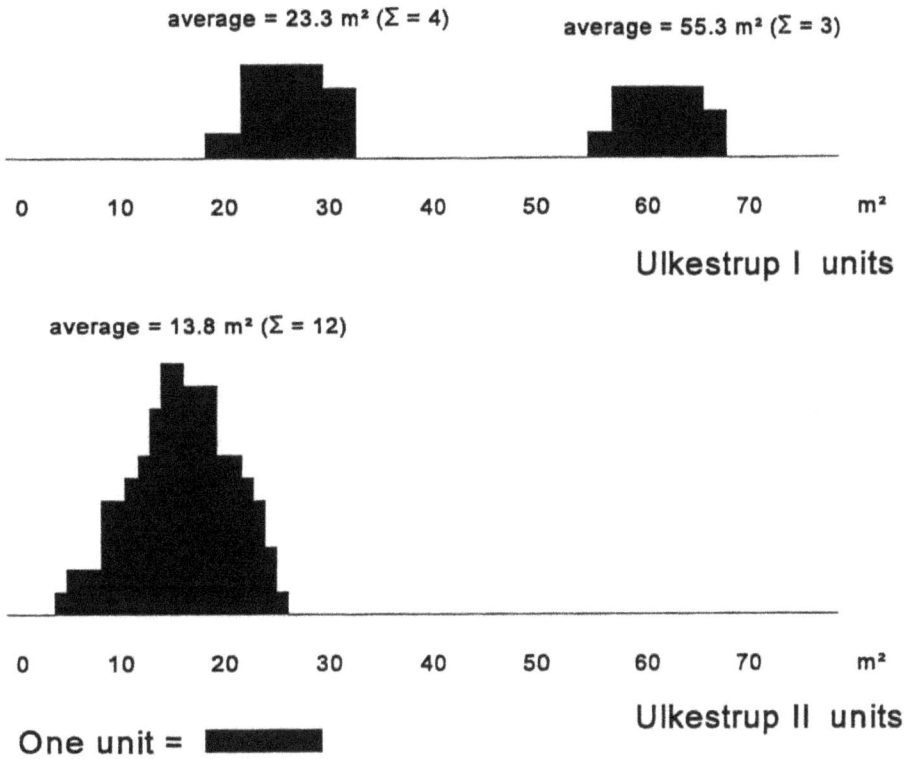

*Fig.19. The sizes of the concentrations related to the different types of units. Each unit is shown as an interval of its estimated area ±5 m². The intervals are 'piled' on top of each other and thus produce a 'smoothing' of the estimated values.*

and IA together, produces a 5.4 units long EESE-orientated vector. The 17 directions involved are in the interval N,NE,E,SE,S,SW. Apparently these sites have been located with protection from western and north-western winds in mind.

Concerning the Ulkestrup IB sites the sum of their directions is a 2.2 units long NNW-orientated vector. The directions are west and north meaning that the sites were leeward orientated from eastern and southern winds. The overlap with the directions of the former group is minimal, and the values support

the differentiation between the IA and the IB sites. Apparently the sites of group II and IA on the one hand and those of group IB on the other have different orientations.

### 3.2.6. Conclusion

It must be concluded that the accessible material consists of three groups of sites which, with regard to their internal organization, have clearly different characteristics.

The small units of Ulkestrup II-type measuring 8-18 m², have a distance of ≤5 m to the shoreline, and have an eastward orientation. Generally, a line through the centres of the hearth and the microlith concentration found here produces an angle less than 50° to the shore-line. Hjemsted is ascribed to this group. The very little concentration of micro blades and waste (approximately 80 pieces found within one 0.5 by 0.5 metre square) is regarded as a substitute for the lacking microlith concentration. Here the total lack of microliths is regarded as a consequence of the very restricted number of worked flint pieces in this find.

The units of Ulkestrup IA-type generally have an area of 20-24 m², a distance of ≤5 m to the water and an eastward orientation. Generally two hearths and two microlith concentrations are located such that the lines through their centres produce angles less than 40° and 20° to the shore-line respectively. Each set, consisting of one hearth and one microlith concentration, is located such that lines through their centres produce angles of 50 to 90° with the shore-line. The hearths are closer to the water than the microlith concentrations.

The units of Ulkestrup IB-type having an area of 54-56 m² are more than 20 metres from the water and are topographically located in positions on north to west orientated edges of plateaus, where the landscape slopes down towards the water. The internal organization seems to have no fixed orientation in relation to the nearby water.

For the neolithic hunter-fisher-gatherers of northern Norway, with regard to the number of hearths and the size of the house pits, Engelstad found the relation between hearth and dwelling area to be an average of approximately 11 m² per hearth (Trash Helskog 1983:84). This is quite comparable to the 13.5 m² per hearth we find for the Ulkestrup II and IA units.

| Site types: | Ulkestrup II-type sites | Ulkestrup IA-type sites | Ulkestrup IB-type sites |
|---|---|---|---|
| Nr. of hearths and microlith concentrations: | 1 / 1 | 2 / 2 | 2 / 2 |
| Area of main concentrations: | 8-18 m² | 20-24 m² | 54-56 m² |
| Distance to water: | ≤5 m | ≤5 m | ≥20 m (special topography) |
| Hearth-microlith angle: | 0-50° (mean=22°,Σ=9) | 50-90° (mean=68°,Σ=6) | 10-90° (mean=51°,Σ=6) |
| Hearth-hearth angle: | | 0-40° (mean=11°, Σ=4) | 5-85° (mean=57°, Σ=3) |
| microlith-micro-lith angle: | | 0-20° (mean=8°, Σ=4) | 10-80° (mean=53°, Σ=3) |
| Direction to nearest water: | N,NE,E,SE,S mean=ESE, Σ=10 | N,NE,SE,SW mean=NE, Σ=7 | W,N mean=NNW, Σ=3 |

*Table 2. General tendencies for the three types of sites.*

# 4. Interpretation of the units

## 4.1. The double pattern as one contemporaneous unit or two overlapping units

Bokelmann accepts the idea of units consisting of one microlith concentration related to one or more contemporaneous hearths. However he interprets the sites of Ulkestrup I-type as representing two similar-ly organized but not exactly contemporaneous units (Bokelmann 1980:327; 1986:149). If his interpreta-tion is correct, however, it remains to explain why the orientations of the hearth-microlith axes differ in the two different situations (3.2.3.). It seems that the hearth-microlith sets on the Ulkestrup I-sites influ-ence each other in a way that can only be explained as a consequence of their contemporaneity.

In our discussions, Bokelmann has suggested that the existence of the 'double-patterns' may be due to prehistoric rules inhibiting the location of a unit in the same place as an earlier one. However the finds of bark floors on top of each other show that the habitation on top of former dwelling units and apparently with a repetition of its spatial organi-zation was not forbidden, as indicated by the finds of Duvensee W.5 (Schwantes 1925:175) and Ulkestrup II. And still his proposal does not explain why the hearth-microlith axis of the *first* habitation unit should be at an acute angle to the shore-line. This is unlikely to be because of an expected second habi-tation?

As we saw (3.2.1.), the Ulkestrup II-type of sites are represented by smaller concentrations of flint (≤18 m²) than those of Ulkestrup I-type (≥20 m²). The

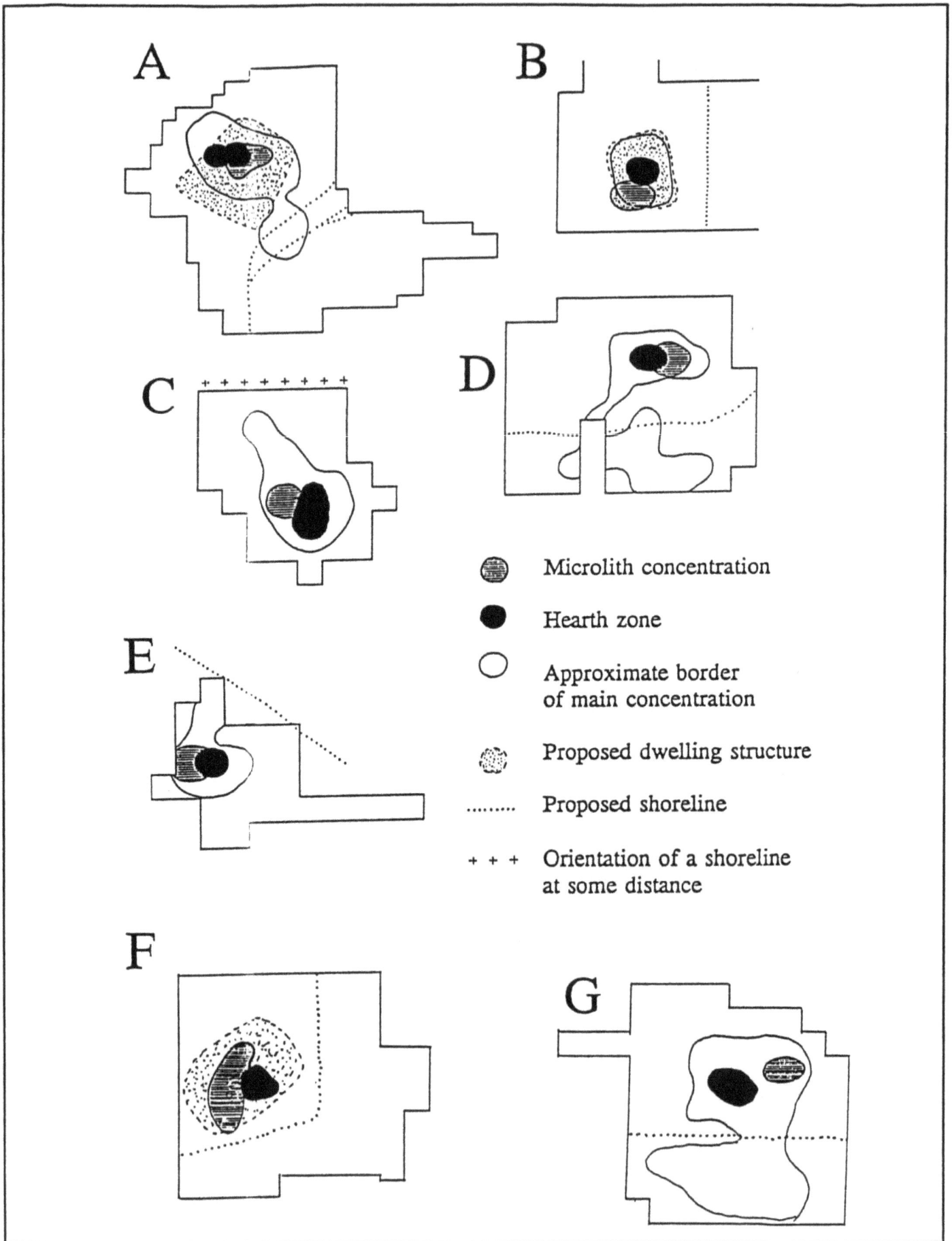

Fig.20. Plans of the distributions of microliths, hearths, lithic waste and proposed traces of dwelling structures. Shore-lines are shown as dotted lines, or, where they are at some distance, as lines consisting of small crosses showing their orientation and the direction to them. The sites are  A: Ulkestrup I; B: Duvensee W.6;  C: Magleby Nor A;  D: Klosterlund 1E;  E: Bare Mosse II;  F: Duvensee W.13; G: Klosterlund 1W.

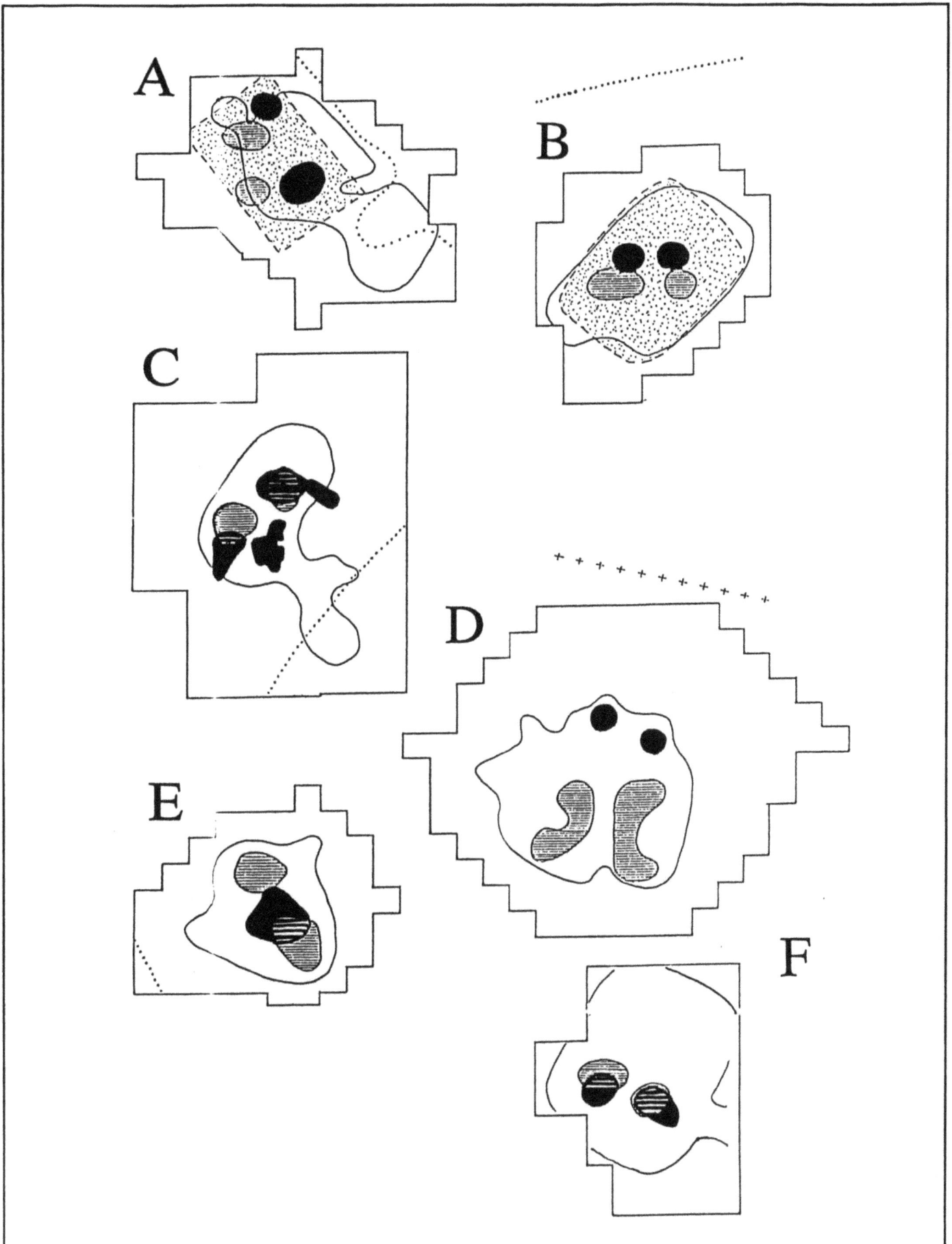

Fig.21. Plans of the distributions of microliths, hearths, lithic waste and proposed dwelling structures. Legend: see fig.20. The sites are A: Ulkestrup II; B: Svanemosen 28; C: Duvensee W.6; D: Flaadet; E: Sværdborg II; F: Bøllund 1W.

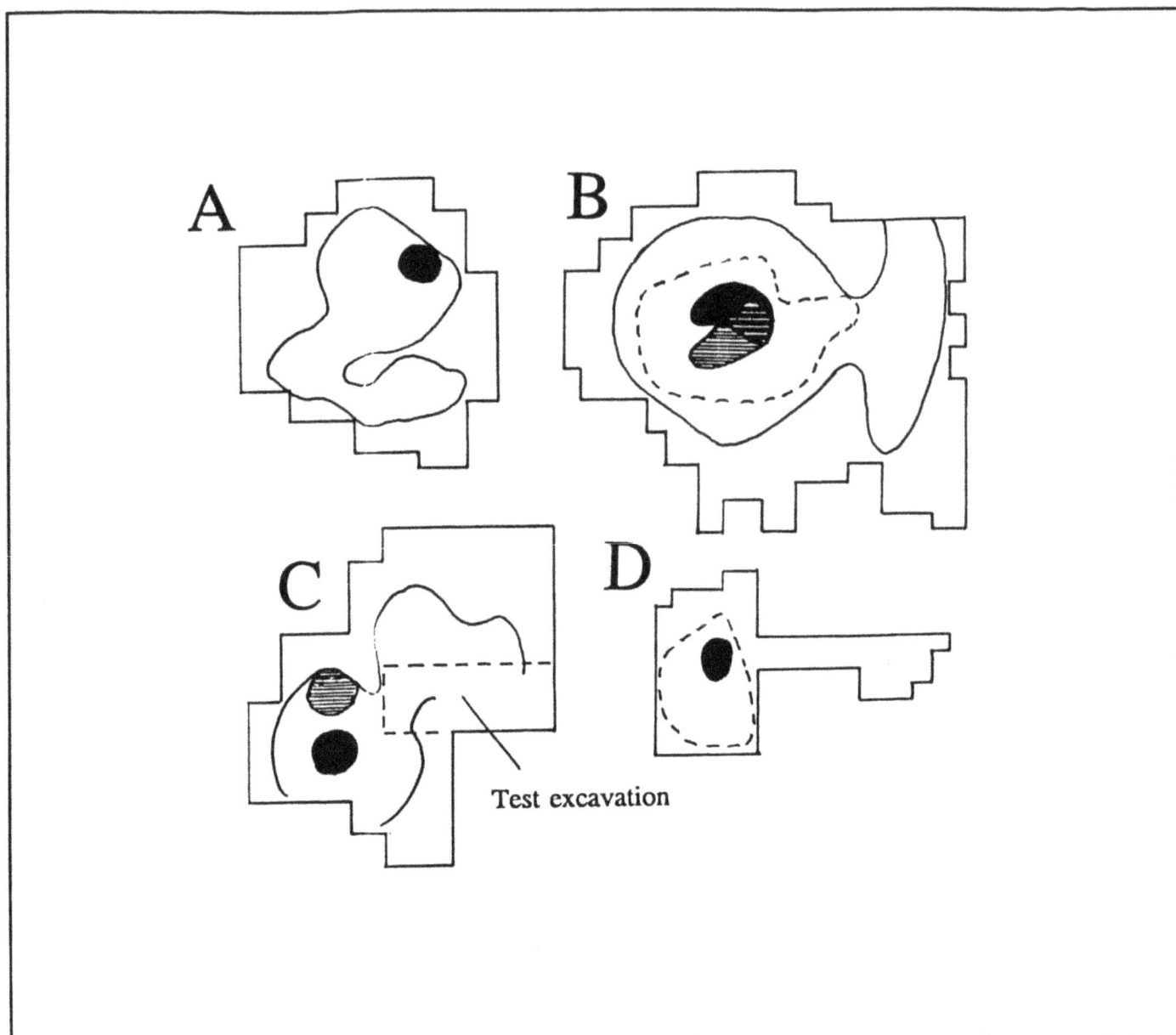

Test excavation

*Fig.22. Plans of the distributions of microliths, hearths, lithic waste and proposed dwelling structures. Legend: see fig.20. The sites are A: Mullerup 1915; B: Barmosen I; C: Draved 35; D: Hjemsted.*

latter *may* consist of two partly overlapping and not exactly contemporaneous concentrations. However the two small units Ulkestrup II and Duvensee W.8 are related respectively to a dwelling structure measuring only 4 by 4 metres and a bark floor even smaller, whereas Ulkestrup I and Svanemosen 28 are related to a bark floor and a shallow dugout pit, both measuring approximately 4 by 6 m. If we accept the structures at Flaadet as representing a dwelling, this was even larger. Thus, our two categories seem systematically related not only to different sizes of their main concentrations, deviating orientations of their hearth-microlith axes, differences in the numbers of hearths and microlith concentrations, but also to physical habitation structures, the sizes of which correspond to that of the main concentrations. Therefore everything indicates that the two different

patterns represent two different dwelling types with different internal organizations, the one containing one and the other two contemporaneous hearth-microlith sets.

## 4.2. The physical structures of the 'units'

The units are central areas on the sites. This is evident from their hearths, bark floors, grey sand lenses and large content of worked flint. The finds at Ulkestrup I and II show that the units were in some cases equipped with superstructures supported by stakes. At Ulkestrup I the line of stakes coincides with a line of noticeable change in the flint density, apparently reflecting the effect of a wall. Parts of the floor had been covered by the bracken *Lastres*

48

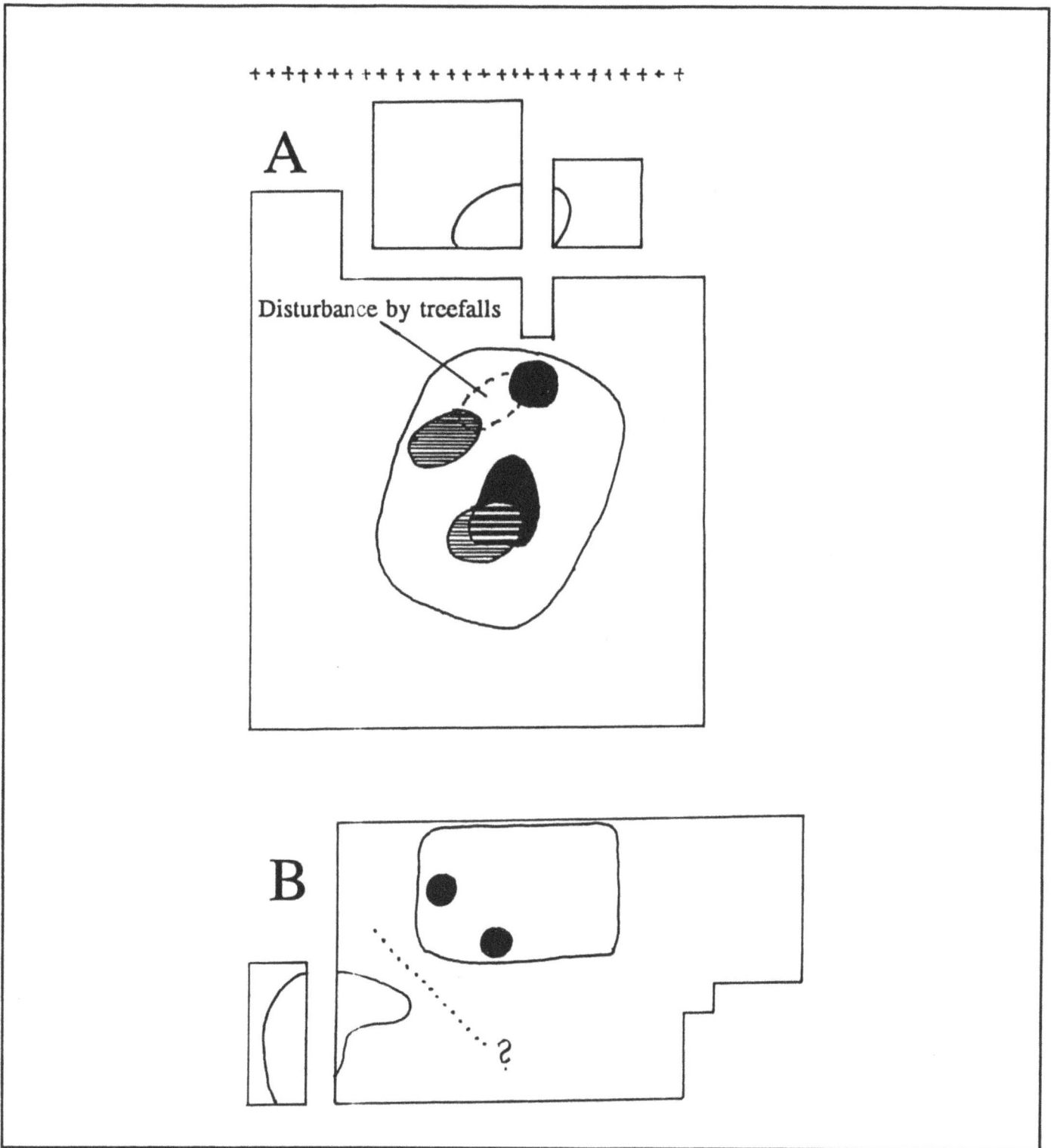

*Fig.23. Plans of the distributions of microliths, hearths, lithic waste and proposed dwelling structures. Legend: see fig.20. The sites are: A: Rude Mark; B: Mullerup 1900 .*

*thelypteris* that may well have served as 'mattress-material' in the sleeping areas. The floor also yielded finds of 'snacks' such as a 'large handful' of seeds of the yellow waterlily (*Nupar lutetum*) and a smaller portion of stones of the edible red cornell (*Cornus sanguina*)(Andersen et al. 1982:12). That numerous hazelnut shells were found in and around the hearth shows that hazelnuts were roasted on the floor. A concentration of bones of fish, birds and mammals is found immediately adjacent to the floor. Apparently they were washed down from its edge. In spite of the bad preservation of bone on the floor itself, these observations indicate that the inhabitants were eating their meals on the floor.

At Flaadet and Svanemosen 28 postholes seem to indicate the existence of a superstructure. In the latter case this coincides with the shallow dugout pit filled with 30 cm of grey homogeneous sand. The main concentration of finds was located 15-25 cm above the bottom of the lens. This must indicate that the activity horizon was here or above this level. A bark floor supported by layers of branches may well have served as a walking surface. Assuming this, sand carried into the structure by the general movement and mixed with fine charcoal particles

(3.1.3.b.)(Andersen et al. 1982:11,12).

There are two possible explanations for the occurrence of concentrations of sharp flints inside the dwellings of the Maglemose Culture: 1) The presence of floors consisting of bark, branches and twigs at both the peat and the solid ground sites can easily have absorbed sharp flints from the walking

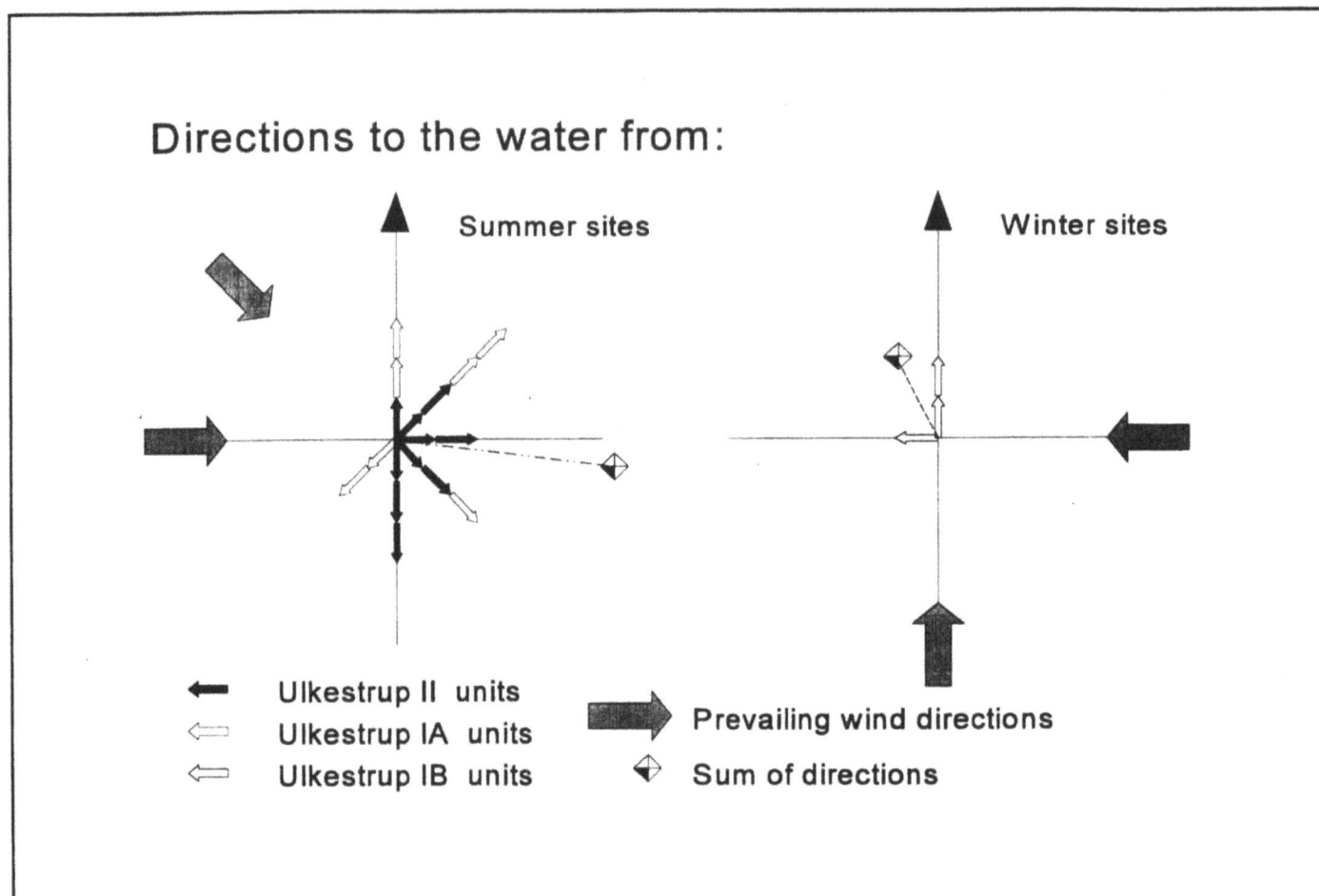

*Fig. 24. The arrows show the direction to the nearest water from the differene types of sites, hypothetically separated into winter and summer sites.*

would sift through the floor and in time fill the shallow pit as a homogeneous grey sand deposit. As mentioned before (3.1.3.b), walking on a surface - even one of loose sand - cannot produce a 30 cm deep homogeneous colouring. Thus, the repeatedly observed grey homogeneous sand lenses seem to reflect the existence in prehistoric times of more sophisticated flooring than the bare ground. A further consequence of the relatively high position of the flint in the grey lens at Svanemosen 28 must be that the main part of the flint knapping was done after the pit had already been more or less filled in by sand. This is evidence of a relatively late phase of the settlement. At Ulkestrup I, the main part of the flint was likewise found in the upper 5 cm of the floor

surface. However, Ulkestrup I, where some flint was evidently cleared out from the floor, shows that cleaning of the floors also appeared. 2) The location of the main part of the flint in the upper part of the lens at Svanemosen 28 may indicate that massive flint knapping was only done inside the dwellings immediately before they were abandoned. These two explanatory aspects do not exclude each other.

Bokelmann does not present any evidence for his statement that the bark 'floors' found hitherto do not represent the inner spaces of dwellings (Bokelmann 1989:17). On the basis of the present analysis this seems unwarranted. He promotes the idea that the little bark 'mats' measuring 0.7 by less than 2 metres

## The chronological relation between the different types of units.

Ulkestrup IA
units ■

Ulkestrup IB
units ☐

8000 B.C.

7000 B.C.

6000 B.C.

Ulkestrup II
units ☐

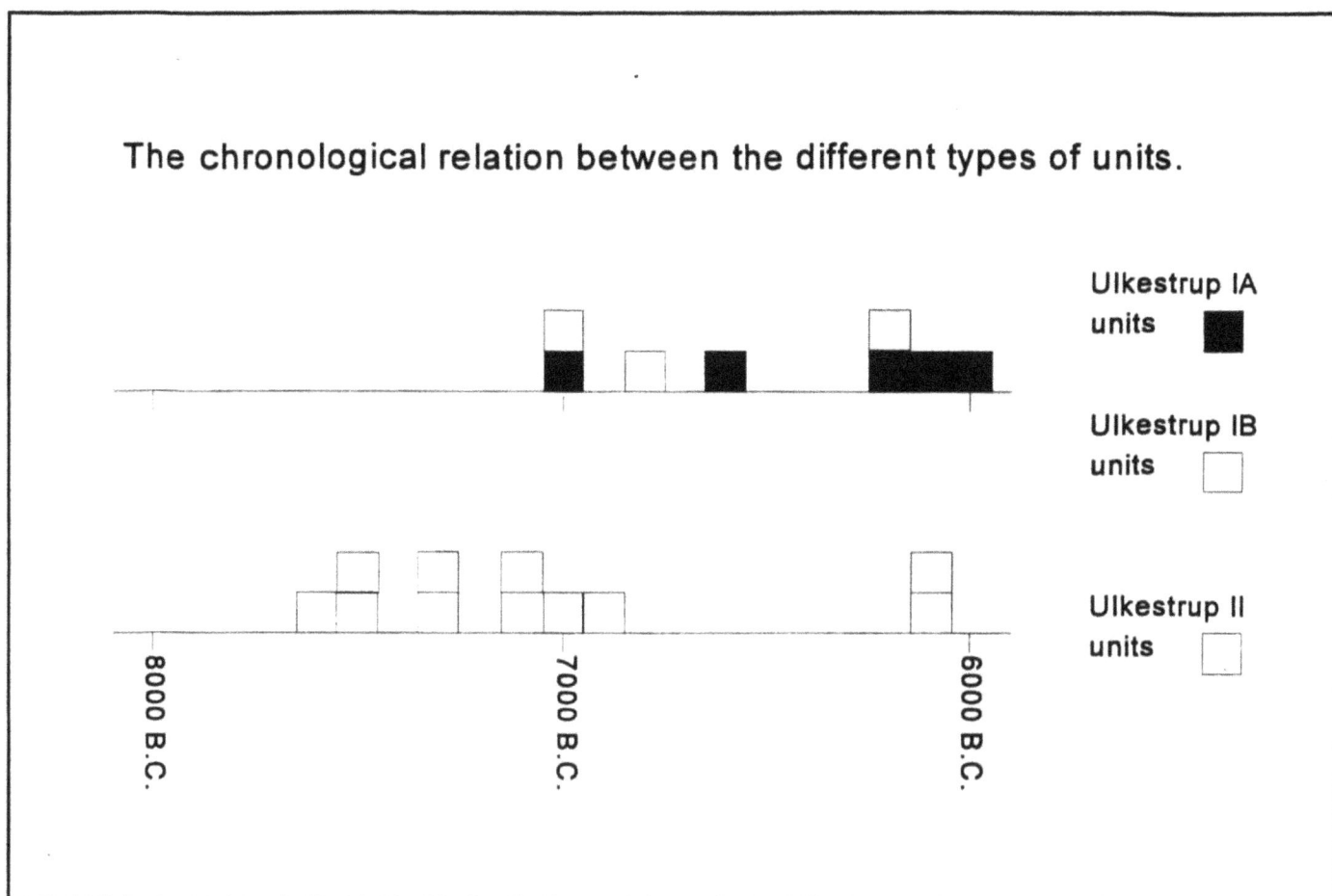

*Fig.25. The chronological relation between the different types of sites distinguished in the analysis.*

found at Duvensee W.13 were peripheral sleeping places, and that the larger 'floors' - including all the main concentrations dealt with here - represent central 'working areas' not employed as dwellings (Bokelmann 1986:160-161). Willkomm's arguments, based on C14 datings, for a possible contemporaneity of the main floor at Duvensee W.13 and one of the little bark mats to the north-west of it by means of a pine cone found on the latter, seem dubious. The basic datings are 6680±160 and 6750±80 (KI-2125 and KI-2126) on charcoal from the main floor and 6790±85 (KI-2378) on charcoal from the hearth connected to the little mat (Willkomm 1986:171). The latter was only 88 by 130 cm, which is rather short for a comfortable bed, even if one sleeps in hocker, as suggested. There were small sharp pieces of lithic waste on the eastern half of the mat, which would make sleeping on it uncomfortable (Bokelmann 1986:153,155,159). Another problem with this interpretation is that the second small mat from the site has a small central hearth which must have made comfortable sleeping on it equally complicated (Bokelmann 1989:19).

The small mats are more likely sitting mats for

activities carried out in the periphery of a camp (and thus may be contemporaneous with other nearby floors/mats/dwellings) or they may be chronologically independent units.

The lack of traces of superstructures in a number of the cases cannot be regarded as decisive, since dwelling structures can very well exist without leaving traces of posts and stakes. Friesheim 2, is an outstanding example of this (Schönweiss and Werner 1977:63). Also the 'tent rings' at Hjemsted, Wierzchowo 6, Deepcar and possibly Granholmen indicate the existence of a type of dwelling structures that did not leave noticeable structural traces below the culture layer (Bagniewski 1990:348; Bech 1966; Radley and Mellars 1964). Dwellings with a superstructure supported by central posts may not have left traces at their periphery. We must also bear in mind that holes from thin stakes thrust into the ground may, after a period of several thousand years, be extremely difficult to distinguish from traces of roots and other disturbances.

Altogether, it seems reasonable to believe that the units dealt with in this analysis represent the dwellings of the Maglemose Culture. If some of the units were without physical screening, they still - due to their spatial organization - must be expected to represent central living areas where the inhabitants slept, ate, and so on. These units must nevertheless be conceived of as 'dwellings'.

## 4.3. Seasonality

Due to the raised water level in the lakes in winter, the sites on the shores must have been uninhabitable (Andersen 1983:179). Where seasonal indicators are preserved from these units, they suggest habitation from the beginning of April to September/October (Andersen et al.1982:169; Bokelmann 1985:13; Bokelmann et.al. 1981:29,30). Also at larger peat sites such as Sværdborg I and Star Carr, consisting of several overlapping units, the period of habitation seems to have been the summer half-year (Bille Henriksen 1976:148; 1980:132; Legge and Rowley-Conwy 1989:227-230). The suggested winter site Holmegård V, located directly on a northern orientated shore, according to a new analysis of the bone material carried out by Philip Jensen at the Zoological Museum of the University of Copenhagen, revealed summer and autumn indicators but no winter indicators (Becker 1953:181-182; Grøn 1987a:311; report from Philip Jensen in The Danish National Museum, A-41156).

The positions of the many sites close to the water undoubtedly reflect the importance of boats as a means of transportation. The paddle and the possible boat-landing place at Ulkestrup I, and the concentrations of heads of fishing spears lost during fishing, found where the water at that time was about 1 metre deep (Andersen 1983:155-158), show the importance of boats in daily life. The typical positions of sites on narrow sand bars jutting into the former lakes (Klosterlund, Lavringe Mose, Star Carr, Åmosen etc.) (Andersen 1983:fig.18; Clark 1954:28; Mathiassen 1937:132; Sørensen 1988:53-55) must reflect that transportation by boat was far more important than land transport in the summer half-year, when these sites were inhabited.

An important question is where we find the winter sites. It has been argued that the Maglemosian winter quarters were located on the coasts of the North Sea and the Baltic, in areas that today are submerged. However, the remains of elks killed in winter approximately 7500 BC were found at Favrbo and Skottemarke, which at that time were clear inland localities (Møhl 1980:5-15). The diet at one of the few known Maglemosian coastal sites, Bua Västergård in Sweden, derived approximately 50% from the sea and 50 % from the forest. The site was located on an island and within reasonable range of hunting/fishing areas consisting of considerably more sea than land (Wigforss et.al.1983:8-13,140,196). On the basis of the content of C-13 in four Maglemosian skeletons, of which only one showed a slight marine content (Tauber, personal communication), it must be concluded that the normal winter diet did not derive from the sea by the northern or western coasts. Apparently the Maglemosians preferred land resources, and also in winter hunted in clear inland areas. We ought thus to find their winter dwellings there.

In winter the shore zones of the lakes might for two reasons be essentially less attractive for habitation. One is that when the water in the lakes froze, their importance as medium of transportation became reduced to something comparable to solid ground, and the bank zone lost its transport-strategical position. Sailing must have been replaced by transport on foot. A second reason is that cold air masses will form just above the ice in calm winter weather, and make the locations in the vicinity of the ice much colder than higher and more withdrawn ones.

According to Knud Frydendahl's reconstruction of the Boreal climate, the predominant wind direction in summer was from the west with a north-westerly tendency (Grøn 1987a:317-318). Bearing this aspect in mind, it is interesting that all Ulkestrup IA and II units are located on shores offering protection from winds with these directions. In winter, eastern and southern wind directions should dominate. And actually the three Ulkestrup IB units are orientated to the north and west, protected from winds from eastern and southern directions (fig.24).

With present hunter-gatherers it is not uncommon that there is a difference in the space available per family in summer and winter dwellings. With the Nunamiut and Mistassini for instance, the maximum area is available in the winter dwellings (Tanner and Binford, personal communication). For the Maglemosian units the difference in available space per hearth-microlith set (13 m² contra 27.7 m²), the different topographical positions, and the systematically different orientations fitting Frydendahl's postulated wind directions, seem to indicate that the Ulkestrup IB units belong to another season than the Ulkestrup IA and II units which were inhabited during the summer half-year. It is likely that the IB units represent the 'missing' winter dwellings.

The preservation of organic matter will, under normal conditions, be minimal at sites withdrawn from the moist/wet areas. This may be the reason why sites with 'winter indicators' are absent from our material.

The picture obtained here of the Maglemosian yearly cycle with summer dwellings on the north, west and to a lesser degree south-shores of the inland lakes, and winter dwellings on the edges of higher plateaus connected to northern or western slopes down to water, is course a simplification of a more complex behavioural pattern. The material contains a number of sites that 'differ' from the main pattern described here, but none of them are related to concrete seasonal indicators or a registration allowing distributional analysis.

From the coastal regions of the Baltic (then the Ancylus Lake, a large freshwater lake), we have sites located approximately 500-1500 metres from its coastline (Becker 1952:152,159; Strömberg 1976: 18). Unfortunately no usable distribution plans are available from these sites. The restricted size of the concentrations and related grey sand lenses found at Tobisborg (7.5, 9 and 6 m²) (Strömberg 1976:14-17) indicates that we are dealing with small Ulkestrup II units. Their western orientation may suggest habitation in the summer half-year.

From Springbjerg, in the Vejle Ådal Valley, three Maglemosian sites were found on the edge of a plateau, connected to a SE-slope, 50 metres above and 100 metres from the bottom of the valley. The present distance to the river is 500 metres (Berthelsen 1944:43-55). The orientation again hints at a summer habitation.

In Jutland numerous accumulations of mesolithic material found by the confluences of watercourses also include Maglemosian concentrations. These may be transitional sites on the main routes of mesolithic man.

## 4.4. The social implications of the spatial patterns

We have seen how the spatial pattern consisting of one hearth zone and one microlith concentration appears to be the basic element of the spatial organization of the Maglemosian dwellings. These basic elements show a clear difference in orientation relative to the shoreline. The hearth-microlith sets of the small Ulkestrup II units have axes more or less parallel to the shoreline. The dual hearth-microlith sets of the larger Ulkestrup IA units, have axes more or less perpendicular to the shoreline. With the Ulkestrup IB units there is no fixed orientation of the hearth-microlith axes relative to the nearby water.

It is obvious that the hearth-microlith sets must reflect an organizational unit of some kind. Traditionally the microlithic pieces would be linked with male activities as a result of their direct relation to hunting, whereas the hearth zones would traditionally be related to female activities such as cooking.

Women from hunter-gatherer societies may hunt with bow and arrow (for instance from the Greenland Eskimos - Jørgen Meldgaard personal communication), but in all hunter-gatherer societies listed by Murdock et.al. in his 'Ethnographic Atlas' hunting is a clearly male activity, with a restricted female participation only in few cases (Murdock et.al. 1962: 390-393,537; 1963:257-259,402,544; 1964:109-110, 203-205,330,421; 1965:117,345).

Males from hunter-gatherers may perform cooking activities on communal occasions, and when they are travelling or hunting without women (eg. Radcliffe-Brown 1964:43-44). An extensive reading of hunter-gatherer literature has revealed no examples where married males under normal conditions prepare meals in the dwellings. The preparation of meals must generally be regarded as a female activity.

Bearing in mind the apparently common and repeated pattern found inside the dwellings it seems reasonable to assume that the microlith concentrations represent locations of male activities, and the hearth zones areas of female activities.

The microlith concentrations are often very small (take up only one m²) and thus most likely represent the activities of only one individual with a fixed position. Whereas one individual may produce spatially large concentrations (like the crescent shaped ones from Flaadet - fig.45C), several individuals with fixed positions in a dwelling space would not be expected to produce concentrations of restricted size.

Where the hearths are well preserved, they appear to consist of a central area (often a shallow pit) approximately 1 metre in diameter, surrounded by a larger area of diffusely distributed sand and charcoal. Thus we must assume that they also represent the activities of a single individual with a fixed position.

The implications are that each of the basic spatial elements we have distinguished as a 'hearth-microlith set' seem to represent the activities of two individuals: one male and one female.

The analysis does not yield any information on the location of individuals not reflected in the distributions of material. However, one must assume that adult male individuals would participate in the hunting, and thus reveal their presence by concentrations of microlithic pieces.

The doors of the dwellings located close to the water seem to have been orientated directly towards it, as at Ulkestrup I (2.1.3.), Klosterlund 1W (3.1.4.) and Svanemosen 28 (3.2.2.), where possible structural remains of the entrances were preserved. In general this is indicated by the position of the often narrow tongues of finds connecting the main concentrations with the waste layers. Thus with the Ulkestrup IA-type units, where the hearths are closer to the water than the microlith concentrations, the female activity areas seem to have been placed closer to the entrance than the males. This fits the observation that females as a basic rule, must be placed next to the entrance in multi-family dwellings of recent hunter-gatherers. In one-family dwellings the man may have his place at the same distance from the door as the woman, but never closer than that. Often the entrance area is related to important female gods (eg. Grøn 1989:10; Paulsson 1952; Ränk 1951).

If we assume that individuals were placed between their 'activity areas' and the outer limit of the dwelling area, then we - in the Ulkestrup I units - have the sequence round the wall: female, male, male, female. From ethnographic sources we know that in all two, three or four family dwellings great concern is taken to avoid man and wife from different families being placed beside each other. In regular dwelling spaces, the standard procedure seems to be to place the families so that the man from each family sits beside the man of the next family, and the wife beside the wife of the next family. Thus sequences like wife, man, man, wife, wife, man etc. are developed (Grøn 1989:102). With uneven numbers of families, curious spatial features are used to solve the problems (eg. Tanner 1979:84-96).

Obviously there are many pitfalls and possibilities of misinterpreting the faint traces of distant prehistoric cultures. However, we have by this analysis revealed a consistency of spatial patterns, related to structural remains of dwellings, as the basis for our conclusions. They indicate the existence of exactly the type of organizational patterns one would expect on the basis of our ethnographical sources. It thus seems reasonable to assume that each of the basic spatial elements (the heart-microlith sets) represents a couple, and that possible children are 'invisible' in the general distribution patterns.

The analysis has brought us to the conclusion that the Maglemose Culture employed both 1 and 2-family dwellings contemporaneously. On the basis of the ethnographical information available, this can hardly be surprising (eg. Jenness 1970:65-76; Rogers 1967a:7; Radcliffe-Brown 1964:412-14).

The chronological relation between the two types of units is interesting (fig.25). The Ulkestrup II units are the only type observed in the Preboreal, whereas the Ulkestrup I units enter and prevail around 7000 BC This must reflect an increase in the size of the households from one to two nuclear families.

## 4.5. The dwellings and settlements of the Maglemose Culture

If the assumptions made above are correct, then we are able to sketch a rather detailed picture of the dwellings of the Maglemose culture and the groups that lived in them.

In summer, northern, western and southern shores of the inland lakes were inhabited. The shores exposed to the prevailing western and north-western winds were avoided. The number of one-family dwellings were approximately double the number of two-family dwellings, meaning that approximately the same number of people inhabited each type.

Whether larger groups split up in one-family units during utilization of predictable stable resources such as hazelnuts in the autumn, as one might expect on the basis of resource-strategical considerations (Wilmsen 1973:6-7), remains to be proved. In the Duvensee Basin the small floors with one hearth dominate, and many of them contain large amounts of hazelnuts indicating that these were specialized hazelnut collection sites (Bokelmann 1971:11; 1981b:29-30; Schwantes 1925:175; 1939:97). The appearance of hazelnut shells on a site in smaller quantities may only imply that they were stored in the autumn and later transported to it. Thus, in smaller quantities, they cannot be taken as a seasonal indicator.

On the basis of the ethnographical information on hunter-gatherers from zones with a temperate climate, the Maglemosian society must be expected to have been organized in 'hunting-groups' numbering from two to five nuclear families (Price 1981:31). Possibly the two-family dwellings occurred more frequently in settlements inhabited by such larger groups than in 'extraction camps' containing only fragments of them.

I have suggested that three camps consisting of three to five contemporaneous dwellings located along the shore with approximately 40 metres between their centres can be observed in Åmosen (Grøn 1987a:308-310,315). A fourth chain of 3 typologically very similar, late Maglemosian concentrations, with 35-40 metres between their centres, is the Springbjerg site overlooking the Vejle Ådal Valley (4.4.). It was excavated by the amateur William Berthelsen in 1942 (Berthelsen 1944:45,53-54). Unfortunately no registration was made of the horizontal position of the finds within each of the concentrations.

With some one and two-family dwellings these chains would give a reasonable number of families. Apart from the southernmost and most problematic site in the chain, at the Kildegård-complex (Åmosen), the four chains run ENE-WSW with an orientation to the SSW, a direction that in summer would provide protection from the prevailing winds, and heating from the sun. It is impossible to prove or disprove the possible contemporaneity between the 'dwellings' in each of the four chains. To try to solve this - among other problems - a research project has been started on mesolithic sites in a submerged bog with good preservation of organic matter. It may here be possible to state exact contemporaneity of wooden structures by means of relative dendrochronology (not necessarily on oak) (Grøn 1990a:84-85).

Whereas the spatial organization of Maglemosian units in chains is not crucial with regard to their exact contemporaneity, the well-documented isolation of the main concentrations of the Ulkestrup IB units, Flaadet and Rude Mark (Skaarup 1979:16,plan 1; Boas personal communication) is a fairly reliable indication of their prehistoric situation. It indicates that the large winter houses with two nuclear families were isolated.

The material contains no obvious traces of assembly camps. Since yearly or half-yearly gatherings of all the hunting groups of one or more bands play an important social, religious and communicative role in most hunter-gatherer societies (eg. Damas 1972: 283-284; Gould 1969:256-257; Gusinde 1931:203; Rogers 1967b:42-47; Silberbauer 1981:195-196), such camps ought to be expected in the Maglemosian material as well. However, the chronological correlation of so many units at one location with repeated habitations every year for a longer interval of time, would imply immense problems for archaeology.

## 4.6. Cultural affinities of the two types of patterns - some further examples

There are indications that Ulkestrup I-type units existed outside the classical Maglemosian area in contemporary mesolithic milieus. In Poland for instance one has probably been excavated at Jastrzebia Gòra 4 with two microlith concentrations

(Domanska 1991:56). In southern Germany, Schön-weiss and Werner at Friesheim 2, in the sand of a river terrace, uncovered the 'shadow' of such a 5 by 5 metres square mesolithic dwelling. This had a shallow wall ditch preserved, which was only interrupted in one corner by what appears to be a diagonal walking path (presumably the entrance). Inside are two hearth structures, located symme-trically around the path. Unfortunately, it has not been possible to obtain information on the exact location of the artifacts (Schönweiss and Werner 1977:60-66).

At Deepcar, north of Sheffield a mesolithic flint concentration, probably of Ulkestrup II-type, was related to a grey culture layer found inside an oval stone structure 2.5 metres deep and 4 metres long NW-SE. The microliths and micro burins were con-centrated in the NW-end and a concentration of burnt flint was related to a possible hearth structure in its SE-end. A little tongue of waste material protruded to the SW. The material is regarded as closely related to the Maglemose Culture and typologically dated to around 7500 BC (Radley and Mellars 1964).

It thus seems evident that the patterns distinguished were not specific to the Maglemosian tradition, but were also employed by the contemporary neigh-bouring groups.

# 5. Discussion and conclusion

## 5.1. The physical frames

An analysis of the available Maglemosian units appearing as restricted and typologically uniform concentrations of material has revealed a number of regularities. By way of these, we now have an angle of incidence allowing us to recognize more possible remains of dwelling structures. Shallow dwelling pits, for instance, in a number of cases seem to reveal themselves as lenses of homogeneous grey sand. Floors composed of bark and branches appear to

types in use simultaneously in the Maglemose Culture: dwelling structures incorporating stake walls, structures with a saddle roof supported by centrally placed posts, and tents.

The Ulkestrup I units appear to have been rectangular or oblong to oval. Internally they have been organized with a diagonal axis of symmetry, roughly perpendicular to the shoreline, where this was very close. It seems that the entrances of the sites close to the shore (IA units) were located on the axis of symmetry facing the water. The Ulkestrup II units appear to have had a trapezoid/D-shaped to an oval outline with the entrance facing the water (fig.26).

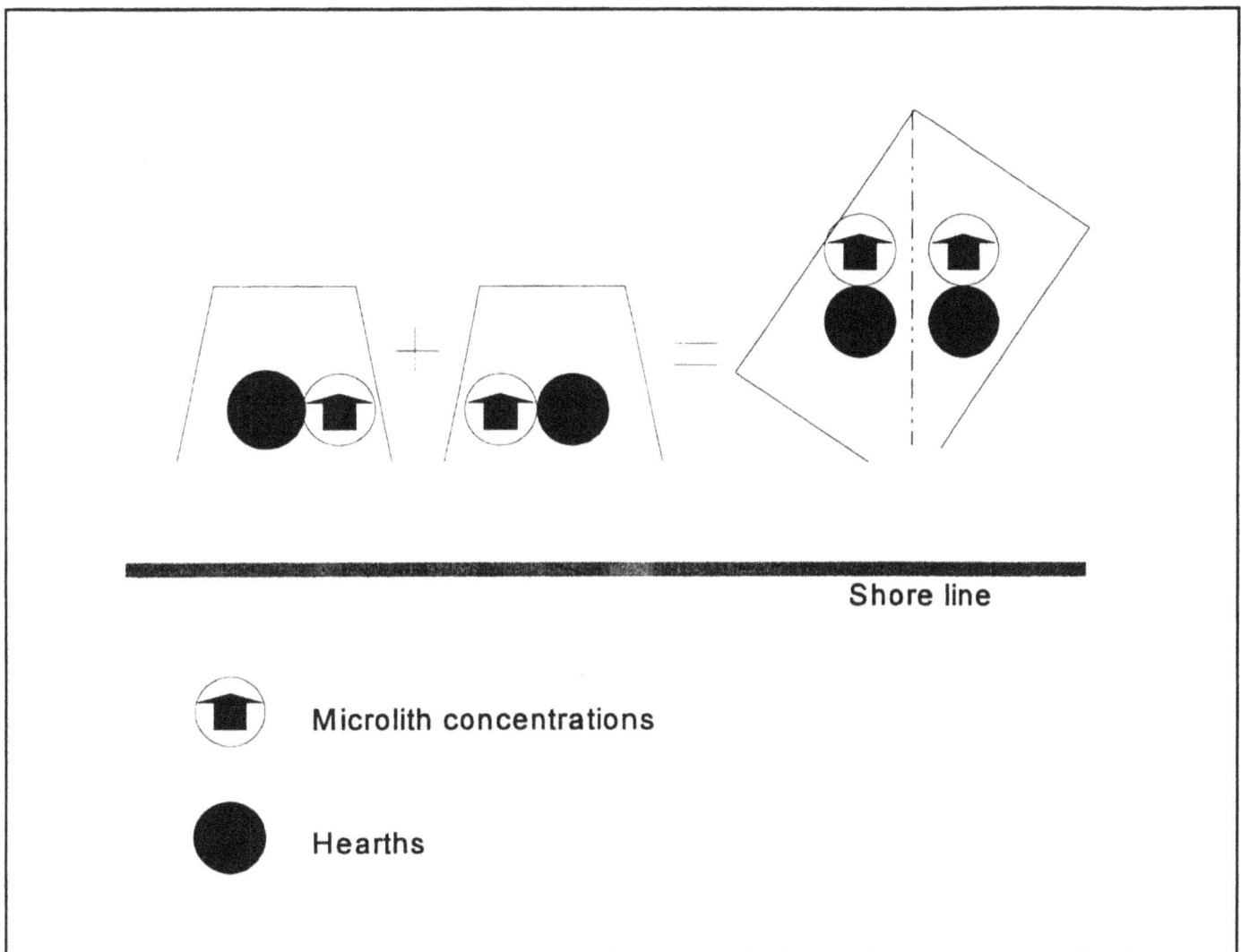

*Fig.26. Model for the organizational relation between the postulated one and two-family dwellings.*

have been the standard here, as well as on the peat sites.

If the interpretations of the structural remains are correct, there were a number of different dwelling

## 5.2. Different types of units and relative artifact composition

A substantial conclusion is that there exist no systematic relation between the type of unit and the

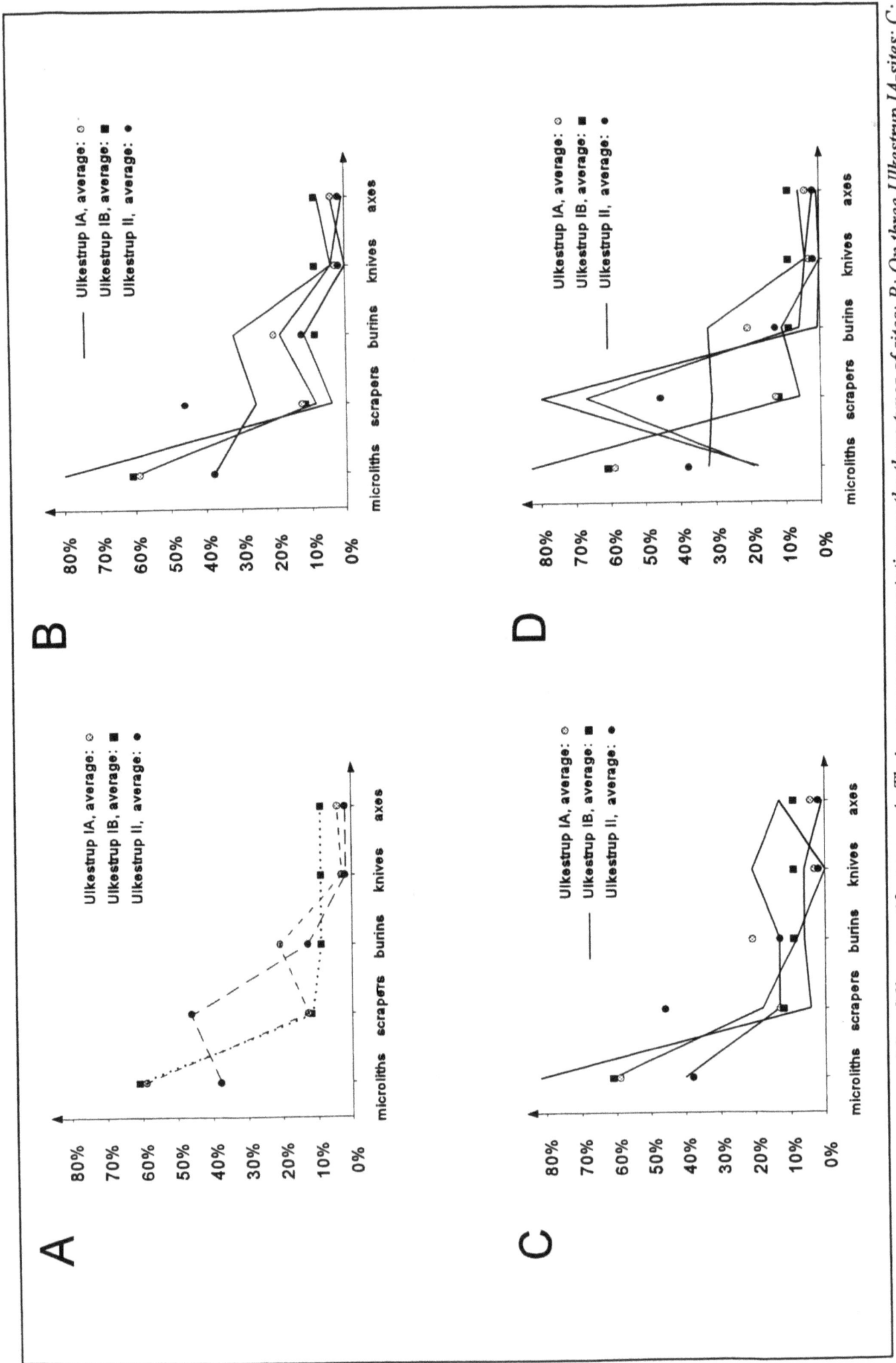

Fig.27. The relative appearance of five different artifact types A: Their average representation on the three types of sites; B: On three Ulkestrup IA-sites; C: On Three Ulkestrup IB-sites; D: On four Ulkestrup II-sites. The average values from A is shown in the other figures by circles, dots and black squares.

composition of artifacts found in it. With some of the units only very little material from the waste layer is included in the published totals, whereas with others, it constitutes a relatively large part. To make the materials comparable, the following is based on counts of the artifacts from the main concentrations which are here regarded as an equivalent of the dwelling area.

Microliths, scrapers, burins, knives and axes as the most important and easily recognizable types indicative of different economical activities, were chosen for this purpose. They total here 100% of the artifact population studied. The graphs express the different amounts in which they occur relative to each other. Fig.27A shows the average values for units of the types Ulkestrup IA, IB and II. Fig.27B,C and D show the relative artifact-composition from the single units of each type respectively. Generally, Ulkestrup IA and IB units are similar. The Ulkestrup II units differ by a rather large relative amount of scrapers and relatively few microliths. This tendency, however, is due to the two Klosterlund sites. Had the information on the artifacts from the Duvensee sites of this type been sufficient to include them, this apparent lack of microliths would have been modified considerably.

Generally the graphs for the units belonging to one site-type differ so much from each other that none of the groups can be regarded as either homogeneous with regard to relative artifact composition, or as differing systematically from the other groups. This is equivalent to the findings of Ericka Engelstad concerning the 'neolithic' hunter-gatherers in northern Norway (Engelstad 1984:19-20).

## 5.3. Social organization

On the basis of a number of assumptions, all open for discussion and revision, the following conclusions concerning the social organization of the Maglemose Culture are forwarded:

1) as expected from the ethnographical parallels (eg. Price 1981:35), the basic social unit of the society seems to be the nuclear family. Spatially the basic unit, the hearth-microlith set, behaves as one would expect nuclear families would do on the basis of the ethnographical information available: in the structures interpreted as multi-family dwellings the females seem to be located next to the door and the adults appear to be organized in sequences of woman, man, man, woman.

2) both one and two-family dwellings were in use, with the former dominating in the Preboreal, and the latter playing a more important role in the Boreal. This indicates a development towards larger households, through the Preboreal and the Boreal. Whether the size of the hunting groups also changes accordingly, or it is just a reflection of change in the internal structure of hunting groups of equal size, is impossible to say before we have more information on the spatial organization and number of contemporaneous dwellings at the settlements.

3) Inland there was a rotation between on the one hand summer dwellings containing one or two nuclear families with approximately 12.8 m² per family and on the other winter dwellings containing two nuclear families with approximately 27.7 m² per family. This allows us to operate with territories of a much more restricted size than if the rotation had been between inland summer sites and winter sites on the coast or the Ancylus-lake.

4) in winter, isolated two-family houses were employed on the edges of plateaus connected to northern to western slopes down to the water and offering protection from the prevailing western and southern winds.

5) in summer, smaller two-family or even smaller one-family dwellings were used on the northern, eastern or southern banks of inland lakes giving protection from the western and north-western winds, possibly in hunting groups of 2-5 families. Other sites which most likely were in use during the summer half year are found in elevated positions near the shores of the Ancylus-lake, and in inland positions related to the river systems.

6) there are no obvious traces of assembly camps in the material, but the idea of such socially important gatherings should not be rejected.

The conclusions obtained sketch the picture of a social organization very close to what one ought to expect on the basis of the ethnographical sources of temperate-climate hunter-gatherer cultures. The nuclear family is the basic unit, permitting dispersal or assembly of the hunting groups according to what is the optimal strategy for resource utilization. The dwellings are one and two-family units, the latter with twice the space of the former, or even more. In the two-family dwelling each family has its own hearth. Inland, large isolated two-family dwellings seem to have been used as winter quarters. A grouping of the families into hunting-groups of two to five families or a bit more in the summer half-year is indicated by the material, but will be difficult to prove.

As we see with present hunter-gatherers, care was apparently taken to place the settlements in optimal positions with regard to wind, sun, transportation etc.

It is a surprising fact that the distributional patterns from so many of the small typologically pure Maglemosian units appear so uniform and so well preserved. With the dwellings located on solid ground this may be due to the fact that some, and maybe all, were placed in shallow dugout pits, protecting the finds from the worst effects of ploughing and other disturbances.

Hopefully, it will be possible to apply similar types of analysis to materials from related cultures, so that a more differentiated understanding of the change and dispersal of cultural tradition in prehistory can be obtained than the traditional one, based mainly on artifact types and reconstruction of prehistoric economies.

## 5.4. Strategy for further research

In the 70's the main aim of archaeology was to reveal the social organization of prehistoric societies as a part of their strategies for adaption and resource exploitation. The means were mainly typological information (artifacts), information on resources utilized (remains of food resources preserved) and ethnographic information of a very general character. To obtain information on the social organization of a prehistoric hunter-gatherer society it has been necessary to introduce, from ethnography, new conventions concerning some general aspects of human spatial behaviour.

In ethnography, such symbolic and practical

organizations of phenomena in time and space are dealt with in their full cosmic (multidimensional) extent (Tanner 1991:39). In archaeology we are only able to excavate reflections of horizontal (two-dimensional) organizational patterns. It is therefore fortunate that interpersonal relations in most cases are reflected at this level.

The present work is based on the sites available from the last 92 years of excavation of Maglemosian sites. The quality of the excavations varies greatly from site to site. However it has been regarded as important to extract a maximum of information, as a basis for further research. Thus, this work must not be regarded as an end in it self, but as a primary step towards distinguishing the development of social organization from the mesolithic to the neolithic.

As a consequence of the poor state of preservation and the mechanical disturbance of the land-based bog basins available today, the number of sites in a state of preservation worthy of excavating to elucidate social aspects must be regarded as extremely restricted. To compensate for this, a new research concept in a couple of well preserved submerged bogs with both mesolithic and neolithic sites is now being developed (Grøn 1990a:83-85; in press A; in press B).

# 6. Catalogue

## 1) Ulkestrup II upper floor

(see section 2.2.)

## 2) Ulkestrup II lower floor

(see section 2.2.)

## 3) Duvensee W.8

The site was located on an former little island in the Duvensee Basin, not far from Lübeck. It was excavated by Dr. Klaus Bokelmann in 1978-1981 (Bokelmann et.al.1981). The site consisted of a rather badly preserved birch-bark floor measuring approximately 3 by 3 m, with a central hearth consisting of sand, ashes, charcoal and partly burnt hazelnut shells. Immediately to the south of this "röststelle" was observed a small but noticeable concentration of microliths. The site contained quite a number of blades and flakes with steep retouch,

lithic waste and good observations of the floor, the hearth and the sediments (Bokelmann personal communication).

From a typological point of view the material from the site seems very uniform (Bokelmann et.al. 1981:25). The presence of flake axes in the Maglemose Culture is not regarded as a problem any more (eg. Johansson 1990:74-77).

The site is dated to 7580±75 BC and by palynology dated to the transition from Preboreal to Boreal. According to Bokelmann the site has been located approximately 2 metres from the contemporaneous shoreline, which ran NNW-SSE to the west of it (Bokelmann et.al. 1981).

No remains of a superstructure were observed. In 1989 Bokelmann states without any arguments that none of the known Maglemosian bark floors (including the Ulkestrup Huts) represent the inner space of huts (Bokelmann 1989:17). It shall be maintained here that the lack of evidence for a superstructure does not necessarily imply that one was not present.

The floor contains one small microlith concentration and one hearth (fig.20B; fig.28A).

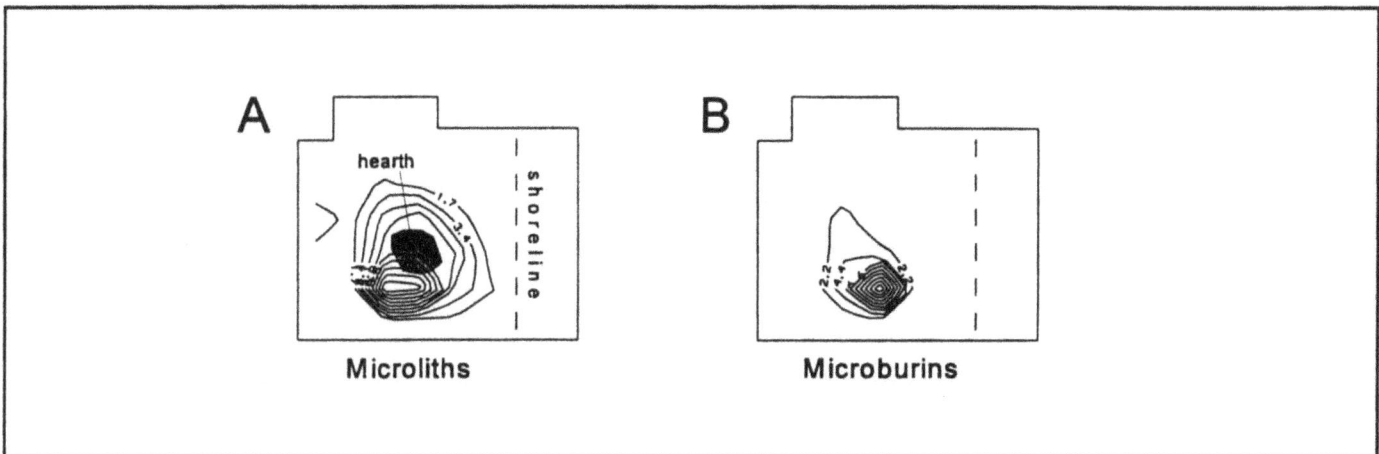

*Fig.28. Duvensee W.8. Distributions. Equidistances A: 1.7; B: 2.2*

micro burins, some flake and core axes and a few burins and scrapers. Apart from the axes this material and the waste was concentrated within the floor area (Bokelmann et.al.1981; Bokelmann, personal communication).

The excavation is of a very high quality with exact three-dimensional registration of all artifacts and the

## 4) Duvensee W.13

For general information on the Duvensee sites see above (3.1.1.) The site was located on an earlier little island in the Duvensee Basin, not far from Lübeck. It was excavated by Dr. Klaus Bokelmann in 1982-1983 and contained the 'relics' of a little pine-bark floor and a large hearth consisting of a 2 by 2 metres

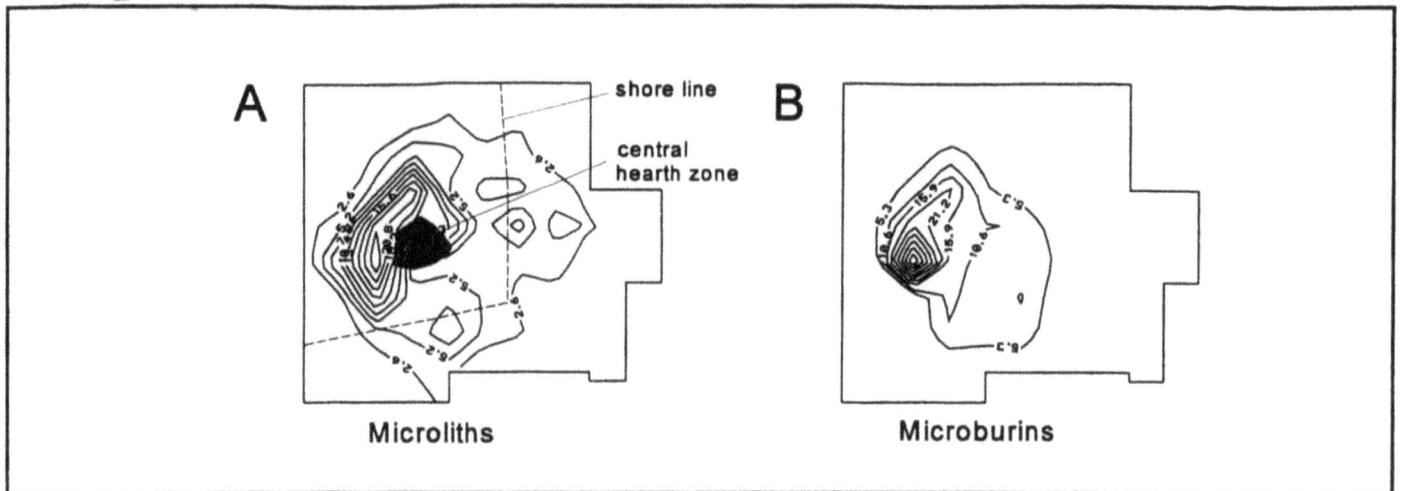

*Fig.29. Duvensee W.13. Distributions. Equidistances A: 2.6; B: 5.3*

large and up to 12 cm thick sand layer with charcoal, hazelnut shells and bark fragments. Its central part measured about 1 metre in diameter. The hearth has been C14-dated to 6980±160 BC and 6750±80 BC (Bokelmann et.al.1985:14-19). From a typological point of view the material from the site appears very uniform, but maybe a bit too young for the C14-dating with the content of 'Sværdborg-triangles' observed (Bokelmann 1985:25).

The excavation is of a very high quality with three-dimensional registration of all artifacts, exact registration of the lithic waste and good observations of the barkfloor, the hearth and the sediments (Bokelmann personal communication).

Information on the distribution of lithic waste has not been available, but the microlithic pieces, the knives and the hearth zone seem to make up a main concentration of 3 by 4 metres with the longitudinal axis NE-SW.

A waste layer deposited in water or in a moist shore zone is found immediately to the south of this concentration. Possibly the shoreline was equally close to the east (Bokelmann 1985:15,17).

A small but noticeable concentration of microliths and micro burins was found immediately to the west of the hearth (fig.29A, fig.20F).

The site must have been orientated towards the water to the south or have been placed with the water equally close from south to east (Bokelmann 1985:17).

## 5) Klosterlund 1E

The site was located on a narrow, sandy, east-west orientated ridge in the peat, a former sand spit jutting into what was then Bølling Lake. It was excavated by Therkel Mathiassen in 1935. The excavation area, which measured 194 m², contained two flint concentrations, one western and one eastern. Here we shall first focus on the latter: Klosterlund 1E (Mathiassen 1937:132-134; Report in the Danish National Museum A37408).

The culture layer was conceived of as one stratigraphical unit, and finds from different levels were not kept separate. Artifacts, blades, micro blades, cores and fire damaged pieces were collected and registered for each square metre, whereas the main body of the "lithic waste" (pieces not conforming to the former groups) were counted and then discarded (a normal procedure at that time). Some artifacts may have been lost. For instance the 16 micro burins found at Klosterlund E1 may seem a small amount for the 42 microliths found there. Meanwhile the general impression is that the major part of the microliths and the larger artifacts have been registered, and thus give a reliable impression of the original distributions.

The site has a clear bipartite character (fig.30A; fig.20D). On the top of the ridge it appears as a 4.5 metres long (east-west) and 4 metres (north-south) broad concentration of flints in a 10-40 cm thick culture layer of grey sand containing little pieces of charcoal and some humus from the covering 20-30 cm of sterile peat. To the south, at an essentially lower level, it consists of a more or less separate

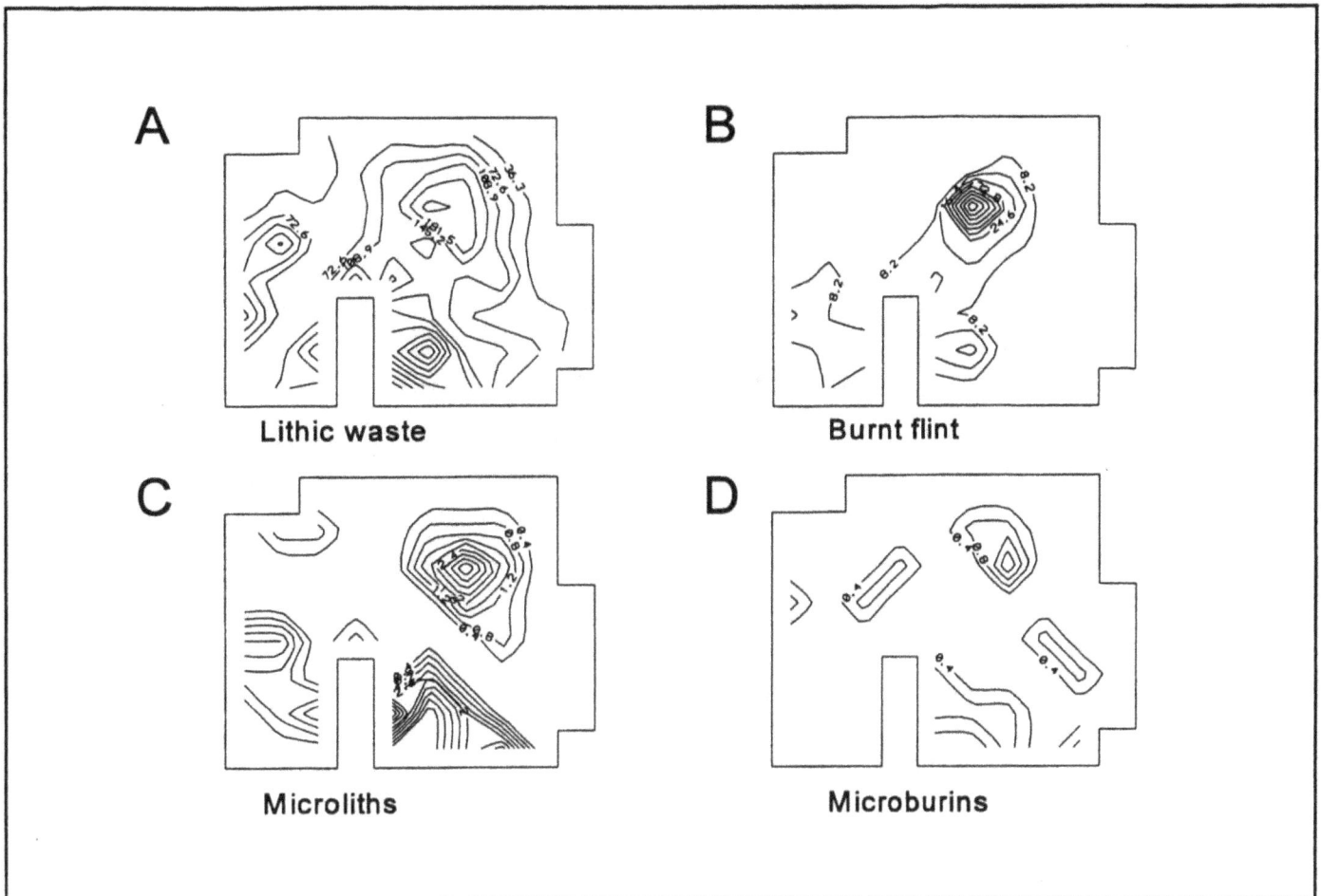

*Fig.30. Klosterlund 1E. Distributions. Equidistances A: 36.3; B: 8.2; C: 0.4; D: 0,4*

concentration of flint embedded in the peat and gytja of the bog. Mathiassen describes how culture layer and the underlying peat here "down the slope" were kneaded together by trampling. At a greater distance from the ridge the culture layer could be seen as a stripe of flints and charcoal in the peat and gytja (Mathiassen 1937:132-134). Clearly the latter must represent a waste layer deposited under moist/wet conditions only a couple of metres from the main concentration.

The flint material "produces a very uniform impression, without the smallest trace of later mixture" (Mathiassen 1937:134). The microlithic material is totally dominated by B.P. type 39, and some B.P. type 40, indicating a rather early typological dating (Brinch Petersen 1967:177). Iversens palynological dating of the site is to the late Preboreal (Mathiassen 1937:183) and fits the C14 dating to 7200-7300 BC uncalibrated (Brinch Petersen 1973:124).

In the eastern part of the 4 by 4.5 metres large main concentration is one small and noticeable concen-

tration of microliths (fig.30C). Immediately to the west of this, exactly in the centre of the main concentration, is a very noticeable and strong concentration of burnt flint (fig.30B).

## 6) Klosterlund 1W

For the basic data concerning the excavation, dating and typology of the western concentration at the Klosterlund 1 site see under site nr.5 in this catalogue.

The western concentration is related to the same shoreline as the eastern one approximately 15 metres to the west of it, and also has a waste accumulation to the south, in the former lake or on its moist shore zone (fig.31A).

The main concentration measures approximately 4 by 4 metres and is roughly rectangular, with the longitudinal axis east-west (fig.31A). It coincides with a lens of the grey sandy culture layer of the site (fig.31D), increasing in thickness from 20 to 40 cm

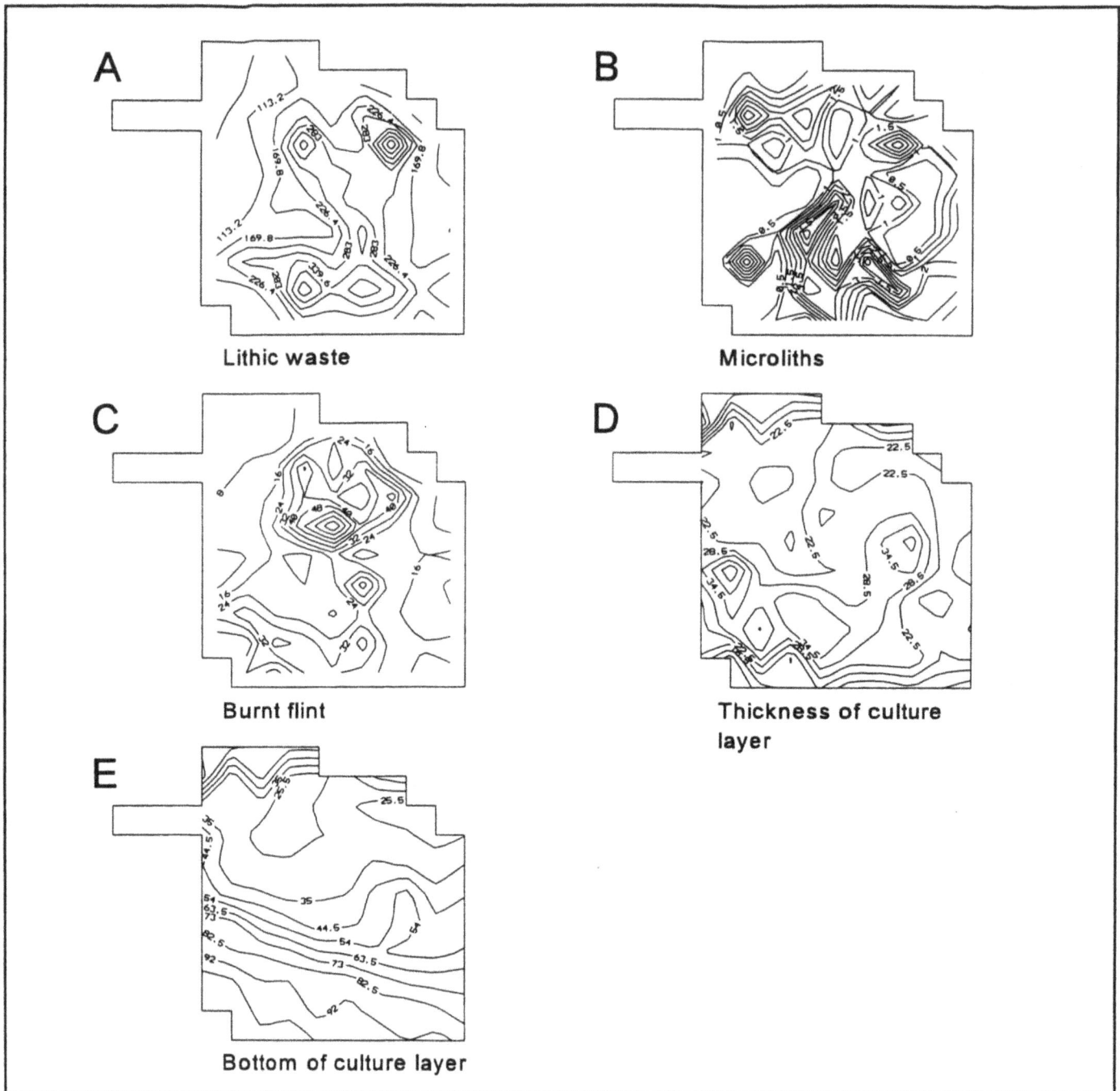

*Fig.31. Klosterlund 1W. Distributions. Equidistances A: 56.6; B: 0.5; C: 8.0; D: 6.0 cm; E: 9.5 cm*

in its central western part. The main concentration is connected to the east-west orientated waste layer by a narrow tongue of material located exactly where the culture layer, according to the levelling, in a north-south orientated zone goes deeper into the underground than in the surrounding area (fig.31E). The phenomenon looks like a walking zone, where material has been trodden into the ground. The shore appears to have been only 1-2 metres from the main concentration.

Only one regular concentration of microliths is found inside the main concentration, in its north-east-corner. Outside, to the west, is a separate concen-

tration of microliths, either a contemporaneous related activity area or an independent chronological unit. The largest concentration of microliths is found related to the tongue connecting the main concentration to the waste layer and in the waste layer itself, and is thus found outside the main concentration.

No direct indications of a hearth were observed in this area, but a noticeable concentration of burnt flint (fig.31C) in the southernmost part of the main concentrations western half, with its centre 2 metres WSW of the centre of the microlith concentration (fig.31B; fig.20G).

The distribution of lithic waste shows two tops inside the main concentration, a smaller one in its western part, and a larger one congruent with the microlith concentration.

The Klosterlund 1W concentration contains one microlith concentration and one hearth zone.

## 7) Magleby Nor A

Since the site Magleby Nor from southern Langeland has not yet been published, the following is based on the excavation report (LMR jnr.11372) which the excavator Jens Bech has kindly let me use. The site was situated on the western side of the northern end of a 200 metres long, to the north 30-40 metres broad and up to 1.5 metres high NNE-SSW orientated island surrounded by peat deposits in the former lake.

In 1983 ploughing revealed Maglemose flint on the site within a 30x40 metres large area. An excavation carried out in 1984 by Jens Bech for Langelands Museum revealed two concentrations of Maglemose flint, a western one (A) (fig.32A) measuring approximately 3.5 by 4 metre, and an eastern one (B). The latter has not been excavated in its full extent (see site nr.19 in this catalogue). We shall therefore focus on concentration A.

The excavated finds were registered in square metres. The plough soil that contained the main part of the finds was sieved with a mask size of 7 mm or less. Some artifacts were found in the up to 4 cm thick sand layer under the plough soil. Under this sand layer was clay moraine. There cannot be much doubt that nearly all of the material has been registered, and that the finds therefore give a reliable impression of the original distributions.

The site is only dated typologically. Apart from a few scrapers, retouched blades, burins, and a single core axe, the microliths make up by far the main part of the tool types in the material. The B.P. type 39 dominates totally. Isoscalene triangles (B.P. type 48) are second, not quite taking up one fourth of the microlithic material. A dating around 7000 BC seems reasonable (Brinch Petersen 1967:177; Johansson 1990:52).

The excavator notes in the report: "The distribution of finds in the area A thus might cause guesses concerning the presence of a tent or hut site", and "For the latter interpretation speaks the very sharp delimitation of the find area".

The site consists of the A-concentration, a small concentration of Maglemosian flint (fig.32A) about 3.5 by 4 metres large. Its north-western part contains a small but noticeable concentration of microliths with 8 in one m² is (fig.32C).

Centrally in the northern part of the A-concentration, immediately to the east of the microlith concentration, indicates a concentration of charcoal particles and a diffuse shallow pit-like structure containing charcoal coloured sand, the existence of a hearth zone of several square metres. A small concentration of burnt flint was observed (fig.32B,C)

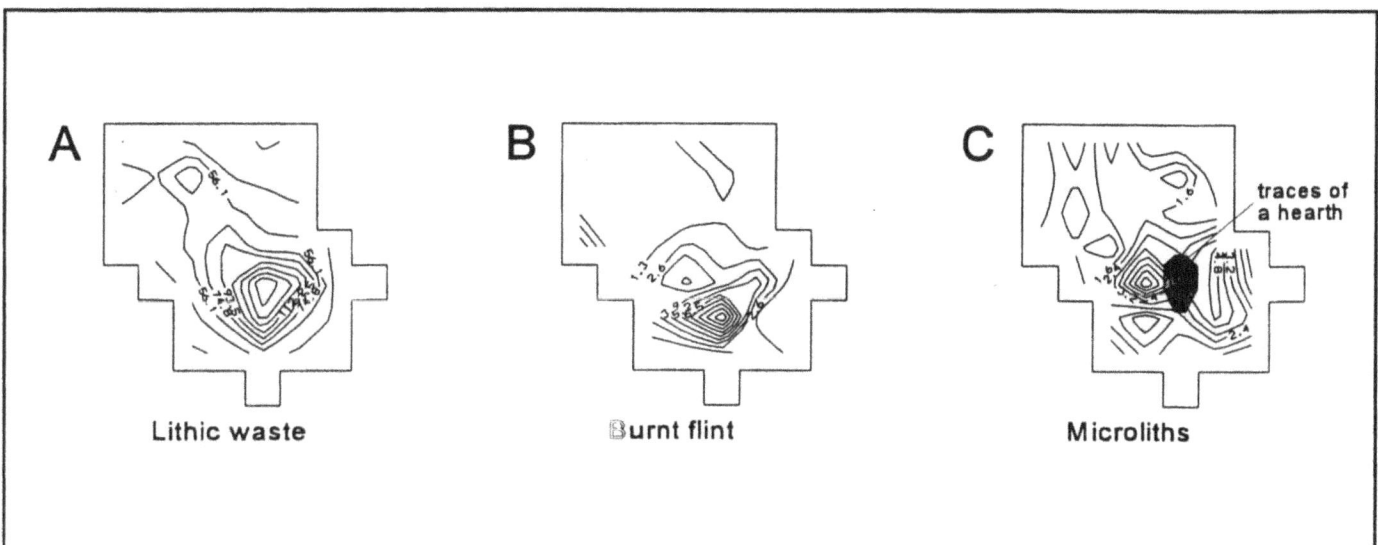

*Fig.32. Magleby Nor A. Distributions. Equidistances A: 18.7; B: 1.3; C: 0.8*

overlapping the southern part of this zone.

From the topography and the geological sections it appears that the A-concentration with a rather high water level must have been related to an east-west orientated shore, whereas a somewhat lower water level would form a shore from west to north of it, at approximately 15-20 m's distance. The peat which might have yielded important information on the water level has decomposed due to the drainage and ploughing of the higher levels of the island.

The distribution of finds inside the excavated area and from the test pits located with less than 3 metres between them, indicates that a tongue of waste projected about 8 metres to the north-west from the main concentration, similar to the

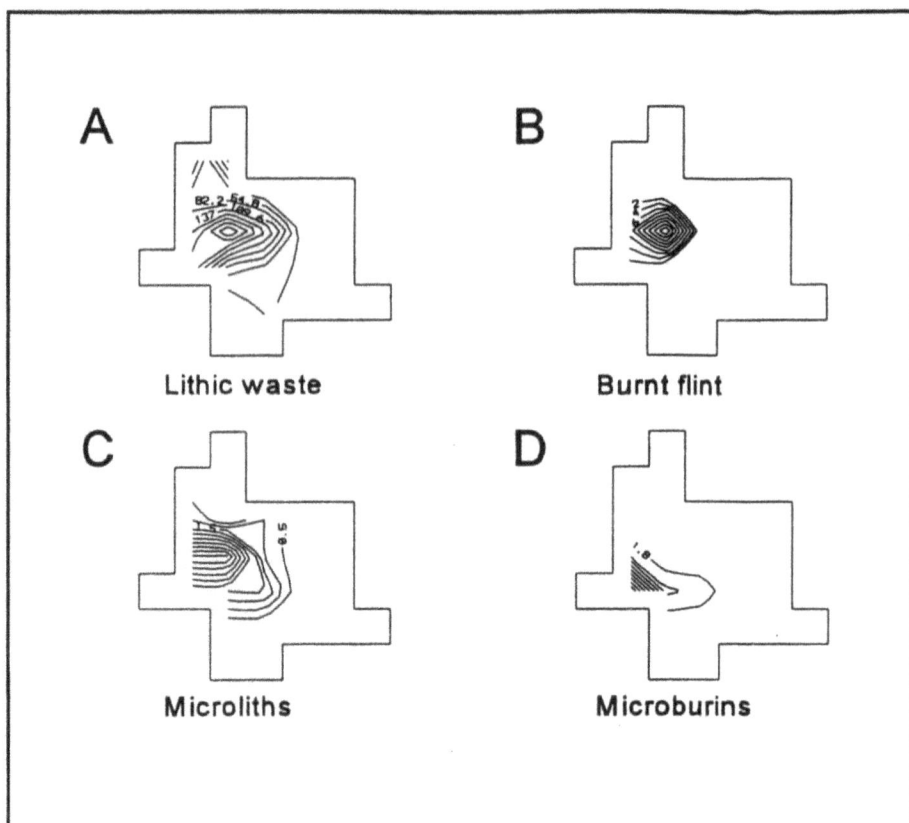

*Fig.33. Bare Mosse II. Distributions. Equidistances A: 27.4; B: 2.0; C: 0.5; D: 1.8*

"waste layers" deposited in water or in moist shore zones known from a number of other Maglemosian sites. This seems to indicate a relatively high water level with an east-west orientated shore a few metres to the north of the main concentration.

Since the settlement already in 1949 was encircled by peat cuttings, it is now difficult to obtain a clear picture of the topography of the contemporaneous surroundings (course of shore, distance to coast etc.)(Althin 1954:51; Skar 1988:87,89,101; Welinder 1971:66-71,73-74,85 plate 1).

## 8) Bare Mosse II

The site was located in south-western Sweden close to Halmstad and excavated in 1949 by Althin. The little, isolated culture layer was discovered at level 165, embedded in the peat about 20 metres from the western edge of the bog, where the site Bare Mosse IV was located. It contained a noticeable and sharply restricted oval concentration of flint approximately 4 by 4.5 metres in section (fig.33A) and 4-5 cm thick. Deviations from distributions published elsewhere are based on my own observations.

The culture layer is C14 dated to 7110±100 BC, which is equivalent to Nilssons BO1. In spite of the fact that the sediments from the levels connected to the culture layer were rather compressed, and thus unsuited for pollen dating, Welinder accepts a palynological dating of them to Nilsson's BO2.

The finds were registered in square metres. Welinder suggests that the large amount of lithic waste in square (-0/+4) may be due to the fact that Althin choose this square for test sieving. However the relative amount of flint pieces smaller than 1 cm is also quite high (more than 70%) in the adjacent squares (-0/+3) and (+0/+2). Thus, the feature does not seem to indicate a noticeable variation in the excavation technique, but a regular concentration of lithic waste. That it has been possible to refit 48% of the artifacts, a quite high ratio (Skar 1988:90), indicates that the excavation in general is of a reasonable quality.

Welinder found some pieces of lithic waste in the gytja in the square (x=+7, y=+7.5), 8 metres to the north-east of the circular concentration, at level -246 to -253 (nearly 1 metre below the culture layer). Because of their lack of patination, which differs from the heavy patination of the pieces from the main concentration, he regarded them as belonging to an older and deeper layer representing the hypothetical site Bare Mosse IV (Welinder 1971:73-75). In the neighbouring squares (x=+8, y=+7,+8) excavated by Althin, some more worked flints including a brown patinated piece were found at a higher level (-221 to -244). Exclusively on the basis of the brown patina of this piece, the flint in this horizon is generally related to a another brown patinated flake found deep in square (x=+8, y=0) to the east of the concentration and pollen-dated to the older part of Nilssons BO1 (Welinder 1971:68,69). This differs from the dating to BO2 of the main concentration, suggested by Welinder.

Skar's refitting, however, has proved that at least one of the unpatinated flints from the north-eastern square (x=+7, y=+7.5) derives from the Bare Mosse II-concentration (Skar 1988:101). This makes it unlikely that the material from Althin's neighbouring square, found at a higher level than the unpatinated pieces and dated to BO1, should be older than Bare Mosse II. Further, it supports Althin's original assumption that the material in the gytja belongs to a water deposited waste layer belonging to the circular culture layer, and thus that the water, to the north-east, was quite close to the main concentration. In similar situations - for instance in Åmosen - it is very often seen that the material from a waste layer is unpatinated whereas the material from the settlement surface is clearly patinated (Andersen 1983:17).

The finds from level -178 to -194 in the *Cladium* and *Phragmites-Thelypteris* peat in square (x=-3, y=7.5), excavated by Welinder north-west of the central concentration, are regarded as belonging to Bare Mosse II. However a find from level -199 is regarded as belonging to the older hypothetical Bare Mosse IV horizon (Welinder 1971:74,75). It seems more plausible that all of this material is waste from Bare Mosse II.

A possibility is that the (somewhat problematic) palynological dating to Nilssons BO2 is wrong, and the C14 dating of the culture layer to Nilssons BO1 is correct. If this suggestion is correct, a coastline running approximately east-west, quite close to the site is indicated, quite equivalent to the view held by Althin. If the brown patinated pieces found deep to the east of the main concentration belong to it, we may have a SE-NW orientated shore. Of course some precaution must be taken because of the character of these data.

With regard to distribution patterns, the microliths (fig.33C) make up a small concentration in the westernmost part of the main concentration, whereas burnt flint (fig.33B) makes up a little concentration in its centre (fig.20E).

## 9) Barmosen I

The site, which was located in the northern part of the bog Barmosen on southern Zealand, was excavated in the period 1967-1971 by a group of amateurs directed by Axel Johansson, himself an amateur and at that time the leader of Sydsjællands Museum in Vordingborg. The work was carried out in collaboration with the Natural Science Department of the Danish National Museum (Johansson 1990:12).

From its typological appearance the material seems to belong to the Preboreal (7500 BC or older), whereas three C14-datings from the hearth point to a date around 6400 BC It must be admitted that the latter dating is difficult to believe, and it appears most likely that the charcoal dated has been contaminated by humus acid as Johansson suggests (Johansson 1990:46-47,53).

The material (fig.22B) appeared as a thin compact layer of worked flint, charcoal, bark etc. under half a metre of peat with an irregular rectangular main concentration measuring approximately 3 by 4 metres and the longitudinal axis orientated NE-SW. Within all of this area were preserved bark pieces found (possibly European aspen), apparently the remains of a bark floor. Centrally was a diffuse hearth zone (fig.34A) measuring 1.5 by 2.4 m, orientated WNW-ESE and consisting of sand mixed with charcoal and containing more or less clayish parts (Johansson 1990:13,16). These are probably parallels to the clay found in other Maglemosian hearths (2.1.2.). The north-eastern part of the main concentration was observed to have a very noticeable and sharp restriction over 1.5 metre (Johansson 1968:108), supporting the impression that the whole concentration represents a dwelling.

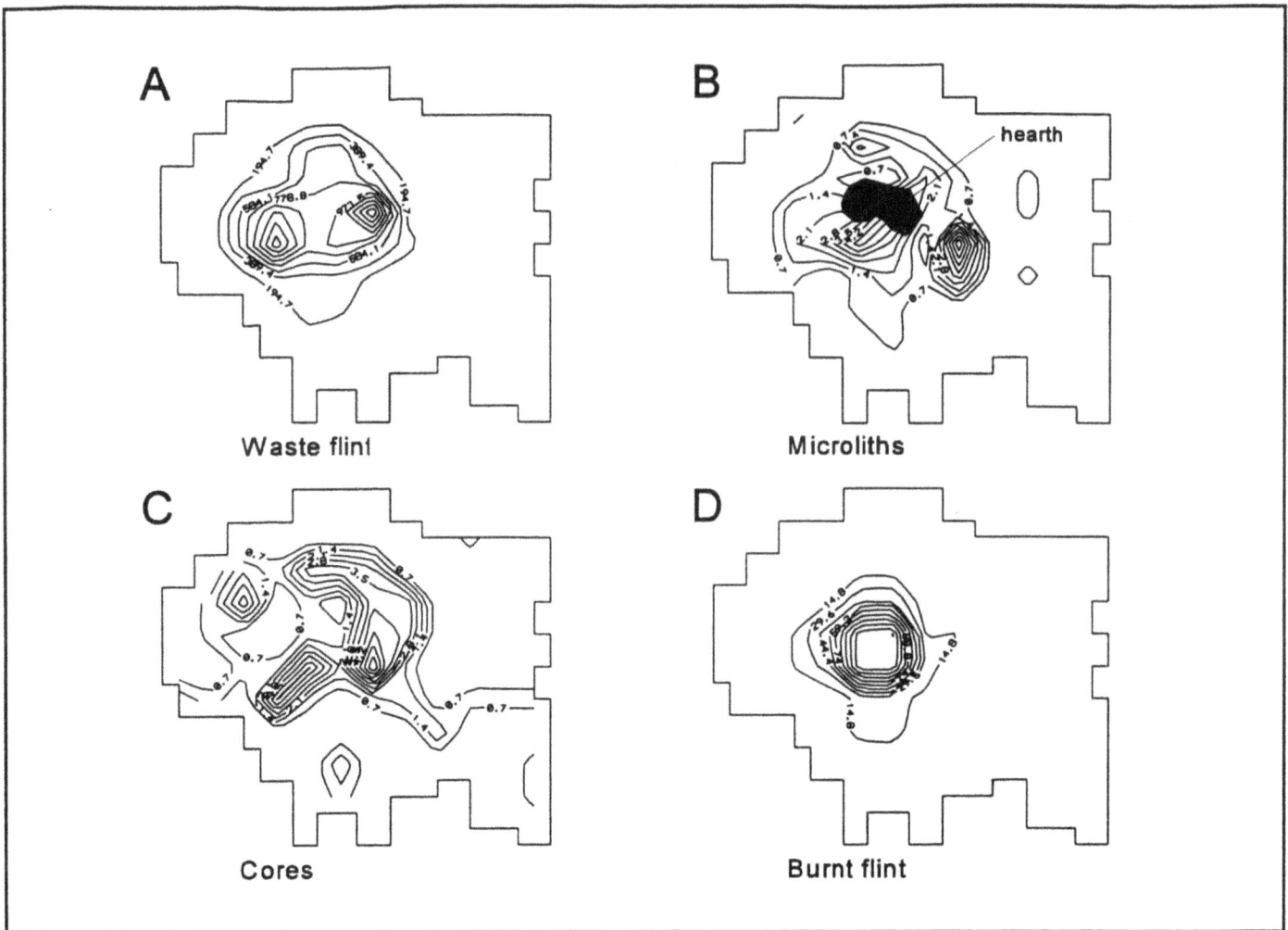

*Fig.34. Barmosen I. Distributions. Equidistances A: 194.7; B: 0.7; C: 0,7; D: 14.8*

According to Johansson there are indications that the shoreline may have been to the south of the main concentration (Johansson 1990:16).

The western part of the culture layer was disturbed prior to the excavation and the waste in the central area was excavated and registered in squares up to 2 by 2 metres (this is also valid for artifacts not recognized immediately and thus escaping exact 3-dimensional registration). Where an amount of material is related to such a 2 by 2 metres square, the interpolation (fig.34) has been carried out as if each of the four squares in it contained ¼ of its total (Johansson's interpolation was made on the same basis, Johansson, personal communication). Such a method of course only gives a very rough approximation to the original distribution and must be taken with all possible precaution (Grøn 1992a;1994).
Johansson notes that to the SE of the concentration were the most finds outside the 'dwelling', thus suggesting that the entrance may have been located on this side (Johansson 1990:16). A north-south orientated tongue of material is connected to the

easternmost part of the main concentration, possibly representing a waste layer deposited in water or a moist shore zone. This may indicate not only that the entrance was to the east but also that the shore was to this side.

Inside the main concentration, in its southern part, is found only one concentration of microliths (fig.34B). The hearth (fig.34B,D) is to the north of this. An eastern microlith concentration was found outside the main concentration on the border of the area with bark and is probably related to the 'waste layer'. Thus it may be regarded as an external feature.

The distribution of the cores (fig.34C) is obviously restricted to the periphery of the main concentration and the bark area, literally following its edge. The external microlith concentration is also clearly outside the area marked by the cores.

The results may indicate that Barmosen I is orientated towards a shore to the east. The site is important as an example of coincidence between a main concentration and a bark floor with a central hearth. Due to the problems concerning registration of the distributions and the lack of information concerning the location of the contemporaneous shore, the site must be regarded with precaution.

## 10) Hjemsted

The site, which is located in the sandy area close to Skærbæk in southern-western Jutland, was uncovered during Per Ethelberg's large scale excavations for Haderslev Museum at the iron age locality Hjemsted in 1986. In the periphery of the approximately 20 acres large excavation area, just on the border of a low moist area, the site (fig.22D) appeared as a 2.5 by 3.5 metres large D-shaped stone ring delimiting a shallow pit containing a lenticular grey homogeneous sand layer with mesolithic flints. The 'flat' side was orientated to the east towards the moist area, and only here did the lens appear a few metres outside the stone structure. The topography indicates that the structure was about 2 metres from the moist area.

Kindly informed immediately by Per Ethelberg and allowed to enlarge the excavation area, I had the opportunity to make supplementary stratigraphical observations by excavating a 1 metre broad ditch from the already excavated structure into the moist area. The site was excavated in ¼ m² squares, all the material being sieved. The profiles and supplementary borings show that the old underground slopes slightly down into the moist area, and that the latter gradually had been filled in by aeolian sand deposits, some of which contained small quantities of ex-

tremely destructed peat allowing no possibilities for a pollen dating.

The lithic material consists of micro blades, a few blades and two atypical scrapers. Technically it is of Maglemosian character, but includes no dating types. We assume that the up to 15 cm thick grey sand lens consisted of sand polluted by charcoal and humus carried into a shallow dwelling pit, during the mesolithic habitation (3.1.3.b.). If thus all of the sand had been exposed to sunlight, and covered relatively quickly after it had been deposited in the shallow pit, TL- and OSL-dating of the lower 10 cm of the layer would be possible. This was carried out by Vagn Mejdahl from the Nordic Laboratory for Thermoluminescence-Dating and gave a (TL-)dating of 7800±700 BC (R-862701) and an (OSL-)dating of 6650±500. These datings are not very precise, but both allow a dating to approximately 7100 BC, in the earlier part of the Maglemose Culture.

Centrally in the southern part of the structure was a very little concentration of blades, micro blades and other pieces of lithic waste (fig.35A). Outside this, the number of worked flints was restricted to a few pieces per square. Only in and immediately around this concentration, worked flints were found deeper than 5 cm into the grey sand lens, indicating that they had been involved in some activities on the spot.

Burnt flints (fig.35B) appeared only in very restricted numbers with a maximum of 10 in one ¼ m²-square. This small but noticeable concentration is located centrally in the northern half. The north-south-profile through the structure shows that the grey sand in the lens here was somewhat darker than

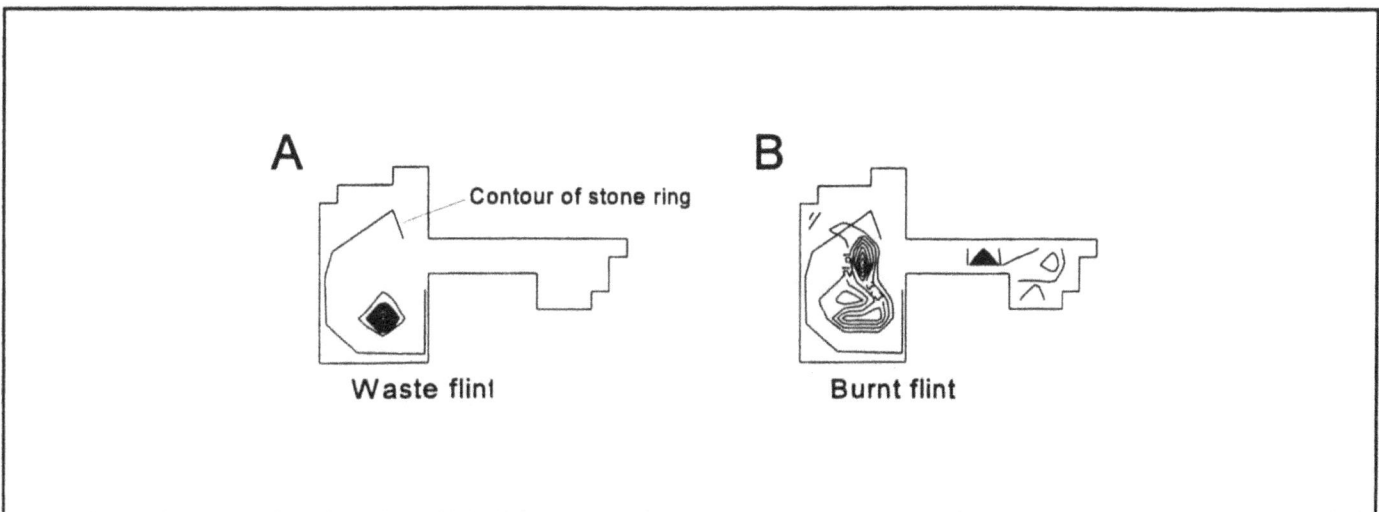

*Fig.35. Hjemsted. Distributions. Equidistances A: 7.9; B: 1.1*

in the southern half, indicating that a hearth was located centrally in the northern half of the structure.

## 11) Draved 35

In the years 1958-1961 4 Maglemosian sites were excavated in the Draved Bog to the west of Løgumkloster in southern Jutland, by C.L. Vebæk and Holger Kapel for the Danish National Museum. As a result of industrial peat digging, mesolithic culture layers appeared down to 40 cm into the sand under the often several metres thick peat cover.

At three of the sites, sb.nrs. 31, 32 and 35, so large areas were excavated that distribution analysis could be applied. They all were excavated in several tempi: first test holes and ditches were made. If these revealed the presence of culture layers, they were connected into a larger coherent area. From the distribution of waste, among other things, I have a rather consistent feeling that the test holes and trenches were less carefully registered and excavated than the supplementing excavation areas. At least the find intensity in a number of cases seems syste- matically smaller in the former than in the latter. In some cases the finds from the survey excavations have not even been related to single m²-squares in the registration.

Site 35 (fig.22C) was located by means of a 2 metres

broad and 5 metres long east-west orientated test ditch (fig.36A). According to the report the top of the sand layer had been disturbed but apparently not partially removed during the peat digging. The interpolation inside the test excavation area is made on the basis of the numbers outside it, since the registration inside is minimal. The site is C14-dated to 7400-7500 BC (report in the Danish National Museum A48213; Brinch Petersen 1973:124).

In the south-west corner of the excavation area is a more or less round concentration of lithic waste (fig.36A) measuring 4 by 4 metres and with its longitudinal axis NW-SE. To the north-east (and east?) of this is a smaller concentration connected to it, presumably a waste layer.

A noticeable concentration of microliths (fig.36B) (the only one present inside the excavated area) was found in the north-easternmost part of this main concentration, whereas a noticeable concentration of burnt flint (fig.36C) takes up a central position in it, 2 metres south of the microlith concentration in centre to centre distance.

The position of the waste tongue indicate according to the observations made above that the structure was orientated towards a nearby shore to the west or NW.

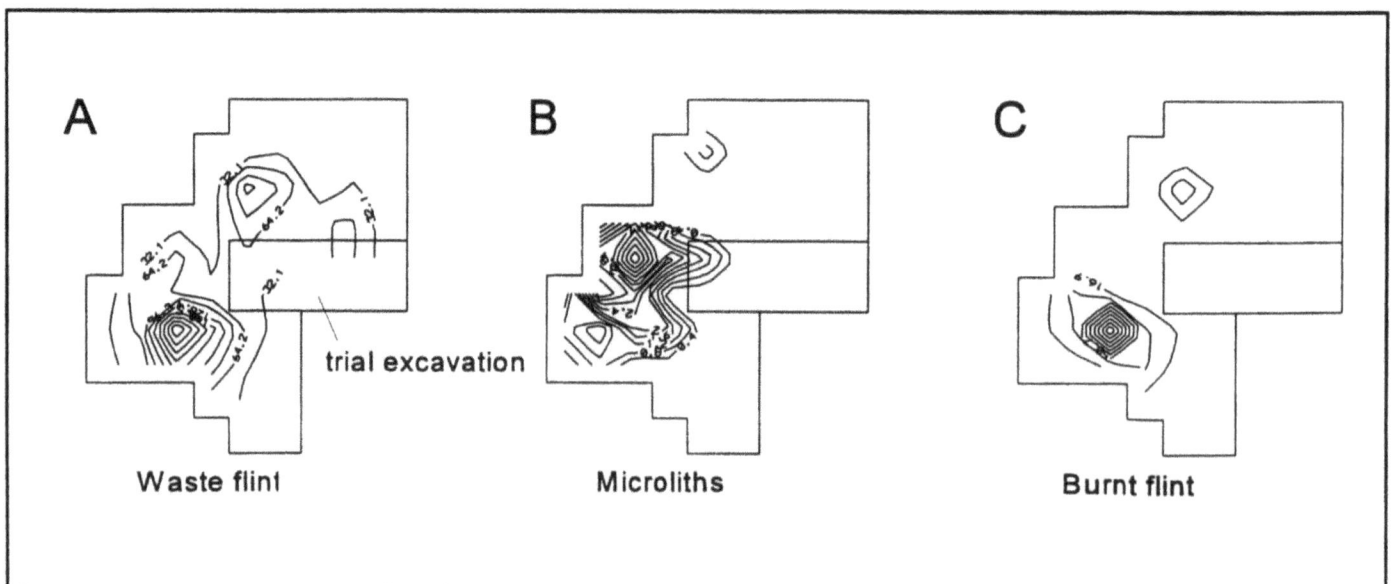

Fig.36. Draved 35. Distributions. Equidistances A: 32.1; B: 0.4; C: 16.9

## 12) Mullerup (Koch and Mathiassen's excavation)

In 1915 Lauge Koch and Therkel Mathiassen, on an islet in the Mullerup Bog, some 120 metres north of Sarauw's excavation, excavated a small Maglemosian concentration (fig.22A) containing remains of birch bark, charcoal, hazelnuts, 3 kg of bone (including bones of fish such as pike), 113 kg of flint (including a couple of recognized microliths) and apparently a hearth (square C: a layer of ashes and burnt flint is reported)(report A28406-10 in the Danish National Museum).

The registration of the material is not very good, and only just allows the reconstruction of a little oval/

## 14) Sværdborg II

Sværdborg II was located in the Sværdborg Bog, southern Zealand. The excavation was carried out by Mogens Ørsnes in 1946. The site consisted of an oblong NE-SW orientated concentration of Maglemosian material measuring approximately 4 by 6 metres (fig.37A; fig.21E). On a palynological and a typological basis the site has been dated to approximately 6200 BC A well-defined limit of the occupation layer was observed at the southern border of the concentration (in the squares 6G, 6D and 6C). During the excavation, artifacts and waste were registered in square metres. All lithic waste, except that from one square, was discarded (Brinch Petersen 1972:43-48,59,70-72).

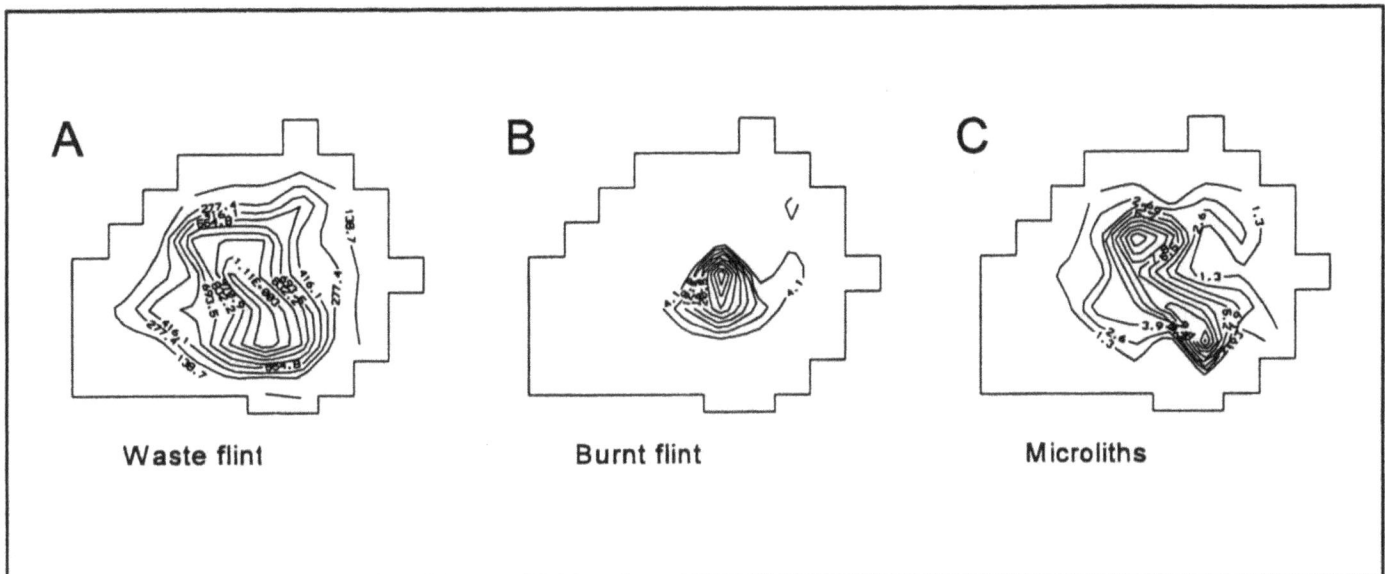

*Fig.37. Sværdborg II. Distributions. Equidistances A: 138.7; B: 4.1; C: 1.3*

rectangular concentration 3 by 4 m, with longitudinal axis north-south and a waste tongue to the west.

The restricted number of microliths observed is most probably due to the lack of experience with this small artifact type at that time. The main importance of the site is that it demonstrates the connection between the remains of a bark floor, a massive concentration of flint 3 by 4 metres and one apparent hearth. Most likely we are dealing with a Ulkestrup II-type unit.

## 13) Ulkestrup I

(see 2.1.)

The site was originally placed on the northern extremity of a large irregular peninsula in the former lake basin. According to the distribution of preserved large bone pieces, mainly found in the south-western corner, the increase in flint density in this direction probably marks the beginning of a waste layer (fig.21E)(Brinch Petersen 1972:48,51,53). The shore must thus have been to the west or south-west of the main concentration, with an orientation closer to NW-SE than to north-south, and not too far from it. Maybe it was separated from the central part of the site by a narrow zone of moist lake marl (Brinch Petersen 1972:52).

The culture layer was apparently only a few millimetres thick. It was positioned directly on the lake marl and in most places covered by 10 cm of peat including 2-4 cm of mud directly upon the layer. It had been disturbed in only three central squares (3C, 3D and 3E) by the production of peat litter (Brinch Petersen 1972:44,52,54).

The microliths (fig.37C) form two small concentrations in the north-eastern part of the main concentration. A line through their centres (approximately 2-3 metres apart from each other) has the direction NW-SE. Between these two, with a slight tendency to the south-west, we find a concentration of burnt flint (fig.37B). Compared to the situation at Svanemosen 28, this may indicate the location of one as well as of more hearths in this area. The position of the burnt flint can be taken as a slight suggestion only that such a hearth/hearths were closer to the water than the microlith concentrations (3.1.5.).

## 15) Duvensee W.6

The location of the site is in the Duvensee Bog, not far from that of Duvensee W.8 mentioned above. The excavation was carried out in 1975 and 1976 by Klaus Bokelmann. The culture layer consisted of flints, charcoal and hazelnut shells, with the main concentration measuring approximately 3.5 by 6 metres (fig.28A). Due to the decomposition of the site, patches of birch bark and remains of larger branches were the only preserved remains of the floor. The preservation of wooden chips to the southeast of the floor indicates that this area was relatively moist and that the water was found in this direction. Most likely the shore was orientated NE-SW only a few metres from the remains of the floor (Bokelmann 1981a:181-183).

The quality of the excavation is very high with a three-dimensional registration of all items, and exact and careful observations of other aspects. Three C14 datings have been obtained from hazelnut shells: 7135±130, 6890±110 and 7140±130 BC (Ki-1111, 1112 and 1113)(Bokelmann 1981a:181).

On the floor were found large blotches of sand with charcoal and hazelnut shells. The blotches seem to make up two hearth zones (fig.21C), of which the northern one was 3.5 metres long north-south and 0.7-1.3 metre broad. Its southern part had a clearly preserved stratigraphy related to a shallow pit only a few centimetres deep. Here its use for roasting hazelnuts could be studied in detail. In the bottom of the pit was found a layer of brown sand - possibly coloured by organic matter from the nuts. Bokelmann distinguishes between a northern zone A to which this hearth and the one of the two microlith concentrations belong, and a southern zone B to which another concentration of microliths and two blotches of sand measuring about 2 metres east-west and 1 metre north-south are related (fig.38B; fig.21C). The latter are interpreted by Bokelmann as two hearths, but may well have made up a 3 metres long north-south orientated blotch together - similar to the hearth from the northern A zone. The thin sandwiched sand and charcoal layers in the profile through the shallow pit in the western part of the northern hearth show that the sand must have been removed from and replaced in this area in connection with the roasting process (Bokelmann 1981a:181-183). Obviously the eastern part of this blotch has served for sand storage (it must be impossible to store sand anywhere without its leaving a sand blotch). A separation of the hearth of zone A into two areas is indicated by its central 50 cm narrow zone. With the less well preserved sand blotches connected to zone B, most likely one represents the hearth zone proper, and the other the area for sand storage.

In 1981 Bokelmann held the opinion that the two zones, signified by a microlith concentration and apparently a hearth each, are contemporaneous. Minor differences in style are explained: "Wahrscheinlich dokumentieren sich hier eher Unterschiede in der Oualität individueller Produktion als strukturelle Änderungen in einem Teil der Jagdwaffen". In 1986, however, he published the point of view that the two zones do not represent contemporaneous units, due to C14 datings to 7150±130 BC (Ki-1111) of the south-western one and 6890±118 BC (Ki-1112) of the north-eastern one. According to the publication of Duvensee W.6, Ki-1111 is 7135±130 (Bokelmann 1981a:181; 1986:149). The distance between the two datings is thus 245 years. The deviation intervals are ±130 and ±110 years, or together 240 years. The gap between the two datings then is only 5 years. Considering the fact that the deviation intervals only mark the ranges within which the corretc datings will be found in 67% of the cases, it must be concluded that these C14 datings

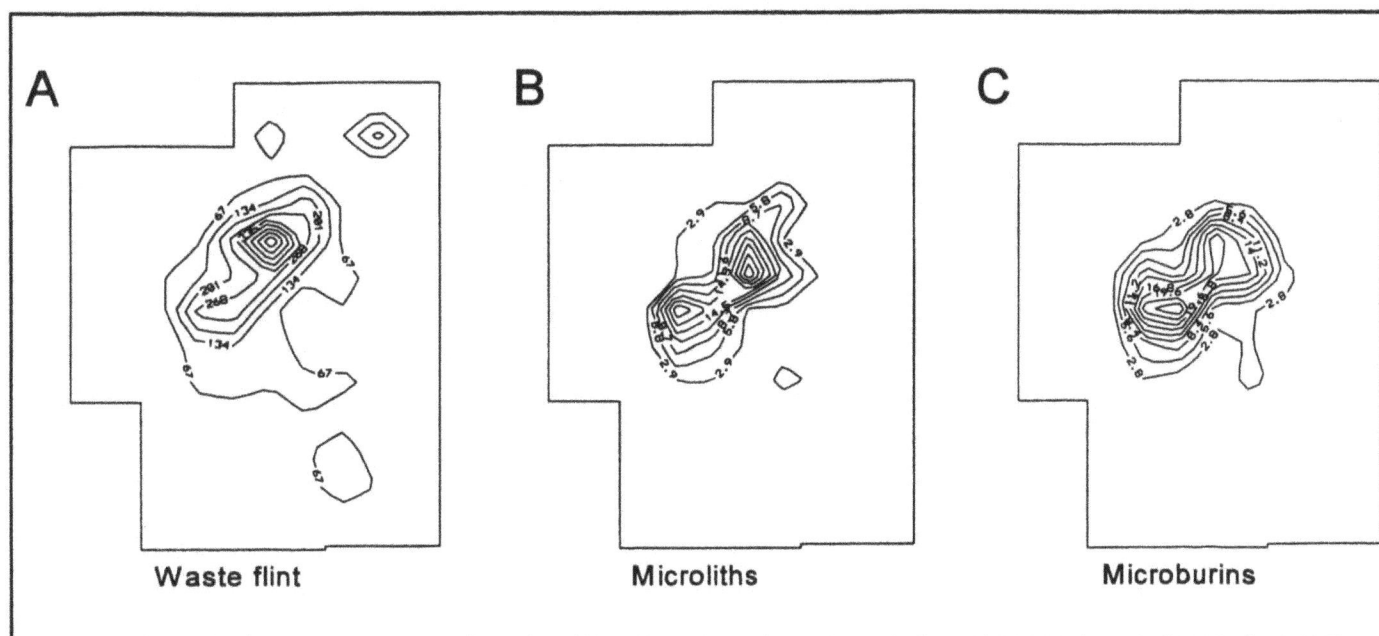

*Fig.38. Duvensee W.6. Distributions. Equidistances A: 67; B: 2.9; C: 2.8*

cannot be used as an argument against contemporaneity. Otherwise we will be forced to accept also that the *upper* bark layer from floor at site W8 dated to 7690±100 BC (Ki-1818) is *older* than the piece found *under* it and dated to 7460±110 BC (Ki-1819)(Bokelmann et.al.1981:25). Here the span between the deviation intervals is 20 years. C14 datings are simply not exact enough for such detailed chronological discussion.

Spatially the microliths make up a pattern with two small concentrations and approximately 2 metres between their centres (fig.21C). One hearth zone belongs to the northern microlith concentration another probably to the southern. These structural features are found inside a main concentration of flint and other kinds of Maglemosian material measuring approximately 3.5 by 6 m. The shore must have been rather close and orientated more or less south-west to north-east, as the wooden chips found to the south-east of the main concentration according to their degree of preservation must have been deposited in a moist shore zone or in shallow water.

## 16) Svanemosen 28

The site was located south-west of Kolding in southern Jutland. One half of it was excavated in 1977 by Erik Jørgensen and Flemming Rieck in collaboration with The Amateur Archaeologists of

Southern Jutland for the Danish National Museum. In 1983 the other half of the site was excavated by the author for Museet på Koldinghus with financial support from The Danish Research Council for the Humanities. The reason for the second campaign was that the already excavated material strongly suggested that the flint concentration represented a typologically pure unit of Ulkestrup II type. The purpose was to investigate the total distributions and to see if the traces of a dwelling were present. Jørgensen and Rieck kindly gave access to their material and entrusted the further excavation to the author.

All material was sieved through a 6x6 millimetre sieve, so that the loss of material can be regarded as minimal. During the first campaign all artifacts were measured 3-dimensionally, whereas the lithic waste was registered in square metres. The culture layer was excavated as one layer and the surface was drawn at the level where worked flints ceased to appear. During the second campaign the excavation was carried out in quarters of square metres and in layers of 5 cm. The material from each unit was kept separate. The preserved sections of the old excavation were registered carefully, and the surface was drawn for each layer.

Svanemosen 28 was located on a north orientated gentle slope down to a clearly visible old bank of the former lake, Svanemosen. The reason for the relatively good preservation of the culture layer is partly

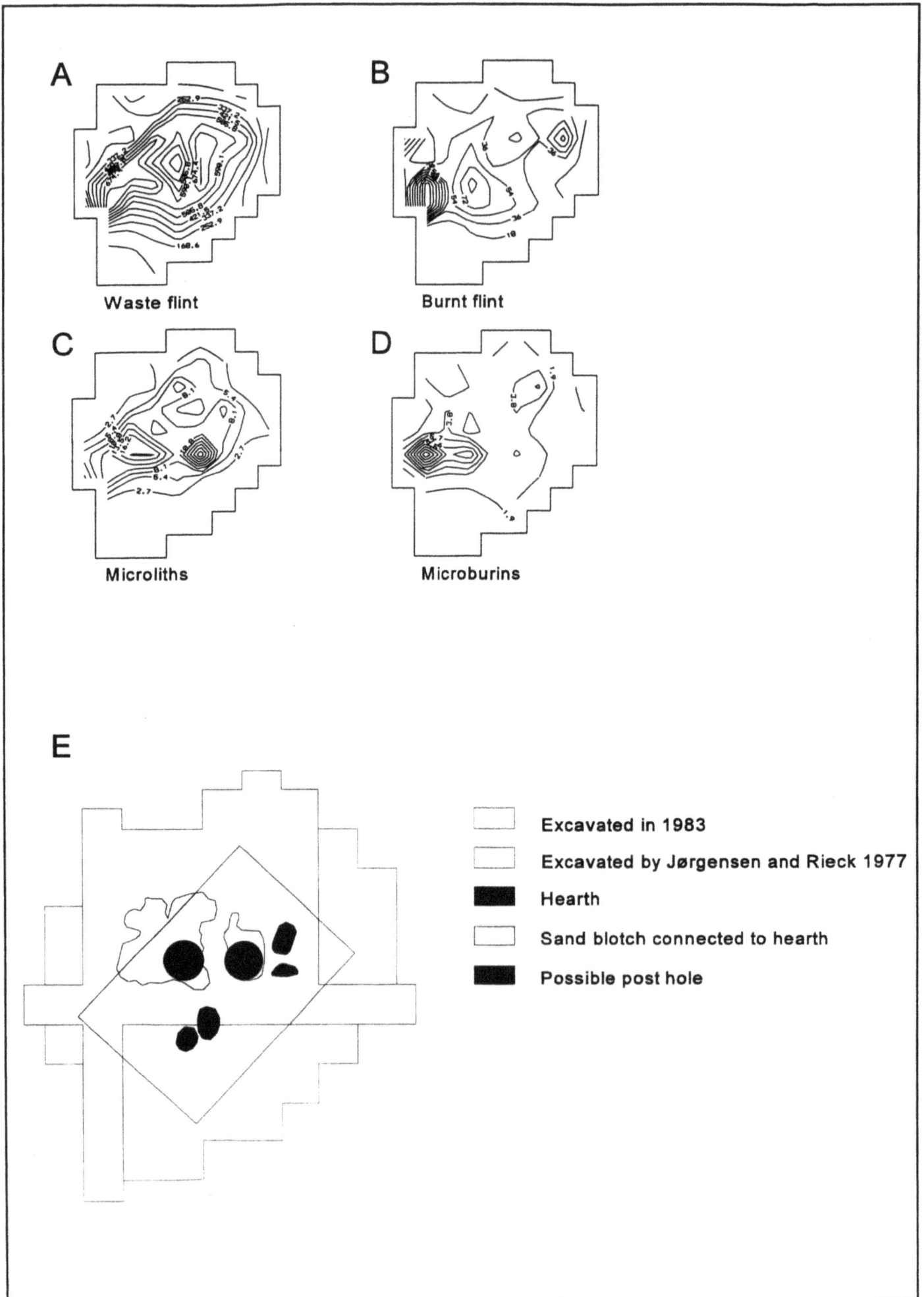

Fig.39. Svanemosen 28. Distributions. Equidistances  A: 84.3;  B: 18;  C: 2.7;  D: 1.9

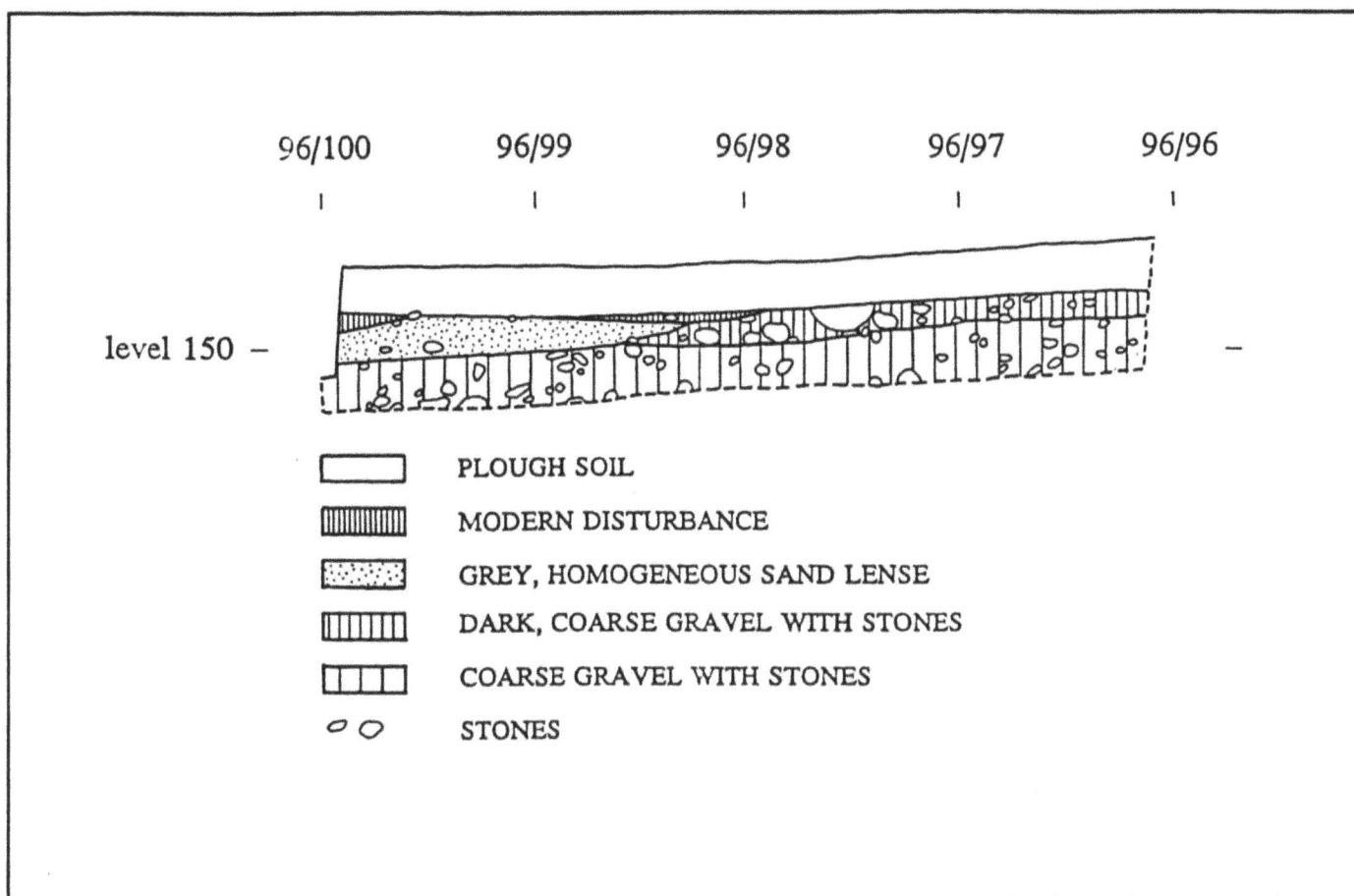

*Fig.40. Svanemosen 28. North-south section through the preserved part of the grey homogeneous sand lens.*

that a protective layer of clay had been washed down from the steeper slope behind the site.

The site can only be dated on a typological basis. The sandy peat outside it was too destructed for a pollen dating, and the amount of charcoal from the culture layer was too small for a C14 dating. The material is typical of very late Maglemosian material from Jutland: occurrence of short scalene triangles and 'triangles' with only the short side retouched, some only 1 cm long. Generally the scalene triangles have an average length of 20.7 mm. A few small trapezoid pieces with retouch on one side and one or two ends are present. Technically the micro burin technique in some of the triangles like with the rectangles is replaced by breaking. A microlith seriation places the site somewhat later than Vinde Helsinge (pollen dated to somewhere around 6300 BC)(Brinch Petersen 1973:125). Altogether a dating to around 6000 BC, into the latest phase of the Maglemose Culture seems realistic.

The site consisted of a noticeable oblong flint concentration with an orientation NE-SW measuring about 5 by 7-8 metres (fig.39A). The concentration was clearly connected to a homogeneous light, grey, sandy lens in the culture layer up to 30 cm thick and measuring approximately 4 by 6 m. To the north, south and east, there was a noticeable change in colour at the edges of the lens. To the west the colour did not change, but the thickness of the layer decreased to 12 cm. The southern north-south section (fig.40) shows clearly that the grey lens, that was nearly free of stones, represents a shallow pit which was dug into an underground consisting of gravel and containing numerous 5-10 cm large stones. Such a shallow pit may well represent a dwelling area.

Interesting is the vertical position of the main part of the flint layer. In the central part, where the lens had a thickness of 25-30 cm (x=96.0-100.0; y=99.5-100.0), adjacent to the east-west-profile, the total number of flints for the 5 cm layers were from the top: 182, 305, 256, 99, 51, 35. This seems to indicate that the floor horizon was at least 15-20 cm above the bottom of the shallow pit, similar to the situation observed with the southern part of the floor at

Ulkestrup I (2.1.1).

Some of the old excavation photos show an oblong north-south orientated coloured zone cutting the border of the lens. We may interpret this as a north orientated walking zone reflecting the position of a doorway orientated towards the lake.

The marked shore of the old lake ran WWSW-EENE about 5 metres to the north of the grey lens (fig.21B). Mapping of the phosphate in the sandy peat of the shallow lake, close to the former shore line, made it possible to observe a tongue of phosphate there. Apparently it reflected a former waterlogged waste layer projecting from the northernmost part of the main concentration connected to the possible walking zone (Grøn 1987b:72). A trench and a test pit confirmed that Maglemosian flints here were embedded in the sandy peat.

During the first campaign, two large and up to 5 cm deep blotches of brown sand (fig.39E) were registered under the culture layer inside the homogeneous lens. The one measured 2 by 2 m, the other 1.5 by 1 m. Photos taken during the same campaign show two brown circular blotches about 1 metre in diameter, each inside one large blotch of light sand measuring 3-4 by 2 m. Often a brown colouring is found under mesolithic hearths (Peter Vang Petersen and Erik Brinch Petersen, personal communication) probably due to colouring by organic matter prepared on the fire. With the brown sand in the bottom of the shallow pit of the one hearth at Duvensee W.6 in mind, an interpretation of these features as the remains of two hearths does not seem presumptuous. Both of the two supposed hearths (fig.21B) are related to a large central concentration of burnt flint (fig.39B). The western one to its centre and the eastern one to its eastern outlier. To the east and to the north-west are two other concentrations of burnt flints just inside or on the border of the grey lens. Apparently they are not directly connected to hearth zones but they may represent material cleared out from them.

In the southern part of the main concentration we find two small and noticeable concentrations of microliths (fig.39C). Their centres are on a line east-west, with 2 metres between them. As with the concentrations from Ulkestrup I, the microlithic sub-types here show systematic 'sub-patterns' related to the two microlithic main concentrations (4.2.).

During the 1983 excavation two 25 cm deep pits, 50 cm in diameter, and with rounded bottoms were found with their centres approximately 50 cm to the south of the central axis of the homogeneous sand lens and 1.25 and 1.75 metre from its south-east end respectively. They were embedded in the culture layer and did not go deeper than this. Their lower 5 cm were made up by a horizon of thin sandwiched layers of charcoal and 'water deposited sand'. Inspection of the plans made during the 1977 excavation showed that apart from the two large brown blotches connected to the hearth zones, two smaller blotches were located with their centres 50 and 100 cm to the south of the central axis of the pit and 1.0 and 2.0 metres from its NW-end. The amateur Niels Boysen, who unfortunately died in 1991, was a participant in the 1977 campaign and reestablished the field surface with his tractor after the excavation. In 1984 he told me that he had used the opportunity to dig deeper in the easternmost blotch because he did not believe that its bottom had been reached. He found that it was somewhat deeper and contained a few pieces of Maglemosian flint. He gave no depth nor diameter. Since the excavators of the first campaign mainly excavated the upper part of the grey sand lens where the finds were, its lower parts may actually have been left untouched. Apparently 3, possibly 4 pits seem to have formed a line approximately 50 cm to the south of the longitudinal axis of the grey sand lens, that is in the direction away from the water. I did not become aware of the possible importance of the pits we found in 1983 and Niels Boysen's information before I found the 4 structures at Flaadet (3.2.4.) in 1989.

## 17) Mullerup (Sarauw's excavation)

The locus classicus of the Maglemose Culture, the Mullerup site in the Mullerup Bog on western Zealand, was excavated in 1900 by Georg Sarauw. According to Sarauw's observations the site (fig.23B) is located on a long north-south orientated low ridge on the bottom of the former lake (Sarauw 1904:155-156). According to the unpublished geological investigations (report in the Danish National Museum A18269) it is clear that the moraine bottom as well as the gytja layers fall away to the south,

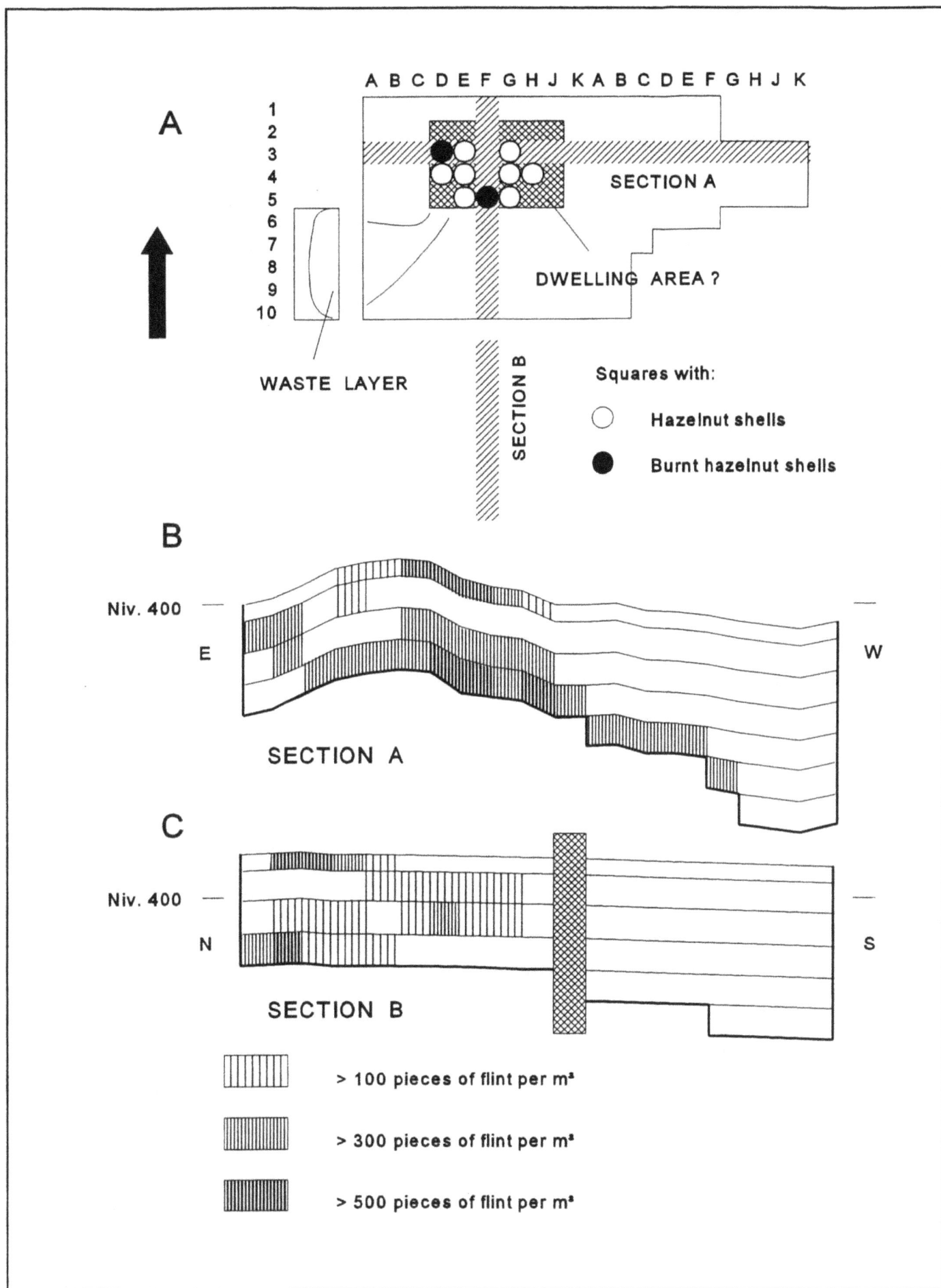

Fig.41. Mullerup 1900. A: the horizontal distribution of lithic waste . The hatched bars show the position of the sections y=3 (fig.41B) and x=F (fig.41C). B and C show the intensities of lithic waste as number of pieces per cubic metre in the two sections.

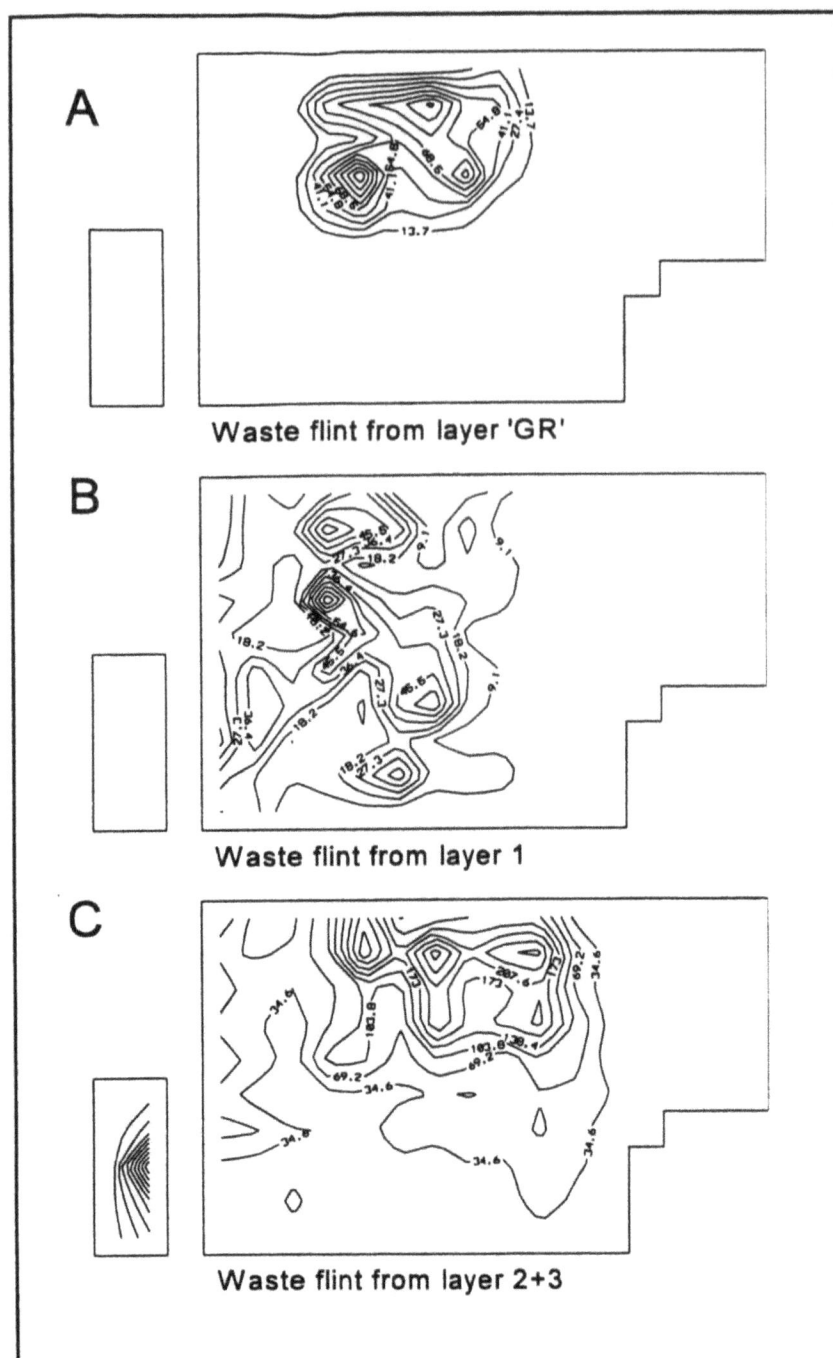

*Fig.42. Mullerup 1900. Distributions. Equidistances A: 13.7; B: 9.1; C: 34.6*

that such separations may be due to the formation of floating islands after the sites were left. Troels-Smith has carried out an unpublished pollen analysis at Mullerup, indicating that 1) either the original settlement surface was in the turf, secondarily lifted by a floating island or 2) there was no regular settlement surface present at the site at all (Troels-Smith (†), personal communication). The sections showing the vertical artifact concentrations (fig. 41B,C) support the idea of a floating island.

The site has later been C14-dated to around 6600 BC (Brinch Petersen 1973: 124,125). It was excavated in m²-squares and in layers of 20 cm thickness, apart from the approximately 10 cm thick turf layer (layer 'GR') which was investigated separately. In the turf is seen a sharply restricted 4 by 6 metres large, east-west orientated rectangular find concentration (fig.42A). The total lack of finds outside this rect-angle is representative according to the excavation report. The first layer (layer 1) below the turf contains relatively few finds (fig.42B), whereas the second and third (layers 2 and 3) (fig. 42C) contain a concentration somewhat larger and more blurred than the upper one, but with the same horizontal location. Most likely, the upper half of the culture layer was lifted up as a part of a floating island.

showing that the site was placed on the southern extremity of this long, low island. The find-yielding layer in the peat showed a clearly decreasing level to the east, west and south from the main concentration (fig.41B,C). The central part of the 'waste layer', to the south-west of the main concentration, consisted of flint, bones, charcoal, hazelnut shells etc. and was clearly water deposited.

Sarauw was not able to account for the fact that material of exactly the same kind and character appeared in two horizontally separated layers (Sarauw 1904:164). Today it is generally accepted

Hazelnut shells are observed in all layers from 'GR' to 3. Meanwhile they are observed in layer GR in 10 conjoining squares in the south-west part of the rectangle. In two of the squares Sarauw noted the presence of burnt hazelnut shells (fig.41A). In the lower layers the distribution of shells is clearly diffuse, and burnt ones are only registered in layer 1, in one of the two squares where they were also observed in layer GR, just above. In spite of the relatively bad conditions of preservation in the turf, this layer contained a noticeable concentration of hazelnut shells. According to their positions inside the rectangle and relative to the waste layer protuding to the south-west, the squares with burnt hazelnuts may well represent two hearth

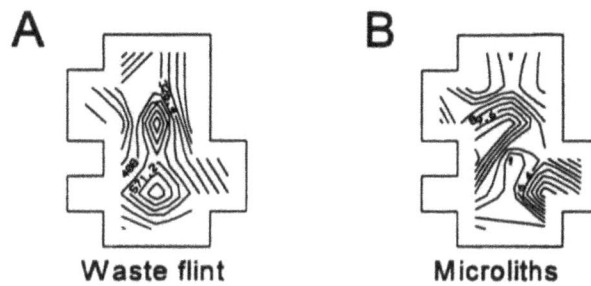

*Fig.43. Stallerupholm. Distributions. Equidistances A: 81.6; B: 1.6*

zones that were lifted with the upper part of a floor.

Sarauw only observed 3 microliths on the site. It must be assumed that a number of this - until then undefined - type were discarded during the excavation as waste. According to Brinch Petersen several microliths were observed on the site at a later occasion (Brinch Petersen, personal communication). Clearly there is no basis for an analysis of the microlith distribution.

With the waste layer orientated to the south-west from its south-west corner of the floor, with what may be interpreted as two hazelnut roasting zones in its south-western part (close to the water) the whole pattern appears to be organized symmetrically around a SW-NE diagonal of the 4 by 6 metres large rectangular main concentration in the turf. Unfortunately Sarauw's observations, registrations and considerations, in spite of the fact that they were splendid for his time, do not help us any further.

## 18) Stallerupholm

The site is located on the top of a very small hill, a former island in a basin NNW of Kolding in southern Jutland. Since the steep south-west side of the island seems eroded by the nearby stream (Blankholm, Blankholm and Andersen 1968:62), it may originally have been positioned on the north-east side of the, then, somewhat larger island. The site is C14-dated to 6370 ±130 BC (Brinch Petersen 1973:124), 300-400 years later than the typological dating suggested by Andersen in 1968 (Blankholm, Blankholm and Andersen 1968:108).

In 1964 and 1965, 24 m² of the site were excavated. Some of the central m²-squares contained more than 1000 pieces and eight of the outer ones contained 700-1000 pieces (Blankholm, Blankholm and Andersen 1968:62-64). From the rough distribution plans and other information published, it appears that we have here a restricted concentration (fig.43A) (Blankholm, Blankholm and Andersen 1968:63-64). However, it is impossible to conclude this for sure because of the limited area excavated. It has also been impossible to check the published distribution of the lithic waste, since a major part of this appeared without any kind of registration codes, mixed in a big box, in the magazine of the Moesgaard Museum (my own observation). The general impression is that the material must be treated with some reservation.

The microliths seem to appear in two small concentrations with approximately 2 metres between their centres (fig.43B), one north-western and one south-eastern, but each on the border of the excavated area and thus not representing a reliable pattern. Therefore, further discussion of the distribution patterns of the microlithic sub-types is omitted here.

No regular 'culture layer' was observed, but the flint was mainly found within a light, grey and fine-grained lenticular sand layer up to 45 cm thick in the centre of the excavation area and 5 cm, or even less, at its borders (Blankholm, Blankholm and Andersen 1968:63). This structure, not described in further detail, appears to have an interesting similarity to the grey sand lens that filled out the shallow dugout pit observed at Svanemosen 28. At Stallerupholm it also coincides with the main concentration of material.

Immediately to the north of the north-western microlith concentration was observed a concentration of charcoal (pieces up to 1-2 cm) and burnt fragments of granite and quartzite in the grey sand layer (Blankholm, Blankholm and Andersen 1968: 64).

Immediately to the east/north-east of the south-eastern microlith concentration was found a pit filled with grey sand containing a lot of charcoal, burnt

zones apparently closer to the old shore than the former two, actually may be present on this site. Whether the elements indicating this spatial pattern are contemporaneous or not, is impossible to decide on the basis of the existing information. The site is regarded as so problematic that its distribution pattern will not be used in the further analysis of distributions. Its importance is in this connection mainly that it is an example of the relation between a main concentration and a grey sand lens.

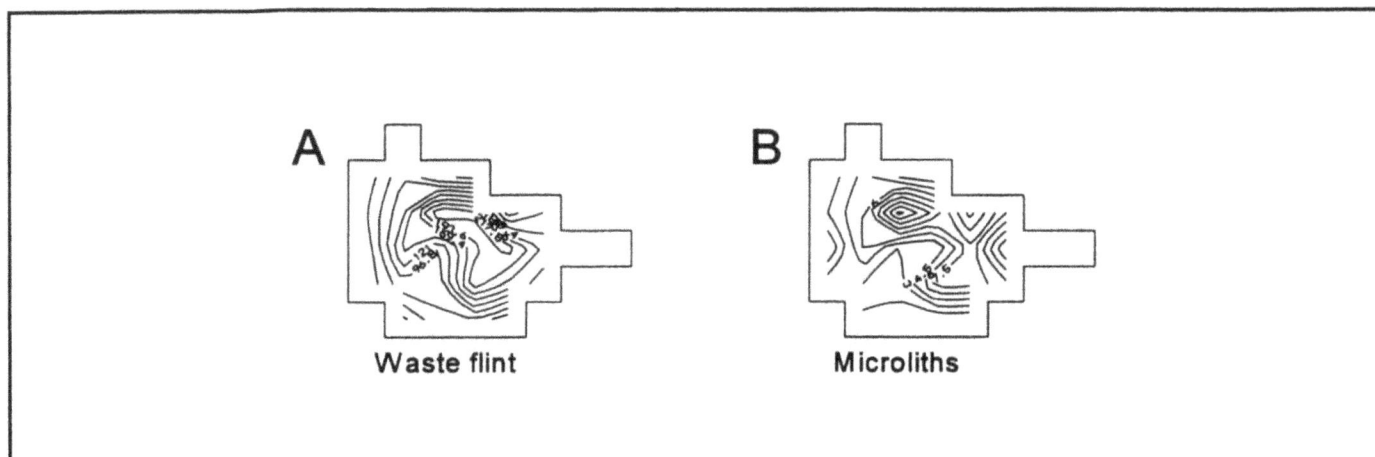

*Fig.44. Magleby Nor B. Distributions. Equidistances A: 24.2; B: 1.5*

flint and 3 triangular microliths. The pit was dug into the light grey sand layer and by Søren H. Andersen related to a Maglemosian phase a few hundred years later than the main part of the material (Blankholm, Blankholm and Andersen 1968:64,108). This subtle typological separation may seem a bit daring on the basis of the C14-dating obtained. Also on the basis of the results from Svanemosen 28 one cannot exclude the possibility that a structure - for instance a hearth - contemporaneous with the main settlement, may appear as a pit in the grey sand lens which at some time may have filled a shallow pit connected to a dwelling.

According to the NNE-SSW oriented profile ditch excavated in 1969, the waste layer seems to be to the north-east of the site.

For several reasons this material must be treated with a certain amount of reservation: the restricted size of the excavation area, not allowing for full observation of the distribution patterns of interest, the lack of registration of some of the excavated material etc. Therefore in this discussion of distributional patterns I only want to hint that two small microlith concentrations close to each other and two hearth

## 19) Magleby Nor B

For the basic data concerning the excavation of the eastern concentration B at the Magleby Nor site see site nr.7 in this catalogue. The B-concentration has the same typological traits and must thus also have a dating around the transition Preboreal/Boreal.

As already mentioned, an essential problem is here that the main concentration of material, estimated to approximately 4 by 5-6 metres, is of approximately the same size as the excavated area, thus restricting our opportunities for proper observation of spatial patterns (fig.44A). The distribution of microliths seems to make up two small but noticeable concentrations with their centres on an ESE-WNW axis with approximately 3 metres between them (fig. 44B). In terms of distribution patterns this fits the approximate east-west oriented shore-line that this main concentration must have been related to, due to its more eastern position than Magleby Nor A (7.7.). However, since the patterns are not uncovered in their totality, the material is too unreliable to support any conclusions concerning the general distribution patterns.

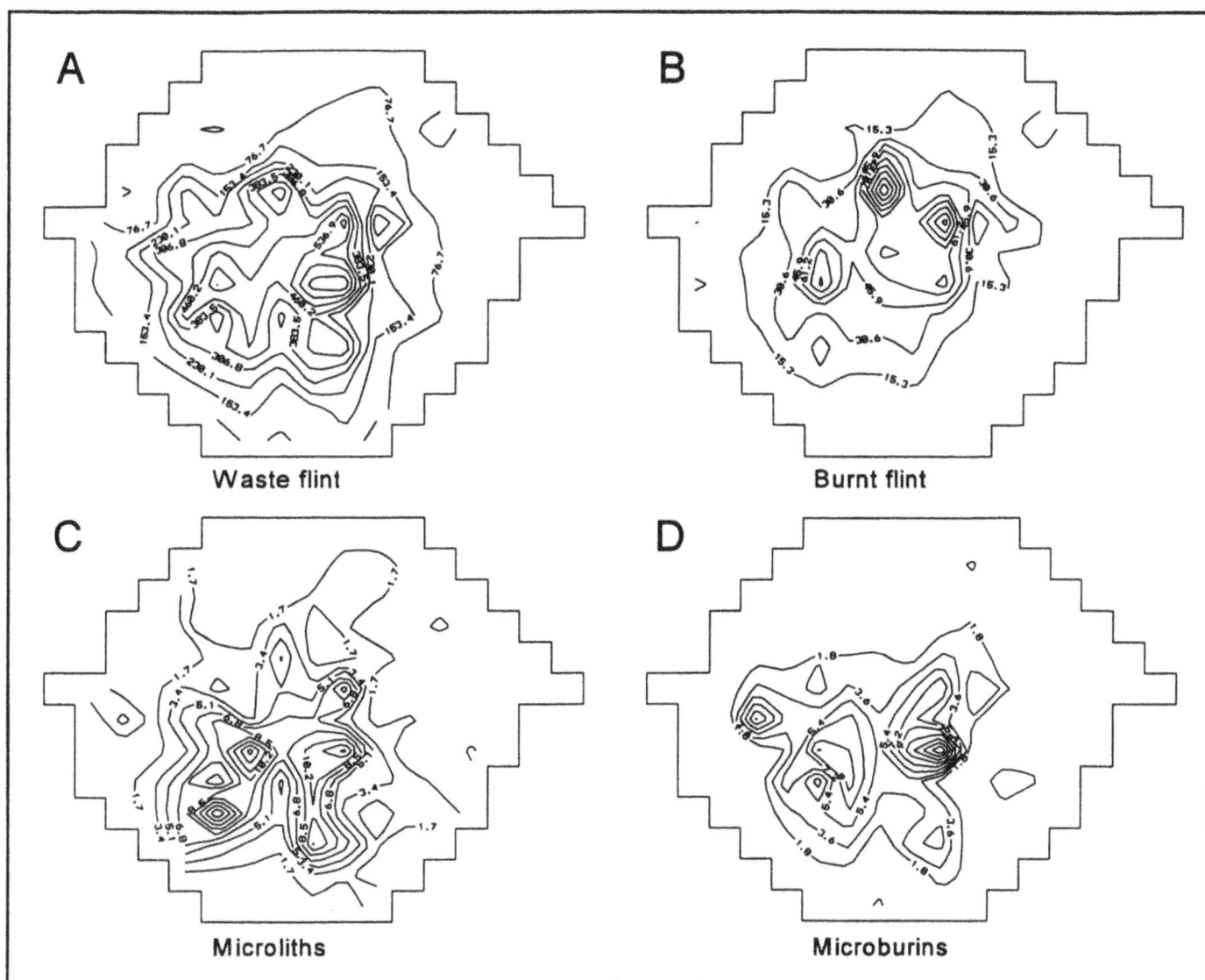

*Fig.45. Flaadet. Distributions. Equidistances A: 76.7; B: 15.3; C: 1.7; D: 1.8*

## 20) Flaadet

Flaadet was excavated in 1973 by Jørgen Holm for Langelands Museum. The site was situated on a little island (Flaadet) in a bog basin on northern Langeland. Originally it was situated about 20 metres to the SSW of, and 1.5 metre above, the contemporaneous shore (Grøn 1987a:311; Skaarup 1979:23-24). During the excavation the finds were registered in m² squares. The material from Flaadet seems extremely pure in terms of typology. This and pollen analysis indicates a dating in early boreal, around or a little before 7000 BC (Skaarup 1979:104).

Compared to other Maglemosian sites Flaadet appears as an enormous rectangular concentration of lithic material with its corners pointing to S,N,E and W, measuring approximately 8 x 8 metres (fig.45A) and containing about 30.000 pieces of flint.

In the part of the concentration most NNE-wards, in the direction of the water, two noticeable concentrations of burnt flint were located (fig.45B) with more than 120 and 150 pieces of fire damaged flint pr. square metre. Their centres are on a line parallel to the nearest shore. To the south-west of these a third, less noticeable concentration, was found.

Concerning the microliths they make up two concentrations (fig.45C) with their centres on an axis parallel to the nearest shore-line (fig.21D). Both concentrations are shaped like crescents around a centre with a very low concentration, producing the impression of two units rather than of four separate ones, as the relatively high concentrations in their ends might indicate. Supporting this interpretation is that the micro burins on the site have a general spatial occurrence coinciding with the microliths, but that noticeable concentrations of micro burins are only found together with the northern concentration of microliths in each crescent (27D). However one must be open to other interpretations of this rather special pattern (fig.21D).

As a consequence of my interpretation of the site as a large rectangular winter house measuring 7 by 8 metres (Grøn 1987a:311-315), in 1989 Jørgen Skaarup and I decided to re-excavate the site to see if faint traces of structures had been overseen in the underground. One of the dangers in square metre excavation is that the underground dries out differently before it has been reached in all squares, and thus may be a difficult medium for finer observations. By removing the plough soil from an already excavated area mechanically and shovelling it clean, it should be possible to get into a better position for observation of structural traces in the underground.

After this operation four grey oval to circular structures, approximately 50 cm in diameter, immediately appeared on a line some 50 cm to the south (that is away from the water) of the central line of the postulated rectangle. The northernmost was located only 10 cm to the south-east of the postulated north-western gable and the southernmost precisely touching the south-eastern gable from the inside (Grøn 1990a:82-84).

The structures consisted of 12-15 cm deep rounded pits with a diameter of about 50 cm in the underground clay filled with sand. They all contained traces of stones recently removed by ploughing, and sandwich-like brown colourings consisting of iron precipitations in the sand. They probably represent cultural phenomena closely related to the site in time. They are interpreted as structural elements related to a dwelling, possibly holes from posts supporting the slightly asymmetrical ridge of a saddle roof (Grøn 1990b:10-12). They parallel the structures observed at Svanemosen 28 (3.1.3.c. and site 16 in this catalogue).

The site contains a clearly symmetrical organization, but differs from most other sites by its relatively large distance to the water.

## 21) Bøllund

The Bøllund site was located on a flat sandy plain on the eastern side of a NNW-SSE orientated valley at a distance of more than a hundred metres from the water course in it. In contrast to the sites dealt with above, this settlement was not directly related to a lake basin. The flint concentration was 250 metres long, NW-SE, more or less parallel to the valley, and 5-25 metres broad.

According to the excavator's report in the Danish National Museum (A38217) the material was typologically very homogeneous. According to Brinch Petersen it must be given a date slightly before Melsted and Vinde-Helsinge, that is about 6800 BC (Brinch Petersen 1973:124,125; 1967:177).

In 1939 a larger concentration from the site (fig.21F; fig.46A) was excavated by L.C. Vebæk for the Danish National Museum. The culture layer was found in the uppermost 10-15 cm of a thicker aeolic sand deposit immediately below the heather cover. Apart from the flint, it contained some charcoal of pine and a certain amount of burnt hazelnut shells. Unfortunately the locations of these objects were not registered.

The excavation technique employed was rather summary, as it appears from the lists of lithic waste and burnt flint per square metre, practically all counts ends with the ciphers 0 or 5. Apart from blades and micro blades the waste was generally discarded. No sieving was employed, and the low number of micro burins seems to indicate that many of these were overseen.

The excavation revealed an approximately 7 (east-west) by 8 (north-south) metres large, more or less rectangular concentration of material, of which the westernmost metre had only been partly excavated. A tongue of material protrudes from the south-east corner to the east, away from the valley and the water course (fig.46A).

The microliths make up two small noticeable concentrations in the southern part of the main concentration with approximately 2 metres between their centres, the one to the ESE of the other, and the western one possibly only partly uncovered (fig. 46B). Because of the summary excavation method, no detailed analysis of the distributions of the microlithic sub-types have been made (smaller types have probably escaped attention to a larger extent than larger types etc.). The locations of the microlith

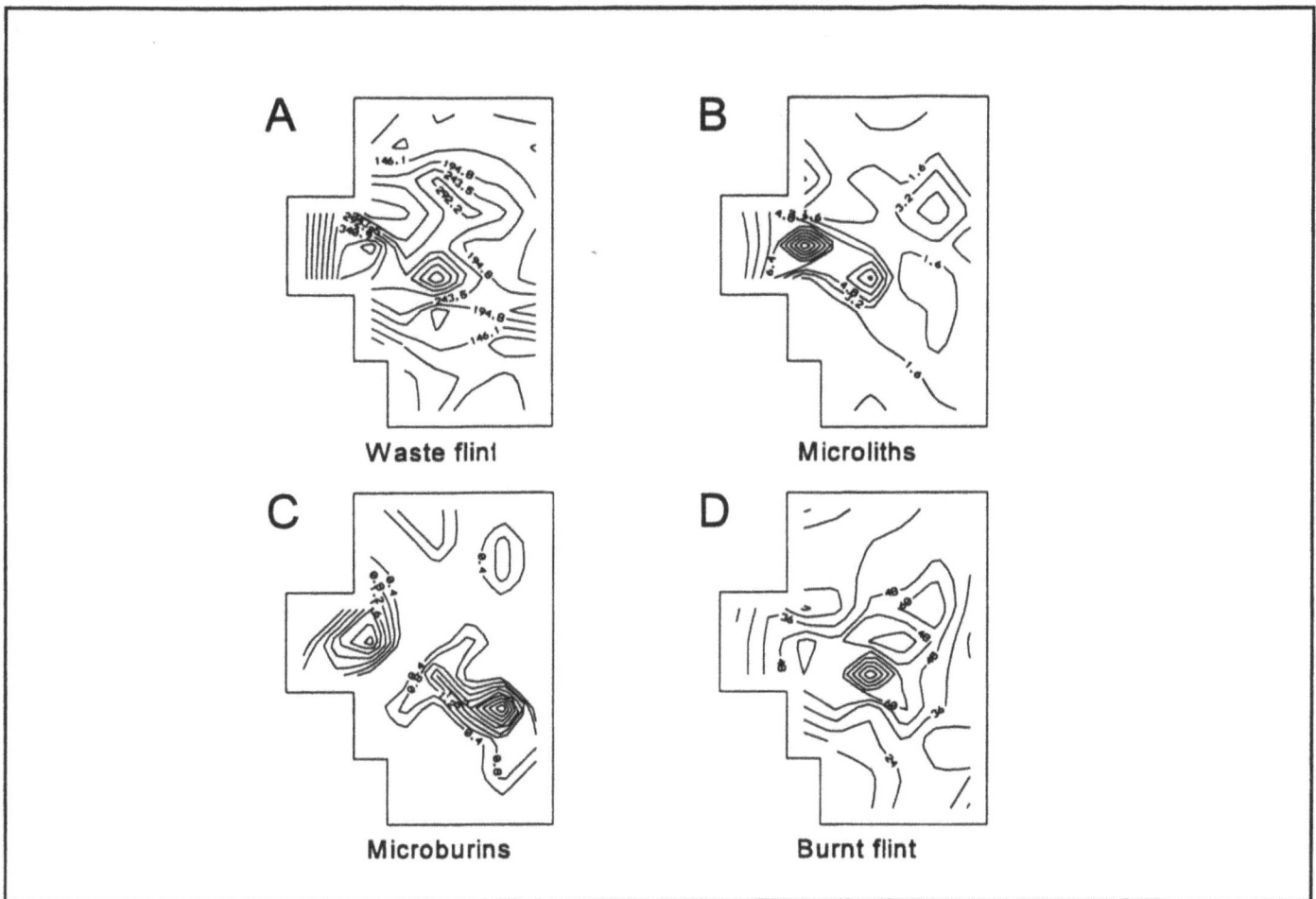

*Fig.46. Bøllund. Distributions. Equidistances A: 48.7; B: 1.6; C: 0.4; D: 12*

concentrations are more or less reflected in two concentrations of micro burins, the eastern one apparently connected to the east-orientated tongue (fig.46C). Also the lithic waste and the burnt flint concentrate in the same two small areas (fig.46A and fig.46D), the latter indicating the presence of two hearth zones coinciding more or less with the two microlith concentrations.

The axes show two concentrations, apparently related to the two microlith concentrations.

In spite of the relatively summary excavation during which, no doubt, micro burins and most likely microliths, escaped registration, some reliable main patterns seem to have been registered. Altogether we get an impression of a very large unit (approximately the same size as Flaadet) with two concentrations of microliths, and two hearth zones arranged in a pattern closely related to the one from Flaadet.

With regard to the orientation relative to the nearest water, the Bøllund concentration diverges from the hitherto observed pattern. A reasonable explanation

may be that a nearby shore was regarded as important for the orientation whereas a distant watercourse was not.

## 22) Rude Mark

The site (fig.23A) appears to have been placed some 200 metres to the south of the shore of, and about 10 metres above the water level of, a large fresh waterbasin (Boas 1987:14,15), south of Århus. It was excavated in 1978 by Niels Axel Boas for Odder Museum. A remnant of the culture layer was observed under the plough soil as a greyish-brown sand lens with a little humus, 10-20 cm thick in the centre and thinning out towards the edge of the excavated area. The excavator suggests that the preservation of this part of the culture layer may be due to the fact, that the site was originally located in a slight depression - possibly created by human activity - in the sandy subsoil (Boas 1987:14).

The concentration of material (fig.47A) measures approximately 6 by 9 metres with a more or less oval

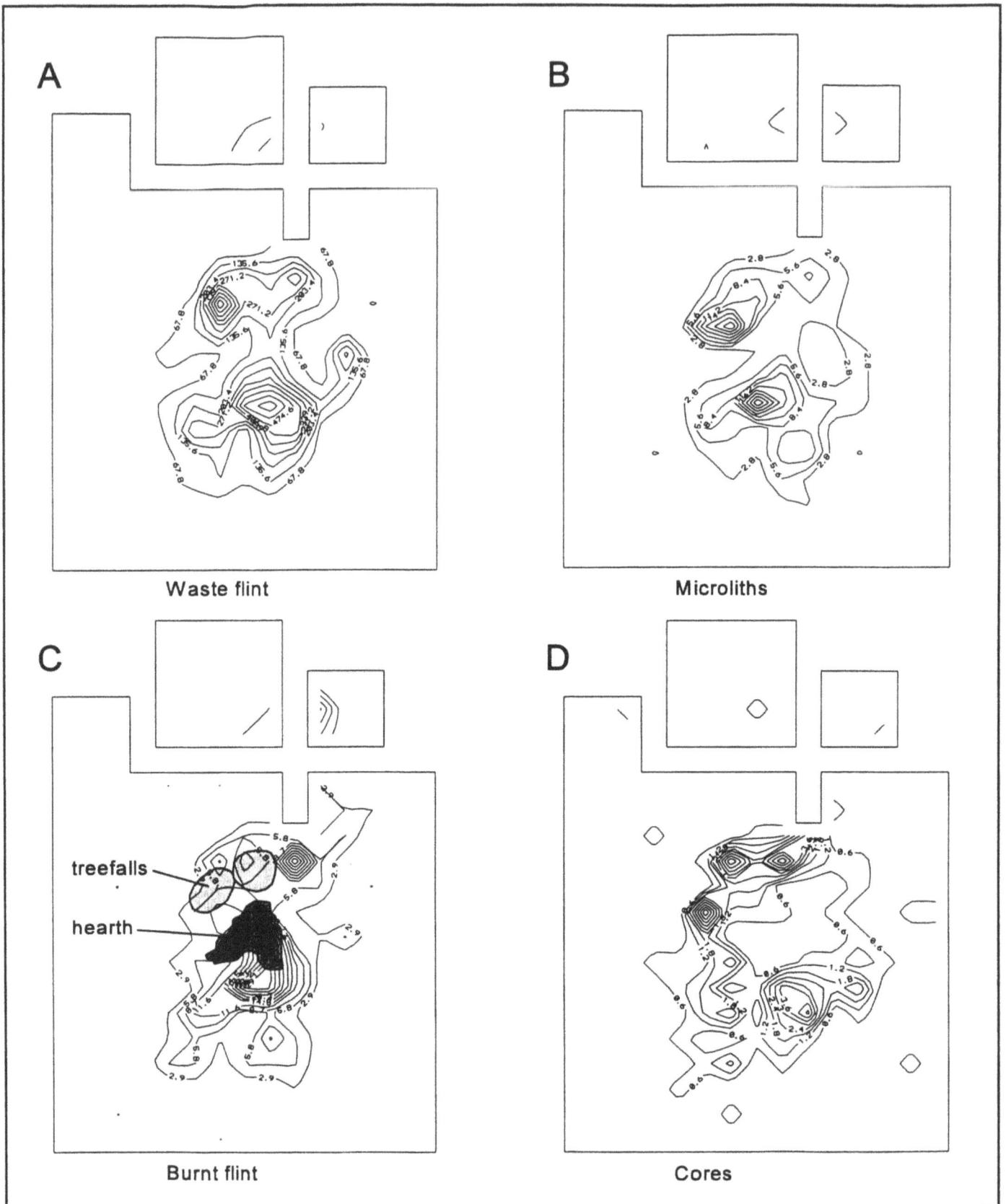

Fig.47. Rude Mark. Distributions. Equidistances A: 67.8; B: 2.8; C: 2.9; D: 0.6

shape and the longitudinal axis orientated approximately NNE-SSW. It has been C14-dated to approximately 6200 BC (Boas 1987:27). Typologically one should think it was a couple of hundred years older.

The material was excavated in m² squares by shovel, and was sieved through a 4 mm mesh. Unfortunately a total of 18 treefall holes 1-3 metres in diameter were observed inside the excavation area (Boas 1987:14-16). This means that we must expect the distribution patterns to be somewhat blurred. On the other hand the excavated area left undisturbed is so relatively large, that the main traits of the distributions can be estimated reliably.

A 2 by 3 metres large and up to 1 metre deep pit (fig.47C) containing reddish and humic sand, charcoal and burnt hazelnut shells was interpreted as the remains of a hearth structure from which an upper hazelnut roasting place might have been partly removed by a medieval furrow between two strip fields passing exactly through this structure (Boas 1987:14-15).

The microliths (fig.47B) show a characteristic distribution with two noticeable and clearly separated concentrations, one related to the northern part of the main concentration and one related to its southern part. Because of the disturbed state of the culture layer the results of a finer analysis of the distribution of the microlithic sub-types would probably be unreliable. Therefore only the main patterns are established.

The hearth structure already mentioned and the concentration of burnt flint related to it (fig.47C), is centred immediately to the east of the southern microlith concentration. The zone immediately to the east of the northern microlith concentration is heavily disturbed by two pits from treefalls. Further to the north-east is a second noticeable concentration of burnt flint, apparently separated from the northern microlith concentration, either originally or due to the disturbing pits from treefalls. This seems to reflect the existence of a partly destroyed northern hearth zone.

The lithic waste (including blades and micro blades)(fig.47A) also makes up two concentrations, each related to one of the microlith concentrations: a northern oblong one orientated WSW-ENE and a southern parallel oblong one.

The distribution of the cores (fig.47D) is interesting in that it seems to outline an approximately 7 by 8 metres large SW-NE orientated rectangle. Centrally is a large empty area coinciding with the location of the two suggested hearth zones.

Rude Mark seems related to Flaadet, with two microlith concentrations and possibly two hearth zones arranged in a symmetrical pattern. As with

Bøllund the axis of symmetry is not orientated towards the nearest water. This again may reflect the fact that the shore is quite distant and thus not so important for the orientation. As at Bøllund and Flaadet the unit is essentially larger than any of the Ulkestrup I-type sites located directly on the lake shores.

## 23) Draved 31

For general information on the Draved sites see site nr.11, in this catalogue. It is impossible to say how representative the registered distributions are since the top of the sand layer containing the mesolithic material here was partially removed by the peat exploitation (report in the Danish National Museum A48212).

The lithic waste makes up a 15 metres long 2-3 metres broad concentration. A concentration in its eastern end may represent a Ulkestrup II-type unit (one concentration of microliths and one of burnt flint on an east-west-axis in a 3 by 3 metres large concentration with a possible waste layer to the north), or the waste layer may also represent another similar overlapping unit. A concentration in its westernmost end 3 by 3 metres large may represent a small unit orientated to the north with a concentration of burnt flint but without a microlith concentration. However, since these structures may partly be due to modern removal of further material, they are regarded as so unreliable that they are not used as a basis for further conclusions.

## 24) Draved 32

For general information on the Draved sites see site nr.11, in this catalogue. The site was covered by up to 2.2 metres protective peat, but unfortunately cut by a drainage channel in its southern part (report in the Danish National Museum A48198).

The site apparently consists of a concentration 3 by 3 metres large containing two concentrations of microliths and some peripheral areas with burnt flint, possibly representing concentrations of this. However, since the excavation proper covers only 4.5 by 5 m, it is impossible to say anything with certainty about the organization of this site.

## 25), 26) and 27) Three concentrations at Star Carr

The site, located a few miles south of Scarborough, Yorkshire, was excavated by Clark in the period 1949-1951. The site is located on the southern extremity of an approximately 1 km long prominence separating Star Carr and Flixton Carr, immediately on the shoreline. The latter had an east-west orientation, and so the site is orientated to the south (Clark 1954:1-4,13,28).

On the basis of the hearths and the existence of smaller concentrations of material inside the large concentration it is possible to distinguish at least three smaller main concentrations: 1) approximately

basis for the determination as a winter site were imported as raw material. The remaining material strongly points to habitation restricted to the period from April to August/September (Legge and Rowley-Conwy 1989:228).

## 28) Hasbjerg II

This site from the Sværdborg Bog in southern Zealand was excavated by Johansson in 1969. It was found on the bog surface in an area where the peat layer containing the culture remains had been ploughed through down to the underlying sand. Apparently the locality was subject to drainage and intensive ploughing at an early date. The moraine

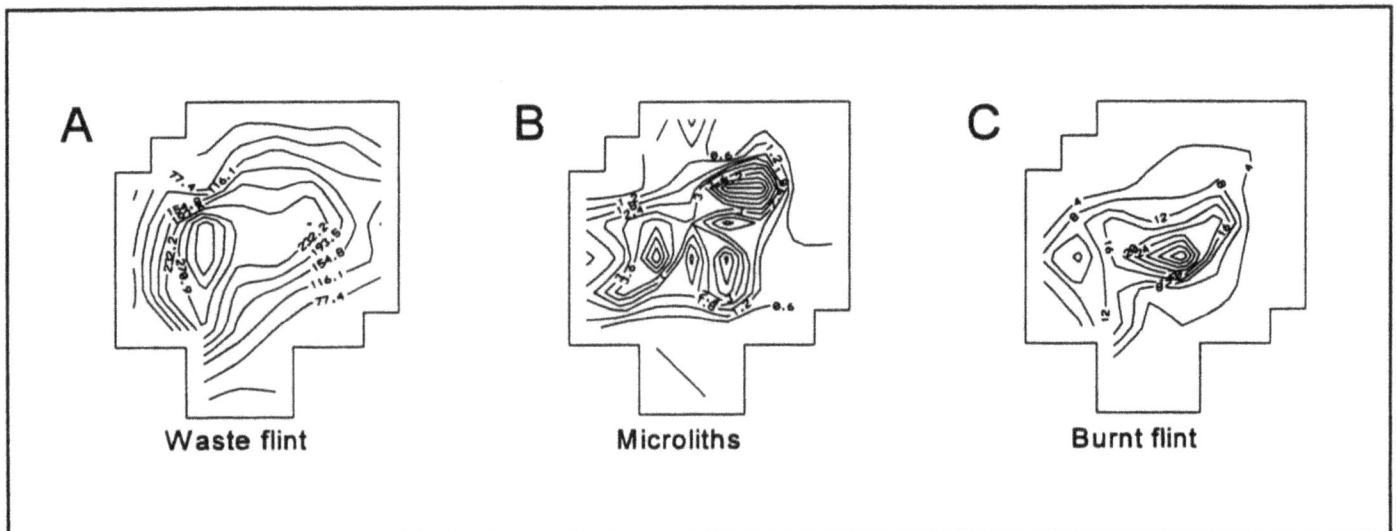

Fig.48. Hasbjerg II. Distributions. Equidistances A: 38.7; B: 0.6; C: 4.0

4 by 5-6 metres (squares F-K and 23-27), 2) 3 by 4-5 metres (squares H-L and 18-20) and 3) 3-4 by 3-4 metres (squares D-H and 14-18) respectively. Immediately the two latter, and smaller, main concentrations seem to contain one concentration of microliths each, whereas the former one may have contained two. Because of an unexcavated row of squares it is impossible to see whether there is one large or two small ones. In all cases the microliths concentrate in the parts most remote from the water (Clark 1954:5,6,11,21). Most likely the excavated distributions reflect the existence of several over-lapping units.

With regard to season, the original determination of the site as a pure winter site (Clark 1954:93-95), has been revised by Legge and Rowley-Conwy. Apparently the red deer antlers that made up the

landscape slopes up to the east, indicating that the site had been related to a shore somewhere to the west of it. On a typological basis the site has been dated to the milieu around 7300-7500 BC (Johansson 1990:52,54).

The excavation was carried out in m² squares. Each square was excavated by trowel, and afterwards the soil was sieved. The heavy ploughing of the site prior to excavation must be expected to have blurred characteristics of the distributions of the larger items, whereas smaller items - such as microlithic pieces - may have been influenced less.

The main concentration appears as a rectangular structure measuring approximately 5 by 7 metres (fig.48A) and with the longitudinal axis NE-SW. It contains 3 small noticeable microlith concentrations (fig.48B), clearly separated from each other and located around a central concentration of burnt flint (fig.48C). According to the excavator, it looks as if some of the flint was damaged during a peat fire (Johansson 1990:54). However such a fire would not be expected to create such a high number of burnt flints within such a restricted zone. The cores show a blurred peripheral distribution along the edge of the main concentration.

We may have here several overlapping main concentrations, or a new, hitherto unobserved, principle of spatial organization. However this heavily ploughed site with its low artifact intensities and lacking information on the position of the shoreline is so poor a basis for analysis that we cannot decide what is the case.

## 29) Tingby

At an old east orientated coast line, close to Kalmar in Sweden, a 3.4 by 8.8 metres large, rectangular dwelling structure containing Maglemosian material was excavated by Ebbe Westergren for Kalmar Lens Museum in 1987. The mesolithic finds were restricted to a 1-10 cm thick occupation layer consisting of grey sand with some charcoal, sharply restricted to the area inside the rectangular structure (Rajala and Westergren 1991:7-9).

To interpret the dwelling structure as mesolithic involves a number of problems. A hearth centrally placed in its NE-end obtained C14-datings of 0±100 and 2240±100 BC. Other datings obtained from features are 690±80, 5700±105 BC and 5240±110 BC. On the basis of the microliths published, a typological dating to the earlier half of the Maglemose Culture around 6500 BC seems appropriate (Rajala and Westergren 1991:13,22).

The main concentration of flint measures 2 by 5 metres with a longitudinal axis NE-SW, and is connected to the south-eastern half of the north-eastern end of the structure and thus occupies only ¼ of the space inside it. It contains a concentration of microliths and looks very much like a Ulkestrup II-type unit (Rajala and Westergren 1991:16-17).

A sample of charcoal pieces collected from the grey sandy occupation layer has produced a dating of

4570±140 BC (Rajala and Westergren 1991:22). This indicates that the culture layer contains charcoal mixed from different periods. The most obvious possibility seems to be that a house has been build on top of a Maglemosian site. Mesolithic material thus has been mixed up with charcoal etc. from a later phase - or phases. The distribution patterns therefore are unlikely to represent the original mesolithic distributions.

## 30) Lavringe Mose

The site is located on the end of a promontory projecting into the Lavringe Bog in central Zealand from the south. It was excavated in 1986 by Søren Sørensen for Roskilde Museum (Sørensen 1988:53-55).

In the Maglemosian layer, according to the excavator directly on an old west-orientated bank, a number of stakes were found, 5-10 cm in diameter, hammered into the ground. None of them were sharpened. They were all placed with their *thin* ends downwards in what Sørensen interprets as a trapezoid structure 5.5 metres long, with a base line of 5.3 and a top line of 2 m, the base being orientated WSW, towards the shore. Bark and branches had apparently been washed away from the structure by wave activity. 5 scalene triangles were related to its northern half. They are so dispersed that we cannot speak of a concentration. Outside to the north were found 1 microlith fragment and two leister prongs, to the east 1 microlith fragment, 1 bone mace and 1 axe, and to the west 1 microlith fragment. The structure is interpreted by the excavator as the remains of a hut (Sørensen 1988:54-59).

A number of comments must be made on this. The structure is not connected to even a slight concentration of flint. The trapezoid, nearly triangular shape, is made up of two lines of stakes. There seems to be no reason that the structure should stop at its postulated back end (the southern rear line of stakes seems to go on to the north-west!). The two lines cut each other more than 8 metres from the base (Sørensen 1988:55). The dwelling shapes indicated by stakes, sand lenses and distributions of material hitherto, have been rectangular/slightly trapezoid to oval. A triangular structure 5.3 by 8 metres clearly diverges from what we would expect at present. This alone is of course no valid reason for rejecting the interpretation.

The basic problem seems to be the chronological gap between the C14-dates of 3 stakes from the structure (7090-6740 BC) and the leister prongs that fit this dating typologically on the one side and the scalene triangles which belong to another Maglemosian phase, some 500 years later, on the other. It must also be noted that the dating from the southern 'wall' (6740±120 BC) and the one from the northern 'wall' (7090±125 BC) are 350 years apart. Even with a tolerant view of their intervals of deviation, the 105 years separating them, seem a bit too much. This at least is a hint that the two lines of stakes are independent of each other in terms of chronology.

That the stakes were not sharpened and were placed with their thinnest end downwards, differs from the Ulkestrup Huts and seems strange for a dwelling structure. It seems logical to let the basis of the structure have the largest dimensions since it has to withstand the strongest forces. With fishing structures, however, it may not be crucial that the thickest ends are downwards. The front fragments of the two bone heads for fishing spears, apparently contemporaneous with the structure, are typically the part of the fishing spears which broke off during fishing, and thus may indicate fishing activities on the spot around 7000 BC. In an area with changing water level, as this is, according to the excavator, it cannot be excluded that stakes belonging to a fishing structure have burnt down, as was the case with a few of the stakes here (Sørensen 1988:54-56).

# 7. Notes

1) Send a 1.4 Mb, 2¼" diskette to:

Ole Grøn
National Museum of Denmark
The Centre for Maritime Archaeology
Postbox 317
4000 Roskilde

And I shall return it with the 'SURFER'-files and some further information.

2) To facilitate their readability, this and the following, automatically produced, distribution plans, are all on the same scale, and have the same orientation. North is always upwards and 4.5 mm on the plans equals 1 m.

# 8. References

Althin, Carl-Axel — 1954: *The Chronology of the Stone Age Settlement of Scania, Sweden. I - The Mesolithic settlement*. Lund.

Andersen, K — 1983: *Stenalder bebyggelsen i den Vestsjællandske Åmose*. Copenhagen.

Andersen, K., Jørgensen, S., Richter, J. — 1982: *Maglemose hytterne ved Ulkestrup Lyng*. Copenhagen.

Ardener, Shirley — 1981: Ground Rules and social maps for women: an introduction. *Women and Space* (ed.) Shirley Ardener. Oxford. 11-34

Argyle, Michael — 1976: *Bodily communication*. London.

Argyle, Michael and Dean, Janet — 1965: Eye-contact, distance and afiliation. *Sociometry* vol.28(1). 289-304

Bagniewski, Zbigniew — 1990: Maglemose-Kultureinflüsse in Mitteleuropa.*Contributions to the Mesolithic in Europe. Papers Presented at the Fourth International Symposium "The Mesolithic in Europe"* (eds.) P. M. Vermeersch and Philip van Peer. 345-353

Barkow, Jerome — 1976: Attention structure and the evolution of human psychological characteristics. *The social structure of attention* (eds.) Chance and Larsen. London. 203-219.

Barton, R.N.E. and Bergman, C.A. — 1982: Hunters at Hengisbury: some evidence from experimental archaeology. *World Archaeology* vol.14(2). 237-248

Bech, Jens — 1966: En boplads og et enkeltfund fra Fyns Maglemosetid. *Fynske Minder 1965*. 161-172

Becker, C.J. — 1945: En 8000-aarig stenalderboplads i Holmegårds Mose. *Fra Nationalmuseets Arbejdsmark 1945*. 61-72

———— — 1952: Maglemosekultur på Bornholm. *Aarbøger for nordisk Oldkyndighed og Historie 1962*. 96-177

———— — 1953: Die Maglemosekultur in Dänemark: Neue Funde und Ergebnisse. *Congrés International des Sciences Préhistoriques 1950, Actes de la IIIe Session*. 180-183

Bernot, Lucien — 1982: The two-door house: The Intha example from Burma - in - *East and Southeast Asia. Anthropological and architectural Aspects* (eds.) K.G. Izikowitz and P. Sørensen. London. 41-48

Berthelsen, William — 1944: *Stenalderbopladser i Sønderkær og Vejledalen*. Copenhagen.

Binford, Lewis R. — 1978: Dimensional analysis of behavior and site structure: Learning from an Eskimo hunting stand. *American Antiquity* vol.43(3). 330-361

———— — 1983: *In Pursuit of the Past: Decoding the Archaeological Record*. London.

Birket-Smith, Kaj — 1929: *The Caribou Eskimos. Material and Social life and their Cultural Position. I Descriptive part*. Copenhagen.

Blankholm, Hans P. — 1991: *Intrasite spatial analysis in theory and practice*. Aarhus.

## 8. References

| | |
|---|---|
| Blankholm, Ruth, Blankholm, Ejner and Andersen, Søren H. | 1968: Stallerupholm. Et bidrag til belysning af Maglemosekulturen i Østjylland. *Kuml 1967*. 61-115 |
| Boas, Niels Axel | 1987: Rude Mark - A Maglemosian Settlement in East Jutland. *Journal of Danish Archaeology* vol.5, 1986. 14-30 |
| Bodu, P., Karlin, C. and Ploux, S. | 1990: Who's who? The Magdalenian flintknappers of Pincevent (France). *The Big Puzzle. International Symposium on Refitting Stone Artefacts* (eds. Cziesla, Eickhoff, Arts and Winter). 143-163 |
| Bokelmann, Klaus | 1971: Duvensee, ein Wohnplatz des Mesolithikums in Schleswig-Holstein, und die Duvenseegruppe. *Offa* vol.28. 5-26 |
| ---------------- | 1980: Duvensee, Wohnplatz 6. *Die Heimat. Zeitschrift für Natur- und Landeskunde von Schleswig-Holstein und Hamburg* 87. Jahrgang, Heft 1Ø, Oktober 1980. 321-330 |
| ---------------- | 1981a: Eine neue Borealzeitliche Fundstelle in Schleswig-Holstein. *Kölner Jahrbuch für Vor- und Frühgeschichte* vol.15, 1975-1977. 181-188 |
| ---------------- | 1981b: Duvensee, Wohnplatz 8. *Offa* vol.38, 1981. 21-40 |
| ---------------- | 1985: Duvensee, Wohnplatz 13. *Offa* vol.42, 1985. 13-27 |
| ---------------- | 1986: Rast unter Bäumen. Ein Ephemerer Mesolithischer Lagerplatz aus dem Duvenseer Moor. *Offa* vol.43, 1986. 149-163 |
| ---------------- | 1989: Eine mesolithische Kiefernrindenmatte aus dem Duvenseer Moor. *Offa* vol.46, 1989. 17-22 |
| Bokelmann, Klaus, Averdieck, F.-R. and Willkom, H. | 1981: Duvensee, Wohnplatz 8. Neue Aspekte zur Sammelwirtschaft im frühen Mesolithikum. *Offa* vol.38, 1981. 21-40 |
| Bordieu, Pierre | 1970: La maison Kabyle ou le monde renversé. Échanges et communications. Mèlanges offerts à Claude Lèvi-Strauss à l'occasionson de son 60ème anniversaire (eds.) Jean Pouillon and Pierre Maranda. Paris. 739-758 |
| Brewer, M.B. | 1968: Determinants of social distances among East African Tribal groups. *Journal of personality and social psychology* vol.10(3). 279-289 |
| Brinch Petersen, Erik | 1967: Klosterlund - Sønder Hadsund - Bøllund. Les trois sites principaux du Maglémosien ancien en Jutland. Essai de typologie et de chronologie. *Acta Archaeologica* vol.XXXVII,1966. 77-185 |
| --------------------- | 1972: Sværdborg II. A Maglemose hut from Sværdborg Bog, Zealand, Denmark. *Acta Archaeologica* vol.XLII, 1971. 43-77 |
| --------------------- | 1973: A Survey of the Late Palaeolithic and the Mesolithic of Denmark. *The Mesolithic in Europe*. (ed.) S.Kozlowski. Warszaw. 77-127 |
| Cahen, Daniel and Caspar, Jean-Paul | 1984: Les Traces d'utilisation des Outils Préhistoriques. *L'Anthropologie* vol.88. 277-308 |
| Canter, David | 1983: The purpose evaluation of places. A facet approach. *Environment and behavior* vol.15(6). 659-698 |
| ------------ | 1984: Putting situations in their place. *Social behavior in context* (ed.) A. Furnham. London. 208-239 |

------------- 1991: Social past and social present: The archaeological dimensions to environmental psychology. *Social Space. Human Spatial Behaviour in Dwellings and Settlements.* (eds.) O.Grøn, E.Engelstad and I.Lindblom. Odense. 10-16

Canter, David and Lee, K.H. 1974: A non-reactive study of room usage in modern Japanese apartments. *Psychology and the built environment* (eds.) David Canter and T. Lee. London.

Chance, M.R.A. and Jolly, C.J. 1970: *Social groups of monkeys, apes and men.* London.

Childe, Gordon V. 1946: *Scotland before the Scots.* London.

Clark, J.G.D. 1954: *Excavations at Star Carr. An Early Mesolithic site at Seamer near Scarborough, Yorkshire.* Cambridge.

Clarke, D.V. and Sharples, Niall 1985: Settlements and subsistence in the third millenium B.C. *The prehistory of Orkney* (ed.) Colin Renfrew. Edinburgh. 54-82

Cziesla, Erwin 1989: Über das Kartieres von Artefaktmengen in steinzeitlichen Grabungsflächen. *Bulletin de la Société Préhistorique Luxembourgeoise.* vol 10, 1988. 5-53

------------- 1990a: On refitting of stone artefacts. *The Big Puzzle. International Symposium on Refitting Stone Artefacts* (eds. Cziesla, Eickhoff, Arts and Winter). 9-44

------------- *1990b: Artefact production and spatial distribution on the open air site 80/14 (Western Desert, Egypt). The Big Puzzle. International Symposium on Refitting Stone Artefacts* (eds. Cziesla, Eickhoff, Arts and Winter). 583-622

Dacey, Michael F. 1968: Modified Poisson probability law for point pattern more regular than random. *Spatial Analysis; A Reader in Statistical Geography* (eds.) B.J.L.Berry and D.F.Marble. 172-179

Damas, David 1972: The Copper Eskimo. *Hunters and gatherers today.* (ed.) M.G.Bicchieri. New York.

Diekmann, Hermann 1931: Ein Mittelsteinzeitlicher Wohnplatz bei Oerlinghausen im Teutoburger Wald. *Mannus* vol.31. 441-445

Domanska, Lucyna 1991: Preliminary results of an analysis of the tool distribution at late mesolithic sites in the Polish Lowland. *Social Space. Human Spatial Behaviour in Dwellings and Settlements.* (eds.) O.Grøn, E.Engelstad and I.Lindblom. Odense. 55-59

Doran, J.E. and Hodson, F.R. 1975: *Mathematics and Computers in Archaeology.* Edinburgh.

Dovido, J.F. and Ellyson, S.L. 1982: Decoding visual dominance: Attributes of power based on relative percentage of looking while speaking and looking while listening. *Social Psychology Quarterly* vol.45(2). 106-11

Doxtater, Dennis 1991: Reflections of the anasazi cosmos. *Social Space. Human Spatial Behaviour in Dwellings and Settlements.* (eds.) O.Grøn, E.Engelstad and I.Lindblom. Odense. 155-184

Eickhoff, Sabine 1990: A spatial analysis of refitted flint artefacts from the Magdalenian site of Gönnersdorf, Western Germany. *The Big Puzzle. International Symposium on Refitting Stone Artefacts* (eds. Cziesla, Eickhoff, Arts and Winter). 307-337

Eliade, M. 1976: *A History of Religious Ideas I.* Chicago.

Engelstad, Ericka — 1984: Diversity in Arctic Maritime Adaptions. An example from the Late Stone Age of Arctic Norway. *Acta Borealia* vol.2. 3-24

Exline, Ralph V. — 1971: Visual interaction: The glances of power and preference. *Nebraska Symposium on Motivation* (ed.) James K. Cole. Lincoln, 163-206

Faegre, Thorvald — 1979: *Tents. Architecture of the Nomads*. London.

Finlayson, Bill — 1990: The Function of Microliths. Evidence From Smittons and Starr, SW Scotland. *Mesolithic Miscellany* vol.11(1). 2-6

Fischer, Anders — 1984: Macro and Micro Wear Traces on Lithic Projectile Points. *Journal of Danish Archaeology* vol.3. 19-46

Fischer, A., Grønnow, B., Jønsson, J.H., Nielsen, F.O. and Petersen, C. — 1979: *Stenalder-eksperimenter i Lejre*. Working Papers. The National Museum of Denmark. Copenhagen.

Fock, Niels — 1986: Et sted i skoven - en verden - et univers. *Jordens folk* vol.21(2). 61-69

Giddings, J.L. — 1952: *The arctic woodland culture of the Kobuk River*. Pennsylvania.

Gifford-Gonzalez, D.P., Damrosch, D., Damrosch, D., Pryor, J., Thunen, R.L. — 1985: The third dimension in site structure: An experiment in trampling and vertical dispersal. *American Antiquity* vol.50(4). 803-818

Gould, R.A. — 1969: Subsistence behaviour among the Western Desert Aborigines of Australia. *Oceania* vol.39. 253-274

Gracheva, Galina — 1989: Nganasan shamans' ways and worldview. *Uralic Mythology and Folklore* (ed.) M. Hoppal and J. Pentikänen. Budapest - Helsinki. 233-238

Grøn, Ole — 1985: Mikroliter som grund för datering. Dags för omvärdering? *Populär Arkeologi* vol.3(3). 22-24

--------- — 1987a: Seasonal Variation in Maglemosian Group Size and Structure. A New Model. *Current Anthropology* vol.28(3). 303-327

--------- — 1987b: Dwelling organization - a key to the understanding of social structure in old stone age societies? an example from the Maglemose Culture. *New in stone age archaeology. Archaeologia Interregionalis* (eds.) J.K.Kozlowski and S.K.Kozlowski. Warsaw/Cracow. 63-83

--------- — 1989: General Spatial Behaviour in Small Dwellings: a Preliminary Study in Ethnoarchaeology and Social Psychology. *The Mesolithic in Europe. Papers presented at the third International Symposium.* (ed.) Clive Bonsal. Edinburgh. 99-105

--------- — 1990a: Studies in Settlement Patterns and Submarine Bogs: Results and Strategy for Further Research. *Contributions to the Mesolithic in Europe. Papers Presented at the Fourth International Symposium "The Mesolithic in Europe"* (ed.) P. M. Vermeersch and Philip van Peer. 81-86

--------- — 1990b: A Large Maglemosian Winter House? *Mesolithic Miscellany* vol.11(1). 7-13

---------        1991: A method for reconstruction of social organization in prehistoric societies and examples of practical application. *Social Space. Human Spatial Behaviour in Dwellings and Settlements.* (eds.) O.Grøn, E.Engelstad and I.Lindblom. Odense. 100-117

---------        1992a: Some comments on the interpretation of Barmosen I. *Mesolithic Miscellany*, vol.13(2). 12

---------        1992b: Maglemosian Microliths and Their Mounting. *Mesolithic Miscellany*, vol.13(2). 9-11

---------        1994: Barmosen I - continued ... *Mesolithic Miscellany*, vol.15(1). 22-24

---------        In press A: Research in Stone Age sites at Submerged Shore Zones. Strategies and Experiences. In *Man and Sea in the Mesolithic.* (ed.) Anders Fischer.

---------        In press B: Neolithization in southern Scandinavia - A mesolithic Perspective. Some suggestions and working hypothesis or - skating on thin ice. In *The Origins of Farming in the Baltic Region.* (eds.) Zvelebil, Domanska and Dennels.

Grøn, Ole and Skaarup, Jørgen        In press: Excavation of a mesolithic dwelling in a submerged wetland. A very preliminary report of an underwater excavation. NewsWARP.

Gusinde, Martin        1931: *Die Feuerland-Indianer*, vol.I. Modling bei Wien.

---------------        1937: Die Feuerland-Indianer, vol.II. Modling bei Wien.

Hall, Edward T.        1969: *The hidden dimension.* New York.

Hartz, N. and Winge, H.        1906: Om Uroxen fra Vig. *Årbøger for Nordisk Oldkyndighed og Historie 1906.* 225-236

Hayden, Brian        1981: *Paleolithic reflections. Lithic technology and ethnographic excavation among Australian Aborigines.* Canberra.

Henriksen, Gitte Bille        1976: *Sværdborg I. Excavations 1943-44. A settlement of the Maglemose Culture.* Copenhagen.

----------------------        1980: *Lundby-holmen. Pladser af Maglemose-type i Sydsjælland.* København.

Howells, L.T. and Becker, S.W.        1962: Seating arrangement and leadership emergence. *Journal of Abnormal and Social Psychology* vol.64(2). 148-150

Jenness, D.        1970: *The life of the Copper Eskimos. Part A, vol.12, A Report of the Canadian Expedition 1913-18.* New York. Reprinted from 1922 version.

Johansson, Axel D.        1968: Barmose-gruppen. Præboreale bopladsfund med skiveøkser i Sydsjælland. *Historisk Samfund for Præstø Amt. Årbog 1968.* 101-170

-----------------        1990: *Barmosegruppen. Præboreale bopladsfund i Sydsjælland.* Aarhus

Johnson, Ian        1984: Cell frequency recording and analysis of artifact distributions - in - *Intrasite spatial analysis in archaeology* (ed.) Harold Hietala. Cambridge. 75-96

Juel Jensen, Helle and Brinch Petersen, Erik — 1985: A functional Study of Lithics from Vænget Nord, a Mesolithic Site at Vedbæk, N.E. Sjælland. *Journal of Danish Archaeology* vol.4. 40-51

Knuth, Eigil — 1984: *Reports from the Musk-ox Way. A compilation of previously published articles with insertion of some new illustrations and with slightly altered radiocarbon dating list.* Copenhagen.

Kroll, Ellen and Isac, Glynn L. — 1984: Configurations of artifacts and bones at early Pleistocene sites in East Africa. *Intrasite spatial analysis in archaeology* (ed.) Harold Hietala. Cambridge. 4-31

Krukowski, S. — 1929: Kronika Konserwatora Zabytkow Przedhistorycznych Okregu Kieleckiego za r. 1924. *Wiadomosci Archeologiczne*, vol.10. 238-254

Kummer, Hans — 1969: Spacing mechanisms in social behaviour - in - *Man and beast: Comparative social behaviour* (eds.) J.F.Eisenberg and W.S.Dillon. Washington D.C. 219-234

Larsson, Lars — 1975: A contribution to the knowledge of mesolithic huts in southern Scandinavia. *M.L.U.H.M.* 1973-1974. 5-28

------------- — 1985: Of House and Hearth. The Excavation, Interpretation and Reconstruction of a Late Mesolithic House. *Archaeology and Environment* vol.4. 197-209

Larsen, Helge and Rainey, Froelich — 1948: *Ipiutak and the Arctic whale hunting culture.* New York.

Legge, Anthony J., and Rowly-Conwy, Peter A. — 1989: Some Preliminary Results of a Re-examination of the Star Carr Fauna. *The Mesolithic in Europe. Papers Presented at the Third International Symposium. Edinburgh 1985.* Edinburgh. 225-230

Leroi-Gourhan, André and Brézillon, Michel — 1966: L'habitation Magdalénienne No. 1 de Pincevent près Montereau (Seine-et-Marne). *Gallia Préhistoire, Fouilles et Monuments Archéologiques en France Métropolitan*, vol. 9(2). 263-385

----------------------- ------------------ — 1972: Fouilles de Pincevent. Essai d'analyse ethnographique d'un habitat magdalénien (la section 36). Paris.

Little, Kenneth B. — 1965: Personal space. *Journal of Experimental Social Psychology* vol.1. 237-247

Lott, D.F. and Sommer, R. — 1967: Seating arrangement abd status. *Journal of Personality and Social Psychology* vol.7(1). 90-95

Löhr, Hartwig — 1990: Serial production of chipped stone tools since Upper Paleolithic times. *The Big Puzzle. International Symposium on Refitting Stone Artefacts* (eds. Cziesla, Eickhoff, Arts and Winter). 129-142

Marshall, Lorna — 1959: Marriage among !Kung Bushmen. *Africa*, vol. XXIX(4). 335-365

Mathiassen, Therkel — 1937: Gudenå-kulturen, En mesolitisk indlandsbebyggelse i Jylland. *Aarbøger for nordisk Oldkyndighed og Historie. 1937.* 1-181

------------------- — 1948: *Danske Oldsager* vol.I, Copenhagen.

Mehrabian, Albert

1968: Relationship of attitude to seated posture, orientation, and distance. *Journal of Personality and Social Psychology* vol.10(1). 26-30

Mellaart, James

1967: *Çatal Hüyük. A Neolithic Town in Anatolia.* London.

Morice, F.A.G.

1909: The Great Déné Race. *Anthropos* vol.IV.

Murdock, George P. et.al.

1962-1965: Ethnographic Atlas. *Ethnology* vol.I:113-134,265-286,387-403,533-545, vol.II:109-133,249-268,402-405,541-548, vol.III:107-116,199-217,329-334,421-423, vol.IV:114-122,241-250,343-347

Møbjerg, Tinna

1991: The spatial organization of an Inuit winterhouse in Greenland. An ethnoarchaeological study. *Social Space. Human Spatial Behaviour in Dwellings and Settlements.* (eds.) O.Grøn, E.Engelstad and I.Lindblom. Odense. 40-48

Møhl, U.

1980: Elsdyrskeletterne fra Skottemarke og Favrbo. Skik og brug ved borealtidens jagter. *Aarbøger for Nordisk Oldkyndighed og Historie.* 1978. Copenhagen. 5-32

Newell. Raymond R. and Dekin, Albert A.

1978: An integrative strategy for the definition of behavorally meaningful archaeological units. *Palaeohistoria. Acta et Communicationes Instituti* Bio-archaeologici Universitatis Groninganae. *vol.XX.* 7-38

Nuzhnyí, Dimitrií

1990: Projectile damage on Upper Paleolithic Microliths and the Use of Bow and Arrow among Pleistocene Hunters in the Ukraine. *The Interpretative Possibilities of Microwear Studies. Proceedings of the International Conference on Lithic Use-wear Analysis, 15th - 17th February 1989 in Uppsala, Sweden.* Uppsala. 112-124

O'Connel, J.F.

1987: Alyawara site structure and its archaeological implications. *American Antiquity* vol.52. 74-108

Ohnuki-Tierney, Emiko

1972: Spatial Concepts of the Ainu of the Northwest Coast of Southern Sakhalin. *American Anthropologist* vol.74(3). 426-457

Parvia, Riitta

1991: The Finish concept of space. A mythical spiritual view. *Social Space. Human Spatial Behaviour in Dwellings and Settlements.* O.Grøn, E.Engelstad and I.Lindblom. 149-154

Paulson, Ivar

1952: The "Seat of Honour" in aboriginal dwellings of the circumpolar zone, with special regard to the Indians of northern North America. *Selected Papers of the XXIX'th International Congress of Americanists* (ed.) Sol Tax. Chicago. 63-65

Petterson, M.

1951: Mikroliten als Pfeilspitzen. Ein Fund aus dem Lilla Loshult Moor, Ksp. Loshult, Skåne. *Meddelande från Lunds Universitets Historiska Museet 1951.* 123-137

Pielou, E.

1969: *An introduction to mathematical ecology.* London.

Praslov, N.D.

1993: Eine neue Frauenstatuette aus Kalkstein von Kostienki I (Don, Russland). *Archäologisches Korrespondensblatt,* vol. 23. 165-173

Praslov, N.D. and Rogachev, A.N. (eds.)

1982: *Paleolit Kostenkovsko-Borščhevskogo rajona na Donu. 1879-1979.* Leningrad.

Price, Theron Douglas

1981: *Mesolithic Settlement Systems in the Netherlands.* Ann Arbor.

| | |
|---|---|
| Radcliffe-Brown | 1964: *The Andaman Islanders*. New York. Reprint of Cambridge version from 1922. |
| Radley, J. and Mellars, Paul | 1964: A Mesolithic Structure at Deepcar, Yorkshire, England, and the Affinities of its associated Flint Industries. *Proceedings of the Prehistoric Society* vol.XXX. 1-24 |
| Rajala, Eva and Westergren, Ebbe | 1991: Tingby - a Mesolithic Site with the Remains of a House, to the West of Kalmar, in the Province of Småland. *Meddelande från Lunds Universitets Historiska Museum* 1989-1990. 5-30 |
| Rapoport, Amos | 1969: *House form and Culture*. Englewood Clifs, N.J. |
| Rogers, Edward S. | 1967a: *The Material Culture of the Mistassini*. National Museum of Canada, Bulletin 80. Ottawa. |
| ----------------- | 1967b: Band organization among the Indians of eastern subarctic Canada. *Contributions to anthropology: Band Societies*. National Museum of Canada, Bulletin 228. Ottawa. |
| Ränk, Gustav | 1949: *Das System der Raumeinteilung in den Behausungen der nordeuroasischen Völker*. vol.1. Stockholm. |
| ------------ | 1951: *Das System der Raumeinteilung in den Behausungen der nordeuroasischen Völker*. vol.2. Stockholm. |
| Sarauw, Georg F.L. | 1904: En stenalders boplads i Maglemose ved Mullerup sammenholdt med beslægtede fund. *Aarbøger for Nordisk Oldkyndighed og Historie* 1903. 148-315 |
| Schwantes, Gustav | 1925: Der frühneolithische Wohnplatz von Duvensee. *Prähistorische Zeitschrift* vol.XVI. 174-177 |
| ----------------- | 1939: *Die Vorgeschichte Schleswig-Holsteins*. vol.I. Neumünster. |
| Schönweiss, Werner and Werner, Hansjürgen | 1977: Mesolithische Wohngrundrisse von Friesheim (Donau). *75 Jahre Anthropologische Staatssammlung München 1902-1977*. München. 57-66 |
| Silberbauer, G.B. | 1981: *Hunter and habitat in the Central Kalahari Desert*. Cambridge. |
| Skaarup, Jørgen | 1979: *Flaadet. En tidlig Maglemoseboplads på Langeland*. |
| Skar, Birgitte | 1988: The Scanian Maglemose Site Bare Mosse II. A Re-Examination by Refitting. *Acta Archaeologica* vol.58, 1987. 87-104 |
| Sommer, Robert | 1959: Studies in personal space. *Sociometry* vol.22(1). 247-260 |
| -------------- | 1961: Leadership and group geography. *Sociometry* vol.24(1). 98-110 |
| -------------- | 1965: Further studies of small group ecology. *Sociometry* vol.28(1). 337-348 |
| -------------- | 1968: Intimacy ratings in five countries. *International Journal of Psychology* vol.3(2). 109-114 |
| Stapert, Dick | 1989: The ring and sector method: Intrasite spatial analysis of stone age sites, with special reference to Pincevent. *Palaeohistoria*, vol.31. 1-57 |

------------        1992: *Rings and Sectors: Intrasite Spatial Analysis of Stone Age Sites*. Groningen.

Stapert, Dick and Krist, Jan S.        1990: The Hamburgian site of Oldeholtwolde (NL): some results of the refitting analysis. *The Big Puzzle. International Symposium on Refitting Stone Artefacts* (eds. Cziesla, Eickhoff, Arts and Winter). 371-404

Steinzor, B.        1950: The spatial factor in face to face discussion groups. *Journal of Abnormal and Social Psychology* vol.45. 552-555

Strongman, K.T. and Champness, B.G.        1968: Dominance hierachies and conflict in eye contact. *Acta Psychologica* vol.XXVIII. 376-386"

Strömberg, Märta        1976: *Forntid i Sydostskåne*. Lund.

Symens, Nicole        1986: A functional Analysis of Selected Stone Artifacts from the Magdalenien Site at Verberie, France. *Journal of Field Archaeology* vol.13. 213-221

Sørensen, Søren A.        1988: A Maglemosian Hut at Lavringe Mose, Zealand. *Journal of Danish Archaeology* vol.6. 53-62

Tanner, Adrian        1979: *Bringing Home Animals. Religious Ideology and Mode of Production of the Mistassini Cree Hunters*. London.

------------        1991: Spatial organization in social formation and symbolic action: Fijian and Canadian examples. *Social Space. Human Spatial Behaviour in Dwellings and Settlements*. O.Grøn, E.Engelstad and I.Lindblom. 21-39

Thomas, Elizabeth M.        1969: *The Harmless People*. London.

Trash Helskog (Engelstad), Ericka        1983: *The Iversfjord locality. A study of behavioral patterning during the late stone age of Finnmark, North Norway*. Tromsø.

Vang Petersen, Peter and Brinch Petersen, Erik        1984: Prejleruptyrens skæbne - 15 små flintspidser. *Nationalmuseets Arbejdsmark 1984*. 174-179

Vebæk, Christen Leif        1940: En Boplads fra den ældre Stenalder i Bøllund. Report in the Danish National Museum A38217.

Welinder, Stig        1971: Tidigpostglacialt Mesoliticum i Skåne. Lund.

Whallon, Robert jr.        1973: Spatial Analysis of Palaeolithic Occupation Areas. *The Explanation of Cultural Change. Models in Prehistory*. (ed.) C. Renfrew. London. 115-130

------------        1974: Spatial analysis of occupation floors II: The application of nearest neighbor analysis. *American Antiquity* vol.39(1). 16-34

------------        1978: Spatial Analysis of Mesolithic Occupation Floors: a Reappraisal. *The Early Postglacial Settlement of Northern Europe*. (ed.) P. Mellars. London. 27-35

------------        1984: Unconstrained clustering for the analysis of spatial distributions in archaeology. *Intrasite spatial analysis in archaeology* (ed.) Harold Hietala. Cambridge.

Wigforss, J., Lepiksaar, J., Olsson, I. U. and Pässe, T.        1983: *Bua Västergård - en 8000 år gammal kustboplads*. Göteborg.

Willkomm, Horst        1986: Bemerkungen zur 14C-Datierungen von Proben des Wohnplatzes 13 aus dem Duvenseer Moor. *Offa* vol.43. 171-172

## 8. References

Wilmsen, Edwin N.

1973: Interaction, Spacing Behavior, and the Organization of Hunting Bands. *Journal of Anthropological Research* vol.29(1). 1-31

Woodman, Peter C.

1985: *Excavations at Mount Sandel 1973-1977*. Belfast.

Yellen, John

1977: *Archaeological Approaches to the Present. Models for reconstructing the Past*. New York.

Aaris-Sørensen, Kim

1984: Om en uroksetyr fra Prejlerup - og dens sammenstød med Maglemosekulturen. *Nationalmuseets Arbejdsmark 1984*. 165-173